# EURASIAN CHALLENGES TO INTERNATIONAL ECONOMIC LAW

## NEW DEVELOPMENTS AFTER BREXIT AND IN THE CONTEXT OF THE COVID-19

Cultures juridiques et politiques
Vol. 18

Cultures juridiques et politiques Vol. 18

Les conceptions du pouvoir, du droit et de l'ordre se réfèrent inévitablement à l'ensemble du système de représentations qu'est la culture de chaque société. Toute forme de culture ayant donc nécessairement une dimension politique et juridique, la collection « Cultures juridiques et politiques » publie des travaux, tels que des thèses, synthèses de recherches, ouvrages collectifs et actes de colloques, se proposant de faire connaître les systèmes politiques et juridiques des pays européens, d'évaluer les grandes tendances des processus d'intégration politique et d'harmonisation juridique en cours dans l'Union européenne et d'éclairer les interférences entre le politique, le juridique et les autres aspects « culturels » dans le contexte de ces processus.

Collection dirigée par Stephanie Rohlfing-Dijoux et Otmar Seul.

AMANDINE CAYOL,
HYE-HWAL SEONG,
REMUS TITIRIGA,
PIERRE CHABAL (EDS.)

# EURASIAN CHALLENGES TO INTERNATIONAL ECONOMIC LAW

## NEW DEVELOPMENTS AFTER BREXIT AND IN THE CONTEXT OF THE COVID-19

PETER LANG
Bruxelles · Bern · Berlin · New York · Oxford · Wien

This book is made possible by the support granted towards the 5th Kazakh-Franco-Korean International Law Conference (May 2021) and the publication of its proceedings by

LEXFEIM Research Centre in Law, Université Le Havre Normandie

DEMOLOMBE Institute, Université Caen Normandie

INHA University Law School, South Korea

AL-FARABI Kazakh National University, Department of International Law

Previous conferences were held in 2014 (Almaty), 2016 (Le Havre), 2017 (InHa), 2019 (Almaty)

Corresponding books were published in 2016, 2017, 2018 and 2020, by Peter Lang PIE, in the series Cultures juridiques et politiques

In French and in Russian

- *Le régionalisme et ses limites: regards croisés franco-kazakhs*, 2016
Russian version edited and published in Kazakhstan in 2014

- *Mutations de société et réponses du droit : perspectives franco-asiatiques comparées*, 2017
Russian version edited and published in Kazakhstan in 2017

In English

- *On the European and Asian origins of legal and political systems: views from Korea, Kazakhstan and France*, 2018

- *The Challenge of change in the legal and political systems of Eurasia and the New Silk Road*, 2020

The book was subject to a double blind refereeing process.


Éditions scientifiques internationales
Brussels 2022
1 avenue Maurice, B-1050 Brussels, Belgium brussels@peterlang.com;
www.peterlang.com

Printed in Germany

ISSN 2235-1078
ISBN 978-2-87574-467-8
ISBN 978-2-87574-469-2 ePub
D/2021/5678/89
ISBN 978-2-87574-468-5 eBook
DOI 10.3726/b19333

**Bibliographic information published by "Die Deutsche Nationalbibliothek".** "Die Deutsche Nationalbibliothek" lists this publication in the "Deutsche National-bibliografie"; detailed bibliographic data is available on the Internet at <http://dnb.d-nb.de>.

CIP available at the British Library and the Library of Congress.

*In memoriam*

*Болат Тұрағұлұлы* БАЙМУХАМЕДОВ

*Bolat Turagulovich* BAIMUKHAMEDOV

*A genuine mind of Kazakhstan*

# Table of contents

## PART II
## REGIONAL AND INTERREGIONAL ISSUES

# Acknowledgements

Amandine Cayol, Hye-Hwal Seong,
Remus Titiriga, Pierre Chabal

The present book blends in the academic wish to understand Eurasian legal evolutions and the need to bring together, in an international conference, colleagues from, this time, five countries (Kazakhstan, France, Korea, Russia, Spain). Professor Bing CHEN (Nankai University, the PRC), an active participant in the 4th conference (2019, Almaty) and book, was unable to present his text *Promotion of data competition in the post- Covid era to the dual-circulation development of China's economy* at this 5th edition (2021, France). The organisers look forward to hosting him at the next and 6th edition (2023, Korea).

Such inter-university research follows a guiding principle: national and regional legal systems and their responses to the challenge of change must be studied both in their slow, institutional evolutions and in their hasted adaptations in times of crises. The need to legislate *en temps réel* must integrate the difficulty to anticipate on further challenges: violence and terrorism, health hazards and pandemics, regime-change and newly elected bold leaderships.

Our thanks are due to our universities. They supported us, in a context of a *Regional Comprehensive Economic Partnership* (2020) touching the Asia-Pacific and Eurasian spaces in a broader perspective than, strictly, international *business* law or even of international *trade* law. Such support helped us mobilise analyses drawing from legal sciences the social sciences at large. International *economic* law encompasses both public law and private law, holistically, by contrast with academic traditions, for example French, where this duality of public and private law serves as a *summa divisio* of and for law scholars and research institutes.

Participants to this (online) 5th edition of the Kazakh-French-Korean conferences see the economic emergence of Eurasia as resulting from economic globalisation over the last sixty years. The post-WWII economic reconstruction of the world yields an extra momentum that is multiplied since the cold-war divide of the planet. With increased competition in Eurasia, trends create and strengthen common regional and economic interests and questions: are consolidated states more successful in the global economy? Are they gaining real competitive advantages?

What are we to make of a development process centred on the Western hemisphere and the USA that seems to be stalling? By 2019–2020, one member has left the EU, a US president has introduced a populist/nationalist economic legacy, the Covid-19 pandemic has hindered the globalisation process. Brexit shows that agreements negotiated over many years or even decades can fast be cancelled. By "exiting", a key-participant of a Union of states creates political and economic uncertainty.

Such lesson is valid for all integrative associations in Eurasia. This continental region gathers half the world population to be economically and regionally merged, the greatest consumer market and productive capacity. Our conference, supported by our universities, brings "geo-legal", and geo-economic backgrounds into an analytical 'thread', probing into whether such a Eurasian economic integration is reachable. Contributors analyse the relation between these events (EU developments, US elections, pandemic) and other Eurasian events (situation in Belarus, progress of the BRI, impact of the Kazakh *Nur Zhol...*) and how this relation may structure international economic dynamics and legal regulations over the continent.

The consequences of Brexit on the EU, the global economy and political stability in Europe and Asia, suggest similar risks for integration associations of Eurasia, bringing attention to the question: how to mitigate their negative consequences for individual states and the entire region?

Such is our progression since, in 2012, during P. Chabal's visit to *al-Farabi* university in Almaty, dean K. Baizakova suggested to 'extend collaboration' to the law department. Within two years, the 1st Kazakh-French law seminar (2014) took place... And since 2015, when during P. Chabal's visit to InHa university, professor Young-Geun Chae triggered the addition of an East-Asian perspective as early as the 2nd seminar (2016), soon to be joined by colleagues from China (2017), Russia (2019) and now Spain (2021).

Thanks are due to the LexFEIM centre in Le Havre, the International Law department of *al-Farabi* Kazakh National University in Almaty, the Inha Law School in Incheon and the DEMOLOMBE Institute in Caen;

to all colleagues and other institutions supporting us beyond budgetary, linguistic or visa complications; and to our publisher, Peter Lang PIE, especially to the directors of the series *Cultures Juridiques et Politiques*.

Success can only be and only is collective.

Рақмет сізге! Merci beaucoup! 정말 고맙습니다!
谢谢! Большое спасибо! Muchas gracias!

***

# Foreword

Innocent Mutabazi

It is a great honour and pleasure for me to write this foreword for the present book edited by prominent experts in legal, political and international studies.

Normandie Université, a cluster of three Norman Universities, two Engineering Schools and one Architecture School, has developed a strategy towards its dedicated international development that included most notably the organisation of such international events, the promotion of excellence of research performed in its academic institutions in order to increase both international visibility and worldwide attractiveness.

Research activities conducted at Normandie Université are structured in five pluri-disciplinary fields. Among these, the cluster "Humanities, Culture and Social Sciences" is a thriving one. Normandy as a region, due to its rich recent history, helps promote peace and friendship among peoples and cooperation among academics.

The present times are characterised by a fast-moving world where information and political actions are dominated by new media and communication tools. This situation can generate a feeling that citizens cannot truly control anything any longer. Law, Political science and International Relations can help, in the pursuit of truth, to contextualise different events in their historic and geographic environment.

The conference *Eurasian challenges to international economic law after Brexit and in the context of the Covid-19* was held during the Covid lockout caused by the on-going pandemics. This prevented the audience from participating "physically" in the conference. However, exchanges by visio-conference were very successful thanks to the dedication of the organisation committee and the quality of the invited speakers.

I thank Pierre Chabal, Amandine Cayol, Zhuldyz Sairambaeva, Hye-Hwal Seong and Remus Titiriga for their efforts to make the workshop successful and for editing the present book to which I wish a large professional success and world-wide audience.

# Preface

Sagyngaliy Aidarbayev

Since the last Kazakh-French-Korean international law conference, held in Almaty in April 2019, there have been dramatic changes in the world.

First of all, the Covid-19 pandemic has become the severest challenge that humanity has faced in the 21st century. Most experts agree that, having become a landmark event, the pandemic will lead to a fundamental shift in the social order and in the way people think. Changes under the influence of the Covid-19 pandemic are already impacting the socio-economic and political-legal spheres of society. Moreover, the world may experience geopolitical and geo-economic shifts that can very well change the place of individual states and regions in the future world order.

In addition, the final stage of the UK's withdrawal process from the European Union superimposed itself onto the coronavirus epidemic. "Brexit" inflicted not only serious political and socio-economic losses on the Union, but reputational losses as well. It also raised the issue of the limits of integration if the world's most successful regional economic integration grouping could face the need to revise the methods of development of its very integration project.

These factors – the Covid-19 pandemic and "Brexit" – thus became a challenge for the entire Eurasian space, specifically in the legal area and for international economic law. This state of affairs raises questions.

Among the host of ongoing international political and legal problems, which are the most relevant for the states and regions of Eurasia, as well as for the entire Eurasian continent, from the point of view of French, Korean and Kazakh researchers? The answers can be found in this book. Indeed, it presents the view of researchers from both the eastern and western extremities of the Eurasian continent, as well as from the center of Eurasia, as to general political and legal issues.

The various problems identified are analysed in three perspectives: “Trade and financial issues”, “Regional and interregional issues” and “Industrial and socio-economic issues”. Yet, existing queries are not limited to these three approaches. Many more are also reflected in the studies presented, such as the problems of the US administration’s trade policy towards Eurasia and China, or the issues of the US military presence in Korea and their operational control over South Korean troops, or the EU experience for the Eurasian Economic Union, as well as WTO issues, etc.

The present book thus presented to the attention of the scientific community provides deeply relevant material for thought as well as for further scientific research.

# General introduction

Remus Titiriga

The book gathers analyses of international economic law (tax law and tax policy, international trade law and international trade policy, international private law, intellectual property law, *e*-services, *e*-transactions, law of personal data protection, matters of security balanced by economic considerations) for actors in Eurasia (states or integrative unions such as the EU or the EAEU) or states interacting with Eurasia (such as the USA). Its chapters focus on the dynamic of international economic law under the impact of events such as a U.S. Presidency imposing a populist/nationalist economic legacy, the Covid-19 pandemic producing tremendous economic upheaval, the Brexit process of the U.K. leaving the EU and other Eurasian relevant events.

Part I covers trade and financial issues. Remus Titiriga, looking at rhetorical change and real continuity in U.S. trade policies toward Eurasia and China, considers that particular rhetoric of political change hides the bipartisan continuity in international trade policies of the U.S. toward China and Eurasia. While the Trump administration took a bolder stance than the Obama administration on trade sanctions and China and other countries, a Hillary Presidency would have used the same such instruments even if under a different rhetoric. Given these continuities (which include a sceptical attitude towards the legal remedies within the WTO), the author considers that the trade war and the sanctions adopted by the U.S. toward China will remain in place or will be strengthened under the Biden administration.

Marie Dumarçay, looking at competition law and the Covid-19 pandemic, focuses on the international (EU) or national (France, Italy, Singapore, etc.) adaptation of rules protecting free competition under the impact of the Covid-19 pandemic. The author notices the increased use of competition mechanisms imposed by the risks of the pandemic. On the other hand, she underlines the 'softening' of the rules about objectives of traditional competition protection.

Young-Hoa Son, looking at Covid-19 and the enforcement of competition law focusing on business combinations, examines the merger and acquisition commercial activities in the context of the Covid-19 crisis. He evaluates what competition authorities worldwide should expect and how specific theories (failing firm defence) should apply in this time of crisis. Failing firm defence theory considers that in the absence of a merger, a company's assets would leave the market, causing a more significant welfare loss than would occur if the merger were permitted. According to the author, most regulators worldwide (in the USA, EU, South Korea) apply the same scrutiny as during the pre-depression period. However, there are practical and procedural opportunities available to informed acquirers and sellers.

Zulfiya Baimagambetova and Assema Akhmetova, looking at international experience in monitoring grain markets under the WTO, examine the regulations of grain trade by grain-producing and consumer countries (US, Canada, Japan – the most supporting countries for own farmers) or economic unions (EU, Eurasian Economic Union) within the framework of obligations assumed when joining the World Trade Organisation (the Agreement on Agriculture). This Agreement is one of the most controversial ones adopted within the WTO framework since, under this Agreement, a state may provide support measures to agriculture.

Looking at the *European Payment Initiative* as post-Covid-crisis adjustment of 'payments instruments', Géraldine Le Labourier-Fleury Le Gros analyses the retail payments (made by non-financial agents to cover current expenses) within the EU. While during the Covid crisis, online payments contributed to health security (payment with no physical contact), they did not offer the best financial security. The author examines how EU member states can find a balance between health security and financial security. Aware of the importance of digital payments at this time of crisis, the European Commission highlighted the need to create an instant European retail payment method and welcomed the European Initiative for Payments – EPI –, launched by several European banks.

Hye-Hwal Seong, looking at the history and the recent changes of short-sale regulation after Covid-19 in Korea, that is the history of "short selling" (sale of securities that an investor does not own) regulations and changes imposed by the Covid-19 crisis in South Korea. Since 2000 in Korea, only "covered short selling" (in which an investor sells stocks borrowed from others through lending transactions) is allowed while "naked short selling" (where one sells when one does not have any own stocks nor has any borrowed stocks) is forbidden. However, short selling has been banned since March 2020 due to the Covid-19 outbreak. Concluding with the desirable regulatory direction, the author argues for the positive function of short selling and the need to resume short selling in South Korea.

Pierre Fleury Le Gros, looking at challenges for the principle of separation of assets provided by Ordinance 2020-317 of 25 March 2020, examines a specific detail of aid (the solidarity fund) put in place by the French Government to curb the impact of the Covid-19 crisis on economic agents. The aid concerns two categories of companies hit by the crisis: i/ single-family enterprises or "business in its own name", and ii/ enterprises with legal personality. The legislator chooses to limit its payment to people whose only source of income was affected by the crisis, excluding from the aid people who have a full-time employment contract in parallel to this activity. Using the 'theory of patrimony', the author covers cases of the contract concluded within the managed company and with another company than that the person manages.

Part II of the book focuses on regional and interregional issues. Ilya Lifshits, looking at tax regulation principles in the European Union (EU) and in the Eurasian Economic Union (EAEU), compares the tax system within the EU and the EAEU. The chapter covers the competencies (or lack thereof) and the harmonisation rules for direct or indirect taxation within the EU or the EAEU. It follows double taxation issues (in an advanced 'communautarisation' process within the EU), tax avoidance (harmonisation of direct taxes within the EU) and the initiatives concerning financial transaction taxes proposal (within the EU). The volume of the tax legislation of the EAEU is relatively modest and limited to indirect taxation in trade in goods and services between the Member states. Consequently, the avoidance of double taxation is covered by legal instruments outside the legal framework of the EAEU. However, the logic of the integration and the functioning of the single market will inevitably lead to greater use of tax regulation at the central level in both unions.

Sagyngaliy Aidarbayev, Aizat Bekzhan and Bakhyt Uderbayeva, looking at the implementation of WTO standards in public procurement: the European Union (EU) experience and situation in the Eurasian Economic Union (EAEU), examine the regulation of public procurement in the EU and the EAEU in the light of the Government Procurement Agreement (GPA), in force within the World Trade Organisation (WTO). As an initiator of the GPA, the EU has experience in applying and complying with it. However, the regulation of public procurement at the level of the EAEU is very conditional since the main rules belong to the national legislation and institutions of the Member states. Therefore, there is considerable interest in getting inspiration and rational adaptation to their specifics of the provisions of the European Union directives in this area.

Catherine Golhen, looking at the Brexit and European regulations of private international law in civil and commercial matters, examines the implication of the U.K. withdrawal from the EU on judicial cooperation in civil matters. The *Rome-I* Regulation and the *Brussels-I bis* Regulation have harmonised the law applicable to contracts, the rules of jurisdiction and the rules for recognising and enforcing decisions among Member states. However, after Brexit and the transition period, these Regulations are no longer binding for the U.K. This creates a legal void in its relations with countries still members of the EU. The chapter formulates solutions to this legal void concerning the law applicable to contracts, the competent court, and the recognition of judgments in Franco-British relations.

Guillermo Palao Moreno, looking at Brexit and international commercial litigation in times of Covid-19, examines the cross-border commercial disputes arising, after Brexit, among businesses established in the EU and the U.K. He analyses, as in the paper by Catherine Golhen, the situation of International Commercial litigation before national courts governed, before Brexit, by the so-called "Brussels's System", *Brussels I bis* Regulation and the "parallel" Lugano Convention of 2007 (Lugano Convention II). In the second part of the paper, the author examines the regime of Alternative Dispute Resolution, focusing first on International Mediation in Commercial matters and further on the International Commercial Arbitration, which seems to be less affected by Brexit.

Fanny Rogue, looking at the legal issues of personal data transfers after Brexit, examines the framework for personal data transfer outside the EU (as is the case for the U.K. after Brexit). In principle, data transfers outside the EU26 are not allowed under the regime of GDPR. However, the Regulation organises a complex system of diverse and hierarchical grounds that may justify the personal data transfer to a third country (such as the European Commission issuing an adequacy decision). Moreover, in a recent case (Schrems II), the CJEU weakened the adequacy decisions adopted by the Commission concerning third countries. Thus, for the author, the framework of the GDPR and the strict interpretation of the CJEU are encouraging data controllers and processors to settle in the EU or elicit third countries to adopt a legislative framework equivalent to the European one.

Looking at the human and commercial challenges of the single European market and of the Asian market, Michel Bruno exposes the disadvantaged position of the EU market in its economic relations with the Asian market. The author underlines that the European market has no joint taxation or social policies, which makes possible the principle of non-discrimination to work only for multinationals that compete with Member states' social and fiscal standards. This European social and fiscal disunity thus undermines the EU's trade policy concerning Asian countries.

Kuralay Baizakova and Fatima Kukeyeva, looking at the modern challenges to the Belt and Road Initiative realisation in Central Asia, analyse the interests of the participants in the *OBOR* and the eventual challenges it might face. China has a clear interest in this initiative as she is the initiator of the process. So do other participant countries in the region that have a clear interest in its success. However, the authors identify several challenges, such as the political instability in the region, the U.S. Strategic interests in Central Asia, the contradictory interests of Russia and China, the risks associated with the threat of international terrorism, etc.

Chan-Mo Chung, looking at GATT principles during Covid-19: focusing on export-restrictions on face-masks, analyses GATT provisions applicable to export prohibitions/restrictions of face-masks during the Covid-19 pandemic. In the first part of the paper, the author examines the regime of such restrictions, covered under GATT provisions (especially GATT XI, XVIII, XX and XXI) and concludes that they are justifiable when imposed temporarily at the time of a critical shortage. However, the author points out that such quantitative restrictions should be limited to the degree necessary and not beyond a reasonable period based on a scientific risk assessment. He also recommends loosening restrictions in a manner phased with the goal of their complete removal.

Tai-Uk Chung, looking at the U.S. military presence in Korea and its operational control over South Korean troops, underlines that the

U.S. military has operational control over the Korean military as United Nations Command (UNC) and Korea-US Combined Forces Command (ROK-US CFC). Therefore, the United States has command over the South Korean army. However, South Korea is also economically dependent on China. Thus, the paper exposes the dilemma on which the future of the Korean peninsula depends: do South Koreans need more military or more economics?

Part III of the book covers sectoral and socio-economic issues. Gulmira Mashimbayeva and Aidana Otynshiyeva, keen on ensuring the right to health in the terms and times of a global epidemics, underline an international dimension in confronting such a health challenge from the perspective of fundamental rights. After examining the frame of the U.N., the authors evaluate the complex relations between the right to health and associated fundamental rights and their eventual collision with other fundamental right during pandemic's taming measures (right to freedom of movement colliding, for example, with the lockdowns or health measures imposed during the pandemic). In a second phase, the authors focus on the WHO and its essential role in protecting health during global epidemics and pandemics.

Amandine Cayol, looking at the development of *e*-health in the context of the Covid-19 pandemic, examines "*e*-health" evolution in France during the pandemic. The health crisis has enabled the development of "*e*-health" as "tele-medicine", whose usefulness has become clear to curb the health crisis and ensure continuity of care. However, this acceleration in "tele-medicine" raised numerous ethical and legal questions. The first group of questions is related to the protection of personal data in the telemedicine process. The second group of questions relates to the respect of patients' rights. According to the author, patients' rights have not been infringed upon, and the deployment of telemedicine strengthened even specific (health) rights.

Yesbol Omirzhanov and Almagul Tusupova, looking at the level of legal consciousness of citizens as determining factor in fighting against Covid-19, examine how the level of citizens' legal consciousness (a developed sense of justice and a high level of legal culture of citizens) influenced the fight against Covid-19 in Kazakhstan. After exposing the facts of the epidemic and measures taken by public authorities, the authors focus on the public reaction and its limits to conclude that during quarantine and after the weakening of quarantine measures, most of Kazakhstan's population adhered to the recommendations of authorities.

Zhuldyz SAIRAMBAEVA and Madina NURTAY, looking at implementing WTO standards in the field of intellectual property into the legislation of Kazakhstan: protecting of intellectual property rights during COVID-19, examine the measures taken by Kazakhstan to implement the requirements of the Trips agreement relative to the protection of intellectual property rights. The analysis covers the situation pre- COVID and post- COVID and the authors develop an argument about the discussions, taking place at the WTO level, about waiving the patent rights of pharmaceutics for prevention, treatment and containment of the COVID-19 pandemic.

Philippe GAST, looking at international and regional evolutions of intellectual property rights', offers a global overview of intellectual and industrial property rights developments. While the literary and artistic property on classical supports is well protected, the situation changes with the *Internet*, which enables the copying and disseminating of copyrighted works. The author examines legal responses such as the EU Directive 2019/790 or the creation in France of the 'High Authority for disseminating works and the protection of Rights on the Internet' (*HADOPI*). Further, the author considers that globalisation created several problems for industrial property, with counterfeit products originating mainly in Asia. He envisaged solutions either with a global tax or a closure of liberal Western markets to authoritarian regimes behind counterfeiting.

Looking at the protection of theatre directors and artistic directors of public *troupe* on filming of the performing arts, Sung-Kee HONG examines the legal regime of performing arts at international and national levels. In the first part of the paper, the author studies the challenges and the answers for the performing arts and filming of performing arts resulting from the lockdowns during the COVID pandemic. In the second part, the analysis focuses on the copyright status of some participants in the filming of performing arts (theatre director vs film director, filming vs choreographer, etc.) in the light of copyright regulations in South Korea, the U.S., Russia, EU and in international treaties (Berne Convention, etc.). Finally, the author proposes the most viable solution to solve a copyright conundrum linked to the evolution of technology.

Odgerel Purevdorj and Erbakhit Badelgaji, looking at Covid - induced challenging losses to a national economy of East Asia: the 2020 economic case of the tourism sector in the Ulaanbaatar area of Mongolia, estimate the economic losses of the tourism field in Ulaanbaatar city in Mongolia during coronavirus-induced restrictions. They focus first on the direct economic loss for the tourism industry. Then, in a second part, the authors examine the indirect loss (experienced by individuals and companies connected with tourism), such as motels, hotels, resorts, camps, museums, cinema theatres, entertainment services, art shows, events and activities, catering industry, festivals and its organising companies, transportation services.

In all, the array of topics analysed, as well as the diversity of analyses provided, justifiy the reader's interest in studying, in one book, three sub-continents.

# Part I

## Trade and financial issues

# Introduction

Hye-Hwal SEONG

The first part of the book browses through the main channels through which international economic law impacts international relations and trade in general. Its seven chapters present a welcome diversity enlightening the present complexity of these issues offset for two years now by a general, sanitary and pandemic situations.

The chapter by Remus TITIRIGA, about the rhetorical change and real continuity in US trade policies toward Eurasia and China, analyses whether the disruptive trade actions of the Trump administration in relation to Eurasia and China would be followed up by the Biden administration. According to the author, the rhetoric of change is addressing an American political audience but hides a bipartisan continuity in the US international trade actions. Trump administration followed in a *crescendo* the antidumping and countervailing duties favoured in the last years by President Obama. Trump administration also took a bolder stance by using other US legal mechanisms (out of WTO but not forbidden by WTO) in adopting trade sanctions against China and other countries. However, according to expert commenters, a Hillary Presidency would have used such legal mechanisms albeit under different rhetoric. There is also a continuity in the escalation of US actions inside the WTO from Obama to Trump who finally blocked the Appellate Body dispute settlement. Given these continuities, the author considers that the trade war with tariffs and sanctions on China adopted by Trump administration will remain in place for the time being under Biden administration.

The chapter by Marie DUMARÇAY researched the law of anti-competitive practices in times of health and economic crisis like this pandemic. The author said the pandemic had raised two types of risk more than ever. On the one hand, the risk of taking advantage of shortage to raise prices abusively on the market of essential products; on the other hand, that business may be tempted to collude through the exchange of information, market sharing, and prices fixing. Accordingly, competition authorities showed more flexibility to protect and support companies in the face of new problems by employing guidelines, communiqués and other announcements, most often of a *soft law nature*. The chapter finally stressed that these tools could play a key role in the development of a more resilient and greener economy that should follow the global crisis.

The chapter by Young-Hoa Son, on Covid-19 and the enforcement of the competition law focusing on business combinations, focuses on how to enforce competition law, especially the so-called 'failing firm defence', for business combinations during the Covid-19 crisis in which many companies go bankrupt or face a crisis in their business activities. The failing firm defence needs three requirements: i/ if a failed company is not acquired by another company soon, it will be withdrawn from the market due to financial difficulties. ii/ There is no more anti-competitive alternative than the proposed merger. iii/ In the absence of a proposed merger, the assets of a failed company will be removed from the market. The author examined a similar situation like the global financial crisis in 2008 and predicts that the business combination approval rate by the competing authority is expected to be about 8 % higher than usual given the positive application of the 'failing firm defence'.

The chapter by Zulfiya Baimagambetova and Assema Akhmetova, on international experience in regulating grain markets under the WTO, suggest that, as a repeated practice, grain-producers (countries or regions) organise support and subsidies to their grain-sectors. Such a practice does entails risks of distortion of market fairness, nit such risks are curtails by the encompassing regulating impact of UN global bodies, once the GATT and today the WTO. Taking in regulations by grain-producing/consumer countries (US, Canada, Japan) or economic unions (EU, EAEU) when joining the WTO's Agreement on Agriculture, one of the most controversial ones adopted within the WTO, may provide support measures to agriculture.

The chapter by Géraldine Le Labourier-Fleury Le Gros on retail payments in times of health-crisis in European Union member-states, shows how the pandemic has brought a great increase of online purchases and, consequently, the volume of distance payments. Then, the article pointed out two things regarding to the change of retail payment: First, the rate of fraudulent transactions is much higher than for card-payments at the sale-counter with cardholder-authentication. Second, since there is no digital payment solution that can be used anywhere in Europe to make any type of retail payment, this situation benefits the major global players in card payment, such as VISA or Mastercard, based in the United States. The author, in this regard, welcomed European Commission's initiative to create a *European* instant retail payment method, to strengthen European sovereignty in the area of payments. The European Payments Initiative – EPI –, launched on 2 July 2020, by 16 European banks. The EPI offers a solution to pay a beneficiary anywhere in Europe, seven days a week, instantly. The objective is to carry out all types of transactions: local payment – at a point of sale –, online payment in the context of electronic commerce and payment among individuals.

The chapter by Hye-Hwal Seong examined the history of short-selling regulation and regulatory changes since Covid-19 and suggested desirable improvement direction of the short selling regulation in Korea. First, he explained the long history of short-selling regulations of more than 400 years in world stock markets and around 50 years in Korean stock market. Next, he showed the regulatory changes in Korea since Covid-19. Among them, it is remarkable that the level of criminal punishment has been significantly increased from a fine of 100 million KRW or less to imprisonment for one year or more, or a fine of three times to five times the illegal profits which is almost the same level as insider trading and price manipulation. His paper argued for the positive function of short selling as well as the backlash of individual investors against short selling should be also fully understood. Therefore, the government should make special efforts to restore the trust of individual investors by expanding the opportunities for short selling by individual investors as much as possible, and clarify whether there is insider trading by institutional and foreign investors through rigorous investigation of large-scale short selling right before an important corporate disclosure.

The chapter by Pierre Fleury Le Gros is about the principle of the "separation of patrimonies" put to the test of the 2020 "Solidarity Fund" in France. Focusing on the challenge to the principle of separation of assets represented by the Ordinance 2020-317 of 25 March 2020, the chapter analyses the detailed implementation of a good idea (a legislation adopted in France designed to alleviate the financial difficulties of companies and businesses hit by Covid-19 induced restriction) provides a critical appraisal of an ambiguity of the law detrimental to the aid that company managers may claim and actually expect to receive. This detailed examination of the "solidarity fund" thus becomes a substantiated critique of the government policy's coherence on the matter. The 'theory of patrimony' enabled the author to explicit his points.

# Continuity and change in US trade policy towards China and beyond

Remus Titiriga

On 20 January 2020, democrat President Biden succeeded republican President Trump, his first months in office enabling us only to begin to decipher his administration's next steps concerning international trade toward Eurasia or China.Various political and ideological alignments and continuities exist in trade policies as the country moves from a republican to a democrat administration due to the weight of *realpolitik* in international relations. The same likely attitude existed in the transition from an Obama's democrat administration to the Trump's republican one. This chapter explores such continuities and eventual changes in trade attitudes in the transition from Obama's to Trump's administrations. It seeks to extend them to the foreseeable actions in this matter to be adopted by Biden's administration.

## I. The main trade tariffs actions of the Trump administration

With the benefit of hindsight, many trade actions seem less radical than the language announcing them. The bold rhetoric of change adopted by President Trump was more daring, in words than in deeds, so as to create leverage for new arrangements or deals. However, continuity of actual trade positions with the precedent administration – President Obama or an eventual Hillary Clinton Presidency – is visible.

### Continuation of anti-dumping and countervailing duties actions

Towards the end of President Obama's second term, the US anti-dumping (AD) and countervailing duties (CD) initiative grew significantly. While this trend reflected evolving economic conditions, it was also due to changes implemented by the Obama administration in the AD and CD regulations or practices. The Trump administration continued and built upon the new methodologies and practices. The outcome was a three-fold increase in the number of AD and CV duties.

## A change of direction by the recourse to unused old US trade remedies

The Trump administration took a more offensive position in trade by using, besides the AD and CD actions allowed by WTO, other US legal mechanisms (out of WTO but not forbidden by WTO agreements) to adopt unilaterally trade sanctions against China[1] and other countries. According to expert commenters, even a Hillary Presidency would have used such legal mechanisms albeit under different rhetoric.[2]

### *A. Global actions*

*Global safeguards law* – Section 201 of the Trade Act of 1974 is a global safeguards law allowing the US President to grant temporary import relief by raising duties or imposing non-tariff barriers on goods entering the US that harm or threaten domestic industries producing similar goods.

On 22 January 2018, President Trump announced tariffs on imports of solar panels from all countries to protect remaining US solar cell and module manufacturers. The 'over the board' safeguard measure was considered since foreign producers, mainly from China, were evading American restrictions on imports from specific countries by spreading their factories around the globe. The US has been pursuing foreign

---

1 Some of these specific US legal mechanisms (such as Section 301 of the 1974 US Trade Act) address only China in the section b of this part.

2 Todd Tucker, a trade expert at the Roosevelt Institute, considered that "Even in a Hillary Clinton administration, you would've seen some of these ideas floated, although probably a bit more artfully". The author of the article, Zeeshan Aleem, concluded that: "Even a long-time free trade proponent such as Clinton might've considered the WTO inadequate for dealing with China". Cf. Z. Aleem "Why Trump's plan to ignore the World Trade Organization isn't as reckless as it sounds", March 8, 2017, at <https://www.vox.com>.

washing-machines makers with AD duties since 2011. On 23 January 2018, the Office of the US Trade Representative announced tariffs on washing machines from all countries. The new measure was needed because foreign producers (mainly from South Korea and China) were evading American import restrictions from specific countries by spreading their factories around the globe.

*National security law: steel and aluminium* – Much of potential US steel and aluminium imports, especially from China, were already covered by highly restrictive AD barriers. At the beginning of 2018, President Trump self-initiated an investigation of whether steel imports were a threat to the US national security under Section 232 of the Trade Expansion Act of 1962. The section enables the US President to act unilaterally if national security is at stake. It seems to agree with the WTO charter, which includes an exemption for such cases (art XXI of GATT 1964). The section was rarely used and never invoked since the WTO appeared in 1995. President Trump also self-initiated a second investigation, this time alleging that aluminium imports threaten national security.

On 8 March 2018, the US administration imposed tariffs on foreign steel and aluminium. Later on, President Trump announced that his administration had reached final agreements (permanent exceptions) with South Korea on steel imports and with Argentina, Australia, and Brazil, on steel and aluminium.

Canada, Mexico, the EU, Turkey, and others have challenged Trump's tariffs at the WTO, considering that their aluminium and steel export pose no threat to America's national security. In the meantime, they have adopted their retaliatory tariffs[3] pushing the Trump administration to bring its own WTO complaints against these measures.

## B. Specific actions of the Trump administration toward China

*Section 301 of the 1974 US Trade Act and tariffs on China* – Section 301 of the 1974 US Trade Act authorises the US President to take appropriate

3 The EU's retaliation (or any other retaliations) does not have a solid legal position at WTO. The EU's lawyers invoked a complex rationale for retaliation under the WTO Agreement on Safeguards. They argued that the US measures, making imported steel and aluminium less competitive, had pushed the products into the EU market in a surge against which the WTO rules allowed the EU to defend itself.

actions to remove any act, policy, or practice of a foreign government violating an international trade agreement or unjustified, unreasonable, or discriminatory, and burdens or restricts US commerce. On 22 March 2018, the US released details of its findings and proposing retaliation for product-dumping, lack of reciprocity on market access, and intellectual property theft by China. The value of the tariffs proposed was based on estimates of the actual economic damage caused by the alleged violations. That was the beginning of a trade war between the two countries only suspended (not solved) with the signature of a "Phase One" trade deal, agreed by the two countries in mid-January 2020.

*"Phase One" trade deal with China* – The deal includes commitments by China to purchase an additional $200 billion worth of US products over 2017 levels in four sectors (manufactured goods, services, agricultural products, and energy) over the next two years. China also made new promises not to manipulate its currency, protect foreign intellectual property (IP), and refrain from forcing foreign companies to transfer technology.

Although the deal includes commitments from China to open up access for US financial services firms and expedite approval for genetically modified foods, it falls short of addressing fundamental structural problems in the U.S.-China relationship. For instance, China's continued use of industrial policy to guide economic outcomes, including industrial espionage and massive subsidies given to favoured companies, are not mentioned.[4]

The agreement also establishes a robust dispute-resolution system that ensures prompt and effective implementation and enforcement. It likewise establishes solid procedures for addressing disputes related to the agreement and allows each party to take proportionate responsive actions deemed appropriate. The United States suspended some of the new tariffs that Trump previously announced.[5]

---

[4] Trump administration officials considered that these concerns would be covered in subsequent talks but announced no immediate plans for a next phase of negotiations.

[5] According to the USTR, tariffs remain in place on about $370 billion out of $550 billion in US imports from China. President Trump has described the remaining tariffs as needed as leverage for negotiations toward a Phase Two deal.

*Other actions with economic connotations adopted by the Trump administration* – After the Covid-19 outbreak, President Trump declared that a second deal with China was not advisable and allowed the US agencies to adopt more than 200 public actions related to China that spanned at least 10 departments.

Among them, actions by the Federal Communications Commission designated the Chinese companies Huawei and ZTE as national security threats. These were followed by sanctions on several other major Chinese technology companies, from top contract chip-maker, Semi-conductor Manufacturing International Co., to Hikvision, the world's greatest surveillance camera maker. That was the beginning of an actual "semiconductor war" against China.

President's executive orders of 2020 banning Chinese-owned applications TikTok and WeChat blocked China's access to large volumes of American data that could be used for intelligence operations or to enhance artificial intelligence tools. Another executive order in January 2021 banned eight Chinese applications, including payment applications such as Alipay and WeChat Pay. Hong Kong goods for export to the US were labelled as made in China by the end of 2020. The decision followed China's imposition of a national security law on Hong Kong and a US decision to end Hong Kong's special status under US Law.

In November 2020, President Trump banned the US investments on a list of 45 Chinese companies deemed as having ties with the Chinese military. The order blocked the flow of American capital, including public pension and retirement funds, into firms that aid the Chinese military. In January 2021, Trump amended the order to ban any Americans from holding securities of blacklisted Chinese firms from 11 November 2021.

## II. The main FTAs concluded by the Trump administration

*De-entanglement from a multinational agreement (TPP)* – If Obama considered that the best way to preserve America's leadership was to embed the US in a network of trade alliances such as the Trans-Pacific Partnership (TPP), Trump had a different position, considering that the international order was not working for America. It was in the US interest to disrupt this order and organise the world around bilateral relations with other powers. The US is the most powerful country that can dictate terms to others on a one-on-one negotiation. Therefore, President Trump withdrew the US signature of the TPP by a simple executive order. The TPP was attacked from across the US political spectrum, especially during the 2016 presidential campaign. Given this US economic mood, a presidency of Hillary Clinton would have also withdrawn the USA from the TPP, proving the continuity of interests between a democrat and republican administration, besides the difference in political rhetoric.

*Renegotiation of KORUS* – The US and South Korea have agreed to a renovation of their bilateral trade agreement. Koreans decided to improve American firms' access to Korea's automotive and pharmaceutical markets while restricting their steel exports to the US by one-third. In the new agreement, the US postponed the 25 % US tariff on trucks until 2041 (scheduled, according to the original KORUS, to happen in 2021). As a result, the US's greatly expanding truck market will be out of reach to South Korean competition for another 20 years.

*Renegotiation of NAFTA* – In his first 100 days, President Trump threatened to withdraw from NAFTA if Canada and Mexico refused to renegotiate. This political rhetoric produced its intended effects since renegotiations began in mid-2017. The resulting USMCA treaty focused primarily on auto exports, steel and aluminium tariffs, and the dairy, egg, and poultry market. After a round of modifications concerning labour, on 19 December 2019, the US House of Representatives passed the USMCA with bipartisan support, followed on 16 January 2020, by the US Senate once more with bipartisan support.

*Negotiations and agreement with Japan* – As the fourth-largest US trade partner, Japan was a priority for US trade negotiations. The recent Japanese free trade agreements (FTAs), with the European Union (EU) and the CTPP (successor to the TPP following the US withdrawal), lowered Japan's tariffs on imports from several countries, placing US exporters at a disadvantage. Also, Japan was a key security partner of the US and did not retort with its tariffs to the US global tariffs on steel and aluminium. An added consideration was the prolonged trade war with China and the need for allies on the American side.

The negotiations resulted in two separate trade deals. The US-Japan Trade Agreement (Trade Agreement) eliminated or reduced duty rates on agricultural and industrial goods and established preferential quotas for US-specific goods. As a separate agreement between the two countries, the US-Japan Digital Trade Agreement (Digital Trade Agreement) provided guidelines on priority areas of digital trade.[6]

## III. Continuity in the escalation of US actions within the WTO from Obama to Trump

The US has a long list of complaints with the WTO's Appellate Body (AB). Most arguments are technical and focus on methodologies to calculate economic harms for applying domestic trade remedies (AD and CV). In successive rulings over many years, AB would have essentially wiped out tools that US trade negotiators never gave up at the negotiating table for WTO. According to US officials, that is a violation of the WTO understanding that it would not take away rights or add obligations to Member nations.

In 2011, the Obama administration blocked the reappointment of Jennifer Hillman, a US member of the AB, out of concern that she was not aggressive enough in issuing dissents of decisions that attacked American trade laws. In 2013–2014, the United States blocked the consensus over James Gathii, an expatriate law professor in Chicago. He would have been the first and only black African on the Appellate Body (representing Kenya).

In 2016, President Barack Obama's administration blocked Seung Wha Chang of South Korea from serving a second term.[7] US accused him of surpassing the scope of his legal mandate in several decisions. That was a clear escalation since, for the first time, it involved the reappointment of a non-US judge. The controversy was settled in November 2016 when Mr Hyun Chong Kim of Korea was appointed to fill that vacancy.

---

6 Congress did not have a formal role in approving the agreement, as the Trump administration used delegated tariff proclamation authorities of Trade Promotion Authority (TPA) legislation to enact the agreed-upon tariff changes. At the same time, the digital trade commitments took the form of an Executive Agreement. Cf. CRS Report RL33436, Japan-U.S. Relations: Issues for Congress, version 10, updated.

7 Cf. M. Elsig, M. Pollack and G. Shaffer, "The US is causing a major controversy in the World Trade Organization", *Washington Post*, June 6, 2016.

In 2017, under President Trump's administration, two AB members' second terms of office were to expire in June and December. According to the Chair's report in April 2017, the replacement process could not be launched because Members diverged on whether the two potential vacancies should be subject to one single selection process or two separate ones. The situation became even more complex as AB member Mr Hyun Chong Kim resigned in August 2017. At the Dispute Settlement Body (DSB) meeting on 31 August 2017, the United States raised the issue about Rule 15 of the Working Procedures for Appellate Review. The United stated considered Rule 15 a priority issue and rejected to launch any procedure before it was solved.[8] Since the US did not find answers to these questions, it starts blocking the nomination of any new member of the AB.[9] It represented a further escalation of the Trump administration, which pursued the dynamic engaged already by the Obama administration. At least three panellists were needed to hear an appeal, and after 11 December 2019, when two of the last members left, the AB ceased to function. However, according to certain commentators, the implications of the AB's blocking were vastly exaggerated.[10]

---

8 According to the United States, the authority to appoint and reappoint AB members belong only to the DSB. The AB cannot extend members' terms through the Working Procedures Rule 15 (allowing an outgoing AB member to complete the disposition of any appeal to which he or she has been assigned). For more details, see Po-Ching Lee, "Appointment and Reappointment of the Appellate Body Members: Judiciary or Politics" in Chang-fa Lo, Junji Nakagawa and Tsai-fang Chen (Eds.), *The Appellate Body of the WTO and Its Reform*, Springer Nature, 2019, p. 267.

9 The US position seems bipartisan: "The US has consciously forced a crisis within the WTO around the Appellate Body because we believed that it had strayed over the years from its mandate and that the crisis was necessary to try to get a role change", according to Robert Holleyman, deputy US trade representative under the Obama administration. Cf. "Donald Trump's block on WTO judges creates 'doomsday scenario' for world trade disputes", *South China Morning Post*, Diterbitkan 23.11, 21/11/2019.

10 "Supporters of Trump's tactics say the negative consequences of the Appellate Body closing have been overly exaggerated. Even if nations cannot appeal, trade complaints can still be raised and potentially resolved formally or informally at lower levels", *idem* note *supra*.

## IV. Continuity and change in the trade actions led by the Biden administration

As a result of the actions of the Trump administration, nearly $400 billion or 16 % of all US imports today face higher duties than they did four years before. In comparison, $100 billion of US exports face additional tariffs imposed in response to the Trump administration's actions.

President Biden has the power to withdraw (as he essentially did in internal policies) executive orders used by President Trump in trade actions. Nothing of that sort has happened yet and, in our opinion, will not happen in the foreseeable future. Mr Biden's team has defined trade agreements to protect American workers, an expression similar to President Trump's trade[11] policy goals.[12]

President Biden has also adopted protectionist attitudes, as seen in his government-procurement actions. For example, he has signed on 25 January 2021, an executive order that updates the Buy American Act. The order seeks to increase purchases of products made in the United States, mainly by tightening rules around federal procurement and giving the government a more significant role in supporting US Businesses.

*Rhetoric of change at WTO* – On 5 February 2021, two weeks after his inauguration, President Biden marked a US return to multilateralism by stopping opposition to nominate Nigerian Ngozi Okonjo-Iweala as the new director-general of the WTO. More recently, in discussions at the WTO over the temporary waiver of intellectual property rules for Covid-19 vaccines, treatments and technology, the US agreed to such a waiver. These are two examples of a 'charm offensive' that precludes nothing about substantive matters at WTO.

*Continuity over the security exception regarding WTO* – The US delegation to the WTO, on 22 February 2021, backed the Trump administration's decision to label Hong Kong exports as "Made in China"

---

11 Yuka Hayashi, "Japan Wants US Back in the TPP. It Will Likely Have to Wait", *The Wall Street Journal*, April 16, 2021.

12 That means continuity of position over FTAs with the Trump administration, which already achieved the maximum possible in this matter. The Trade Promotion Authority (TPA), under which Congress authorizes the President to conduct trade negotiations is set to expire in July 2021. Without the renewal of TPA, no trade negotiations can start. We doubt that Biden administration will search or will be in a position to secure a new TPA after July 2021.

and recognised that the WTO had no right to intercede in the matter because the organisation's rules permit countries to take any action to protect their "essential security interests".[13]

This position aligns with the Trump administration's, which invoked the same security exception concerning tariffs adopted under Section 232 of the Trade Expansion Act of 1962.

*Continuity of actions about WTO's Appellate Bodies* – On the real important issue of the blocked Appellate Bodies (AB) at WTO, the continuity with Trump's policies is unquestioned. In her confirmation hearing, held in March 2021, Katherine Tai, the new US Trade Representative, showed no intention of departing from the Trump-era attitude toward the dispute settlement mechanisms.[14]

With the AB inactive today, more than 19 WTO cases are in limbo, allowing the countries involved to continue practices rejected by lower panels. Six of the pending appeals were filed by the US, and three were filed against the US. One involves a lower panel of the September 2020 decision that the US's unilateral tariffs on over $200 billion of imported Chinese goods violate WTO rules (Trump's USTR officials obstructed that decision with an appeal to the blocked AB).

We suggest that under the Biden administration, the AB will remain blocked until honest discussions about a profound reform of the WTO could start.

*Continuity of position toward China* – Biden officials have indicated that his administration would continue with President Donald Trump's strict approach to China but have emphasised working with allies to

13 According to the US delegation, "The situation with respect to Hong Kong, China, constitutes a threat to the national security of the United States".... "Issues of national security are not matters appropriate for adjudication in the WTO dispute-settlement system". Cf. B. Baschuk, "Biden Picks Up Where Trump Left Off in Hard-Line Stances at WTO", *Bloomberg*, 22 February 2021.

14 As she explained: "Over the years, the appellate body has overstepped its authority and erred in interpreting WTO agreements in a number of cases, to the detriment of the United States and other WTO members."... "In addition, the appellate body has failed to follow existing rules created to ensure that disputes are resolved in a timely manner. Reforms are needed to ensure that the underlying causes of such problems do not resurface and that the appellate body does not diminish the rights and obligations of WTO members". Cf. E. Wragg, "Slim chances for the WTO appellate body despite US return to multilateralism", *Global Trade Review*, 3 March 2021.

counter the regime, which they say is different from the Trump administration. The administration is currently reviewing Trump's China policies and has yet to detail concrete plans for responding to the challenges posed by Beijing. Meanwhile, Republican lawmakers have increased pressure on Biden to continue Trump's hardline stance toward the regime.

We suggest that the tariffs and the sanctions on China adopted during the Trump administration will remain in place for the time being. Eventually, Biden administration, in coordination with US allies, might add several sanctions and tariffs related to the human rights infringements by China.

*

In conclusion, President Trump was not the 'generator of change' but just a symptom of changes happening within the US society and the world. Like any democratic leader, President Biden will move forward and follow this evolving economic mood of the US population. We believe that there will be no 'going back' to the USA's earlier economic world or trade attitudes.

# Anti-trust law in times of sanitary and economic crises

Marie DUMARÇAY

More than a health crisis, the COVID-19 pandemic has turned into a global economic and social hazard that requires competent decisions to protect free competition. This required adapting practices to different degrees. In the European Union (EU) as in many regions where the economy is inspired by liberalism, at least in part, undistorted competition is designed to be a catalyst of economic and technical progress, lower prices and, *ultimately*, consumer welfare. This free competition – with specialised authorities such as the European Commission in the EU or the Competition Authority in France, must ensure its preservation and exclude any behaviour whereby companies collude/abuse their dominant position to distort/restrict it.

Facing the pandemic, such public authorities had to adhere strictly to this dual restriction provided for by EU law (art. 101 § 1[1] and 102[2]

---

1 [1] The following shall be prohibited as incompatible with the internal market: all agreements between undertakings, decisions by associations of undertakings and concerted practices which may affect trade between Member states and which have as their object or effect the prevention, restriction or distortion of competition within the internal market, and in particular those which: (a) directly or indirectly fix purchase or selling prices or any other trading conditions; (b) limit or control production, markets, technical development, or investment; (c) share markets or sources of supply; (d) apply dissimilar conditions to equivalent transactions with other trading parties, thereby placing them at a competitive disadvantage; (e) make the conclusion of contracts subject to acceptance by the other parties of supplementary obligations which, by their nature or according to commercial usage, have no connection with the subject of such contracts.

2 As art. 102 TFEU states, "The abuse by one or more undertakings of a dominant position within the internal market or in a substantial part of it shall be prohibited as incompatible with the internal market in so far as it may affect trade between Member states. Such abuses may consist in particular in: (a) Directly or indirectly imposing unfair purchase or sale prices or other unfair trading conditions;

TFEU), which sanction collusions and abuses of dominant positions, respectively. The emergency context resulting from the health crisis has given rise to or accentuated a twofold risk: i/ the risk of taking advantage of this situation and the shortages it entails to make 'the most of it' through collusive mechanisms or mechanisms aimed at exploiting a position on a market that is particularly under pressure by increasing prices in an abusive manner; ii/ and the risk that economic operators may be tempted to collude through the exchange of information, market sharing, and the aligning of prices, for example, as a response to the serious economic and financial crisis that has affected certain sectors.

Public authorities in charge of protecting the market were thus to play an essential role from the start of the crisis. "Protecting" and "accompanying" businesses are – without turning away from the traditional objectives of protecting free competition – the key words of their actions. Some authorities set up units entirely dedicated to these issues in order to provide responses as adapted as possible to the crisis and the emergency context. The authorities already had procedural instruments at their disposal which gave them a certain degree of flexibility in preventing and dealing with possible infringements. However, some of these instruments were revised in order to meet the dual objective of "protecting" and "supporting" operators in the face of new problems or problems made more acute by the crisis.

While pursuing their original mission of market protection, the authorities have had to demonstrate a greater flexibility in their practices. The extent and swiftness of their efforts have been unanimously praised. In addition to the necessary material and procedural adaptations that are more a matter of daily practice, they had to adjust their action and communication strategy. It remains to be seen whether the health crisis could lead to a more lasting change in their understanding of compliance with competition rules. Although the modalities of their interventions bear

---

(b) Limiting production, markets or technical development to the detriment of consumers, (c) Applying unequal conditions to equivalent services to business partners, thereby placing them at a competitive disadvantage, (d) Making the conclusion of contracts conditional on the acceptance by the partners of additional services which, by their nature or according to commercial practice, have no connection with the subject-matter of such contracts. Not related to the subject matter of the contracts".

the stamp of diversity, the fact remains that their action has essentially taken a dual and complementary direction.

More than ever, the authorities have increased their regulatory actions by issuing guidelines, *communiqués* and other announcements, most often of a *soft law of nature*, in order to support market players who are considering arrangements to respond to the shortages caused by the health crisis or to deal with the economic crisis. In order to support economic operators, they have also made some substantial adjustments to their apprehension of potential infringements of free competition, which maybe suggests that some of them will more fundamentally redirect their policies that had hitherto been essentially geared towards protecting the market (I). Hence, the question is what meaning and scope one can give to these more or less profound shifts, especially since the next step will be, as the OECD stressed, to support or "stimulate a more resilient, inclusive and green economy"[3] (II).

## I. The increased use of competition regulation mechanisms

The global crisis has given rise to a double anti-competitive risk. The first stems from the economic shocks of supply and demand for specific health products and from the various calls for cooperation from the public authorities. The second risk, linked to the economic crisis, could encourage certain operators to form so-called "crisis" collusions. In order to reconcile these different issues with the traditional objectives of market protection, the authorities have had to mobilise more or less formal mechanisms by borrowing from the field of regulation.

Some have privileged the implementation of more or less general frameworks, implicitly based on the compliance policies developed by the companies (A). Others have opted, possibly cumulatively, for the implementation of individualised procedures to support the actors considering the implementation of cooperation agreements required or imposed by the crisis (B). Whatever they may be, these instruments are flexible.

---

3 OECD, OECD Competition Policy Responses to Covid-19, in Combating Coronavirus (Covid-19), 27 April 2020, available on the OECD website, p. 2.

## A. The increased use of compliance mechanisms

Driven by a liberal dynamic, the control of collusions and abuses of dominant position is now based in most legal systems on an *ex-post* control. It is therefore up to the companies themselves to assess *a priori* the validity of their agreements and practices. These practices – while sometimes contrary to free competition – are nevertheless likely to escape any sanction if the accompanying efficiency gains compensate for the infringement.[4] In recent years, the competition authorities have increased the number of measures aimed at enabling companies to adapt their behaviour to the requirements of competition policy, through the publication of notices, *communiqués* and other guidelines. In the EU, some authorities have even developed policies to encourage companies to set up or strengthen their competition law compliance programmes,[5] including by considering rewarding the companies committed to undertake such a programme – regulated by a "contentious protocol" – with a reduction of the fine.

Unsurprisingly, new problems arising from the Covid-19 crisis led regulators to make massive use of all the levers of *advocacy*. They have often acted individually, thus reminding us of the imperatives of competition policies[6] but also indicating the main lines of their policies for supporting operators faced with the problems arising from the crisis through press-releases, guidelines or announcements. The activity of the French,

---

4 The individual exemption of the anti-competitive agreement is provided for in French law, but also in art. 101 § 1 TFEU. According to the latter, "(...) the provisions of paragraph 1 may be declared inapplicable: – Any agreement or category of agreements between companies, – Any decision or category of decisions of business associations and – Any concerted practice or class of concerted practices which contributes to improving the production or distribution of goods or to promoting technical or economic progress, while allowing users a fair share of the resulting benefit, and without: (a) imposing restrictions on interested companies that are not indispensable to achieving these objectives, (b) giving undertakings the possibility, for a substantial part of the products concerned, of eliminating competition".

5 M. Dumarçay, "L'entreprise: Anticiper, gérer et digérer un contentieux - Variations autour des programmes de compliance", in *La systématique des contentieux concurrence en Europe*, under the direction of G. Godiveau, Bruylant, 2021.

6 This is evidenced by a warning from the Irish Competition Authority (Irish Competition Authority, CCPC warns businesses must act independently when setting prices during the reopening phase, Press Release, 1 July 2020).

Singaporean,[7] Brazilian,[8] Hong-Kongese[9] and American[10] competition authorities are cases in point. The Australian competition authority more recently published its competition policy priorities in an economic climate characterised by these new issues.[11] They have also worked at a collective or regional level to promote coherent support for businesses.

The European Competition Network, which brings together all the regulators of the Member states, issued a joint declaration on the application of competition law during the coronavirus crisis.[12] The effectiveness of such approaches is based on a double dynamic. The first aims to make companies responsible by reminding them of the rules and sanctions provided for by competition law, including in times of crisis[13] The second deals with specific support for companies encountering difficulties arising from the context.

Whatever the dynamic envisaged, compliance with competition regulations depends on the ability of companies to regulate their market behaviour on their own or with the more or less formal support of the competition authorities.

---

7 Singapore Competition Authority Guidance note on collaboration among competitors in response to Covid-19, Press Release, 20 July 2020.

8 Brazilian Competition Authority, About Collaboration between Companies to Confront the Covid-19 Crisis, Provisional informative note, 6 July 2020.

9 Hong Kong Competition Authority, Competition Commission cautions participants in anti-epidemic programmes to comply with Competition Ordinance, Press Release, 14 August 2020. In the same sense, see Singapore Competition Authority Guidance note on collaboration among competitors in response to Covid-19, Press Release, 20 July 2020.

10 Joint FTC-DOJ Antitrust statement Regarding Covid-19, March 24, 2020, available at ftc.gov.

11 ACCC 2021 Compliance and Enforcement Priorities, Committee for Economic Development Australia (CEDA), 23 February 2021.

12 Joint statement by the European Competition Network (ECN) on application of competition law during the Corona Crisis.

13 For the practice of the Dutch authority, Procedural Release, 18 March 2020, e-Competition, No. 93817; US DOJ, Cautions Business Community Against Violating Antitrust Laws in the Manufacturing, Distribution, and Sale of Public Health Products, Press Release, 9 March 2020, e-Competition, No. 93788.

## B. The resurgence of the mechanisms for the authorisation of cooperation agreements

The health- and economic crisis saw the return of more or less formal mechanisms of prior authorisation for certain agreements. Without over-generalising here, the legal exception system replacing the notification of agreements for individual exemption (as envisaged in European procedures before Regulation 1/2003) remains in principle. But the national authorities or the Commission itself have sometimes invited companies considering setting up cooperation agreements that might raise difficulties with regard to the competition rules to contact their services in order to establish a framework to support their implementation while limiting the harm or risk of harm.

For example, the European Commission developed a framework enabling companies operating in the health or pharmaceutical products sectors under pressure to set up cooperation agreements in order to respond to supply and demand shocks. To be sure, if the Commission set up this type of mechanism to accompany the agreements, it is also to better control them. This is often extended by the setting up of monitoring mechanisms. For the Commission, there is no question of granting authorisations with a general scope or purpose. The mechanism is individual and detailed and gives rise to the issue of a "comfort letter",[14] which is limited to agreements aimed at responding to shortages in the pharmaceutical and health products sector that are brought to its attention.[15] These agreements cannot in any case justify possible horizontal price agreements, which are identified as the most serious concerns. So far, the Commission has issued two such comfort letters.[16] This shows how sparingly it uses the instrument.

---

14 These administrative letters – which the Court of Justice has previously defined – inform the undertaking concerned of the Commission's opinion that there are no grounds for action by the Commission in respect of the practices in question and that the case may therefore be closed (ECJ, 10 July 1980, Case 253 and 1 to 3/79, Procureur de la République and Others v Bruno Giry and Guerlain SA and Others [1980] ECR 2327, speculative pages 12 and 13).

15 Commission Notice Temporary framework for the assessment of anti-competitive practices in cooperative ventures undertaken in response to emergency situations arising from the current pandemic of Covid-19, 2020/C116/02, C/2020/3200, OJ C 116l, 8 April 2020, pp. 7–10.

16 Comfort letter: coordination in the pharmaceutical industry to increase production and to improve supply of urgently needed critical hospital medicines to treat

Other authorities have adopted a more massive approach to this type of mechanism, giving them a much wider scope of application. The practice of the Australian Competition Authority (ACA) is a case in point.[17] The ACA increased the number of authorisations for cooperation agreements covering all economic sectors. Genuine sectoral authorisations are issued. In this context, the ACA has adopted – following the example of its Greek counterpart[18] – a broader approach to the authorisation mechanism, not limiting it solely to practices intended to respond to the needs arising from the health crisis but including – and in a relatively massive manner – those intended to combat the economic crisis.

For its part, the French Authority also envisaged a procedure of this nature, which it uses sparingly. In one year, it has issued one *communiqué* and one announcement aimed at setting up practices or cooperation agreements in response to the economic and financial difficulties encountered by certain professions or economic sectors. One of these aimed at setting up a project for concerted action of the distributors on a film release schedule when movie-theatres reopen. At other times, such an action would probably have drawn the ire of the authorities. However, this yields to the idea while providing the framework for its implementation, which must necessarily be temporary. As long as operators comply with the conditions specifically laid down by the Authority, their concertation agreement should probably be covered by an individual exemption, which would in principle exclude the imposition of a financial penalty of up to 10 % of the author's worldwide turnover. In this context, the approach adopted by the authorities is more informal.

---

Covid-19 patients, 08/04/2020, COMP/OG – D(2020/044003); Comfort letter: cooperation at a Matchmaking Event – Toward Covid-19 vaccines upscale production, 25/03/2021, COMP/E-1/GV/nb (2021/034137).

17 See in particular: Australian Competition Authority, Private and Public hospital can continue cooperating on Covid-19, Press Release, 9 July 2020; Australian Competition Authority, Supermarkets authorised to continue cooperating on Covid-19 response, Press Release, 3 September 2020; Australian Competition Authority, Oil Companies authorised to secure fuel supplies during Covid-19, Press Release, 10 September 2020; Australian Competition Authority, Energy industry cooperation authorised with strict conditions, Press Release, 17 September 2020; Australian Competition Authority, Virgin Australia/Alliance Airlines, Press Release 241/20, 19 November 2020.

18 Greek Competition Authority, Commission Implementing Regulation in the wine sector, Press Release, 15 July 2020.

This is not even a question of the Authority granting an authorisation. The objective is rather to provide an analysis-grid to guide companies and limit the risks of more serious infringements of competition law and therefore of a penalty. Consequently, the French approach does not appear to signal a return to a system of *a priori* control. The approach of certain authorities is sometimes more protective. The authorisations issued in Australia, for example, formally protect companies that follow the guidelines against any risk of prosecution before the competition authorities and the judge for damages.

These more protective instruments call into question the traditional objectives of anti-competitive practice law (II).

## II. The 'softening' of the rules pertaining to traditional objectives of competition

Through more or less significant adaptations of the practice of the competition authorities, the health and economic crisis has apparently questioned the very foundations of competition policies. Although a certain shift in standards and their interpretation has been observed in some cases (A), the authorities seem to be reluctant to depart too much from the objectives traditionally attached to the law on anti-competitive practices (B).

### *A. Lowering the standards for the prohibition of competition law infringements*

Driven by the "ordo-liberal" influence, the European system places the opening-up of the market at the heart of the economy, with one or more independent bodies in charge of controlling its effectiveness. This was the basis for the European doctrine on collusions and abuses of dominant positions within the framework of the Treaty of Rome, their prohibition being a condition for the very construction of the common market. Moreover, free and undistorted competition leads to prices being set solely by the interplay of supply and demand.

The crisis and the temptations of abusive practices occasionally called into question the "natural laws" of the market, prompting certain states to intervene directly to regulate the prices of products in markets under pressure. This was the case, for example, in France for the sale of surgical masks[19] and hydro-alcoholic gel.[20] Other systems preferred the virtues of the market, even if it meant that the regulator intervene in the context of emergency procedures to stop abusive pricing practices for products having become "essential". The case of Italy, Greece or Hungary are good examples.[21] However, the risks relating to excessive pricing practices remained essentially within the competence of the competition authorities. These approach such practices as representing an abuse of exploitation, which is one of the forms that abuse of a dominant position can take (in addition to abuse of predation). Some authors saw it as – subject to confirmation by the courts – an "unexpected revival of the ordo-liberal doctrine".[22]

Above all, the attention to draws to the use of instruments aimed at authorising, in a more or less formal manner, certain cooperation agreements, particularly in the area of information exchange, in order to respond to the risks of shortages of products that become "essential", and even more so the authorisations intended to accompany the practices adopted in response to the economic crisis. Classically, antitrust-law allows exemptions where the economic or technical progress – in the form of efficiency gains – brought about by the agreement or practice benefits consumers or end-users. On this point, the Commission takes a flexible view of the traditional precepts of collusion law in the context of the "comfort letters" it issues for cooperation agreements responding to shortages of health or pharmaceutical products, the latter being of obvious interest to end-users.

Competition as a means is not alien to the European approach. Indeed, some say it makes it unique. Thus, it is not certain that this should be seen as a "pure and simple" rupture from the spirit of European

---

19 Decree of 10 July 2020 on the sale prices of hydro-alcoholic gels and solutions and surgical masks for single use.

20 Decree of 5 March 2020 on the sale prices of hydro-alcoholic gels; Order of 4 April 2020 on the sale prices of hydro-alcoholic products prepared by pharmacies and pharmacies for internal use.

21 Press Release, ICA: Coronavirus, the Authority intervenes in the sale of sanitizing products and masks, 27 February 2020, en.agcm.it; Hellenic Competition Authority, The Interim result of HCC's investigation on health and hospital equipment during COVID-19 pandemic, Press Release, 11 September 2020; Hungarian Competition Authority, Vargapeptide, Press Release Vj/22/2020/63, 28 July 2020.

22 C. Mongouachon, "Towards the end of an 'ordoliberal' model of market regulation?" *RLC*, 2021, 103, p. 7, spec. p. 10.

competition policy. Perhaps this is a question of an evolution – admittedly constrained by circumstances – in the ways in which competition policies and other public policies are linked. The environmental issues that the Green Deal[23] wishes to place at the heart of European policies in support of a resilient economy could prolong or renew[24] it.

### B. The crisis agreement as a limit to the bending of standards regarding the prohibition of infringement

The more or less "watered-down" forms of authorisation covering cooperation agreements in certain sectors particularly affected by the crisis could be accompanied by a clearer shift in the traditional rules of the law against anti-competitive practices. It is probably for this reason that they are by no means generalised to all economic sectors, and that they are allowed under certain conditions in Europe and within the Member states. In this sense, they are an exception. They could also constitute the limit to the modification of competition policies.

Systematically, the authorities insist that they are in no way to justify possible horizontal price agreements. Therefore, a consensus seems to be emerging – subject to future confirmation – in favour of excluding in principle the admission of crisis collusions. The context could encourage companies in a sector – possibly under the influence of the professional bodies representing them or even certain public policies – to establish agreements or practices aimed at restricting their production or reducing their capacities in order to increase their profitability and prevent market-penetration by new operators during the crisis. The question is whether the competition authorities should be more lenient in dealing with such infringements. As is well known, such horizontal collusions are particularly serious infringements of competition law. The authorities, for instance the OECD, seem *a priori* hostile to collusions.[25] However, the OECD accepts that "any exempted collusion should be allowed for a limited period of time, subject to review against pre-defined criteria".

---

23 Competition Contributing to the European Green Deal – Call for Papers, available on the Commission's Green Deal website.

24 M. Dumarçay, "Développement économique durable et solidaire et droit de la concurrence. Vers une alliance raisonnée?", *RDAI/IBLJ*, 1/2021, p. 101.

25 OECD, OECD Competition Policy Responses to Covid-19, in Combating Coronavirus (Covid-19), *op. cit.*

Such seems to be the approach of the French competition authority. Its press-brief on the distributors' plan to agree on a release-schedule for films, when movie-theatre reopen, states that "as the law stands, (…) a temporary agreement of this type is likely to constitute a collusion prohibited by national and European competition law, but it could, however, benefit from an individual exemption in the event of a dispute, provided that it meets a certain number of criteria".[26] The welfare of the consumer or end-user is not far away, however, as the Authority envisages a possible individual exemption in the event of a litigation procedure if it can be proved that the agreement between film producers would contribute to promoting economic progress. The preservation of the diversity of the cinematographic offer and the wider distribution of artistic works would be likely to support the latter. The economic progress is assessed here in qualitative terms. In order to escape the prohibition, such an agreement will necessarily have to be neutral for cinema exhibitors and not be detrimental to spectators. Finally, individual exemption should only be considered in the event of litigation if it is demonstrated that the crisis context offered no alternative to concertation between distributors. The Authority's approach to the issue of "crisis collusions" takes the form of an advice, not of an authorisation.

*

In conclusion, such an approach could lay the foundations or inspire the mechanisms for accompanying actors who consider implementing cooperation agreements in the service of environmental policies that may affect competition. This is at least what the Authority's practice could suggest.[27]

---

26 Press Release, Following a referral by the *Médiateur du cinéma*, the *Autorité* issues an opinion on a consultation project for distributors on a film release schedule when cinemas reopen, April 16, 2021; Opinion, 21-A-03 of April 16, 2021 on a referral by the *Médiateur du cinéma* for an opinion on a film release schedule in cinemas.

27 ADLC, Press Release, "The Authority takes stock of its activities and outlines its action for 2021", 23 Dec. 2020.

# Covid-19 and the enforcement of competition law: Focusing on business combinations

Young-Hoa Son

This chapter analyses what competition authorities around the world expect and how practical theories such as failing firm defence are applied in times of crisis. This will help companies have a successful M&A during this uncertain period.

The Covid-19 pandemic has reached since December 2019 a total of confirmed cases of 129,495,677 and 2,828,643 deaths, that is a mortality rate – as of 1 April 2021 – of 2.184 %. The combination of economic instability in general and the recent pandemic worsened structural problems:[1] i/ the demand for products necessary to limit/treat the spread of the pandemic skyrocketed; ii/ the supply channel collapsed; iii/ in order to prevent the spread of diseases and control their outbreak, self-isolation measures were taken for infected people and the general public; iv/ business restriction measures for businesses were implemented.

The collapse of demand means that many companies and shops are unable to continue to pay their employees. They had to lay off workers whose incomes collapsed and faced serious liquidity crisis especially in the areas of construction, transportation and restaurants. To avoid economic collapse, companies were encouraged to rework and adopt new ways of working, such as working from home, as much as possible. Various forms of financial support were provided to companies in need (e.g., tax moratorium, credit facilities, capital injection)[2] – see *infra* P. Fleury's chapter.

---

1 M. Boyer, "Competition, Open Social Democracy, and the Covid-19 Pandemic", CIRANO Papers, 2020pe-15, 2020, p. 4.

2 F. Jenny, "Competition Law and Health Crisis", *Concurrences* 2–2020, *Competition law and health crisis*, p. 4.

The global Merger and Acquisition market (M&A) also suffered by the Covid-19 pandemic. In the first quarter of 2020, the world M&A decreased by 28 %, the lowest level since 2016.[3] In the first half of 2020, M&A volume and deal size decreased by 13 % compared with the same period last year.[4]

The recession provides a unique environment for M&A activities. M&A levels across the world economy are on the decline,[5] but M&A can become more important than ever, as it offers a unique opportunity to acquirers who want to provide the necessary lifelines for companies facing difficulties or take advantage of sluggish ratings. Speed, which is always essential in business transactions, can be an even more important factor in M&A. To that end, it is important to evaluate regulatory risks, especially competition laws. Most regulators around the world apply the same level of scrutiny as during the non-depression period, but there are practical and procedural opportunities available to sufficiently consulted acquirers and sellers.

## I. Failing firm-merger defence in the USA and in the EU

The global health emergency caused by the Covid-19 pandemic impacts lives and economic activities around the world. The effects of the outbreak are already evident in many sectors; other aspects take time to focus. Among the many unknowns are how many companies affected will be able to overcome the crisis, some will eventually close down, and how they can continue to maintain their failed companies (or their assets) in the marketplace.

If there is a causal relationship between mergers and expected competitive risks, then mergers that are expected to lead to anti-competitive effects should be prohibited. In some situations, the competitive

---

3 P. Barbaglia, and G. Roumeliotis, "Global M&A dwindles as coronavirus batters world's economies", Reuters, 2020. 3. 31. <https://www.reuters.com/article/us-global-m-a-review-coronavirus/global-ma-dwindles-as-coronavirus-batters-worlds-economies-idUSKBN21I0LT>.

4 B. Levy, "Global M&A Industry Trends Fierce competition ahead for dealmakers shaping the post-pandemic economy", <https://www.pwc.com/gx/en/services/deals/trends.html>.

5 Kane Wu, "Coronavirus Takes Toll on Global M&A as $1 Billion Deals Disappear", Reuters, 2020. 4. 20.

environment in the market after the merger may not be as anti-competitive as the competitive environment in the case of bankrupt companies leaving the market. In such a case, even if the post-merger scenario is less competitive than the pre-merger scenario, the merger should be approved.[6]

## A. In the United States of America

The failing-firm defence is that mergers are permitted if certain requirements are met, as in the USA v. Citizen Publishing Co. case,[7] despite the increased concentration of the market and the effect of inhibiting competition. Certain requirements are set out in Section 5 of the Horizontal Merger Guidelines of the United States 1992.[8] (i) the imminent risk of bankruptcy, (ii) the lack of realistic prospects for a reorganisation, and (iii) the absence of other acquisition candidates with less competitive inhibitory effects. Even if it is not a failed company, the current market share may overstate the importance of future competition despite its high level of market share and concentration. In order to ensure failing firm defence, the company claiming the requirements bears the burden of proof.

In the USA, failing division defence[9] and failing firm defence or weakened firm defence are recognised as variations of failing firm defence.[10]

### Covid-19 and failing-firm defence

The standards for establishing failing firm defence remain the same even in times of crisis. However, the facts necessary to make a defence are likely to occur during the economic downturn. For example, on 1 May 1 2020, the DOJ announced it would allow Prairie Farmace to buy milk processing plants from bankrupt Dean, noting that the collapse of school and restaurant milk demand is creating a "raucous period in

6 OECD, Roundtable on Failing Firm Defence, 2010, p. 11.

7 United States v. Citizen Publishing Co., 394 U.S. 131(1969).

8 Echihomi, Tadashin Tanno, and Hideya Hayashi, "Business Combination Examination and Economic Analysis", Joint Research Centre for Competition Policy Research, 2005, p. 12.

9 DOJ and FTC, Horizontal Merger Guidelines § 11 (2010).

10 OECD, Roundtable on Failing Firm Defence, 2010, p. 124.

the dairy industry."[11] FTC Chairman Noah Phillips recently said, "Due to Dean's financial difficulties and the lack of alternatives to acquire the plant in a timely manner, Prairie Farmace acquired it". Due to the collapse of milk demand from schools and restaurants, the problematic factory will probably close in the absence of Dean's financial difficulties and alternative buyers to purchase the factory in a timely manner. Noah Phillips recently acknowledged that there is a high possibility of more defences against bankrupt companies in the wake of the current COVID-19 crisis.[12]

## B. In the European Union

In 1991, the EU Commission rejected the failing firm defence in Aerospatiale-Alenia/deHavilland[13] This defence was first discussed in 1994 in Kali Salz/Mdk/Treuhand[14] and the EU Commission established three conditions for the successful failing firm defence in the merger review.[15] The EU Commission amended these standards in the following arguments. BASF/Eurodial/Pantochim[16] in 2001.This criterion was reflected in the 2004 horizontal merger guidelines.[17]

---

11 U.S. Department of Justice, Press Release Justice Department Requires Divestitures as Dean Foods Sells Fluid Milk Processing Plants to DFA out of Bankruptcy; Department Also Closes Investigation into Acquisition of Other Dean Plants by Prairie Farms, 2020. 5. 1. <https://www.justice.gov/opa/pr/justice-department-requires-divestitures-dean-foods-sells-fluid-milk-processing-plants-dfa>.

12 ABA Antitrust Law Section, "Where Do Vertically Integrated Digital Platforms End?", 68th Antitrust Virtual Spring Meeting, 2020. 4. 29. <https://www.youtube.com/watch?v=f5dkjj1GDnc>.

13 Commission Decision of October 2, 1991 in Case M.53 Aerospatiale/Alenia/De Havilland.

14 Commission Decision of July 9, 1998 in Case M.308 Kali+Salz/MdK/Treuhand.

15 Takeshige Sugimoto, "EU Competition Law: Recent Trends and Future Outlook" (Focusing on fields other than Cartel Affair) in Seminar *EU Competition Law: Recent Trends and Future Outlook 2014*, 2014. 6. 17, p. 60. https://en.sandkbrussels.com/news/seminars-lectures/lecture-eu-competition-law-recent-trends-and-upcoming-prospects-focusing-on-areas-other-than-cartel-/

16 Commission Decision of 11 July 2001 in Case M.2314 BASF/Eurodiol/Pantochim.

17 Guidelines on the assessment of horizontal mergers under the Council Regulation on the control of concentrations between undertakings (Horizontal Merger Guidelines), OJ [2004] C 31/5, § 90.

The EU Mergers Regulation (EUMR) does not explicitly mention the principles of failing firm defence.[18] The EU Commission will assess the impact on competition intensively, taking into account the degree to which failed companies are effectively competing in the market. From this point of view, the acquisition of a failed company is presented as a rescue merger and can be the only viable way to keep corporate assets in the market.[19]

The EU horizontal merger guidelines set out principles for recognising the theory of failing firm defence and set out three criteria for their application. i/ If a failed company is not acquired by another company in the near future, it will be withdrawn from the market due to financial difficulties. ii/ There is no more anti-competitive alternative than the proposed merger. iii/ In the absence of a proposed merger, the assets of a failed company will be removed from the market.[20]

Due to successful claims of the failing firm defence, the criteria for evidence that the parties must meet are very high, and the EU Commission's economic analysis is complicated. Indeed, in the EU, the defence of failed companies is only allowed in four cases. The four cases are The Kali Salz case,[21] BASF/Pantochim/Eurodiol case,[22] Nynas/Shell/Harburg Refinery case,[23] and the Aegean/Olympic II case.[24]

---

18 J. Buhart, and D. Henry, "Covid-19 and EU merger control: Time to loosen the FFD straitjacket?", *Concurrences* 2–2020, *Competition law and health crisis*, p. 39.

19 O'Melveny Alert, "The Failing Firm Merger Defence in Times of Economic Turmoil: Past Lessons and the Covid-19 Crisis", 2020. 4. 23.

20 Horizontal Merger Guidelines, OJ [2004] C 31/5, § 90; Joined Cases C-68/94 and C-30/95, Kali and Salz; Commission Decision 2002/365/EC in Case COMP/M.2314 – BASF/Pantochim/Eurodiol, pp. 157–160.

21 Case IV/M308 Kali und Salz/MdK/Treuhand [1994] OJ L186/30.

22 Case No COMP/M.2314 – BASF/Eurodiol/Pantochim [2002] OJ L132/45.

23 Case No COMP/M.6360 – NYNAS/SHELL/HARBURG REFINERY.

24 At the time of 2011, the EU Commission banned the acquisition of Olympic Airlines by Aegian Airlines on the basis of EU merger regulations because it could have had a quasi-exclusive effect on the Greek air transport market. (Aegean/Olympic I case. European Commission, Press Release Mergers: Commission blocks proposed merger between Aegean Airlines and Olympic Air, 2011. 1. 26. <https://ec.europa.eu/commission/presscorner/detail/en/IP_11_68>). The Aegean/Olympic II case concluded that Olympic Airlines would soon be forced out of the market in the absence of such transactions, due to the changing market conditions (promoted by the ongoing economic crisis in Greece), rapid decline in target companies' competitiveness and financial conditions. (European Commission, Press Release Mergers: Commission approves acquisition of Greek airline Olympic Air by Aegean

Furthermore, the EU Commission made it clear that it would continue to apply strict merger management standards in times of crisis in 2008.[25]

However, in the counterfactual scenario, it is suggested that clarification is likely to be used as a decisive practice for the EU Commission if it clarifies that pursuing combination transactions does less harm to competition than removing the assets of the merged entity's assets from the market.[26]

### *Special measures due to Coronavirus/Covid-19*

On 16 March 2020, the EU Commission announced "Special Measures Due to Coronavirus/Covid-19" on its website.[27] The EU Commission (DG COMP to be exact) recommends informing customers, competitors, suppliers, and third parties of the transaction by electronic means due to difficulties in collecting information, considering the requirements caused by the outbreak.[28]

As failing firm defence are often raised in the event of a large-scale economic crisis, if the Covid-19 crisis worsens, discussions on bankrupt company defences are expected to increase in the EU Commission. However, the Commission is very strict in applying this principle, and a very small number of cases of the failing firm defence have been cited under the EU merger regulations (EUMR). Indeed, despite the recession of the past, the Commission has shown no flexibility or relaxation in the application of the principles of failing firm defence.[29]

The precedent is that the EU Commission can persuade the merged companies through an appropriate fact-finding analysis that takes into

---

Airlines, 2013. 10. 9, p. 1. <https://ec.europa.eu/commission/presscorner/detail/en/IP_13_927>).

25 OECD, Roundtable on Failing Firm Defence. 2010, p. 187.

26 Case No COMP/M.2876, NewsCorp/Telepiù, Decision of 2003. 4. 2.

27 European Commission, SPECIAL MEASURES DUE TO CORONAVIRUS / Covid-19. <https://ec.europa.eu/competition/mergers/information_en.html>.

28 *Ibid.*

29 The EU Commission has repeatedly said that the application of EU Merger controls cannot be mitigated and that social concerns such as employment should be addressed by instruments specifically designed for them (P. Ranta, "The Failing Firm Defence in EU Merger Control and the Effects of the Economic Crisis on its Development", Master's thesis University of Helsinki, 2016, p. 76).

account their financial difficulties, whether they apply the formal failing firm defence or a more relaxed version of their defences. The economic difficulties posed by the Covid-19 epidemic imply that the time has matured for more flexible use of this principle. It is highly likely that the EU Commission will exhibit some flexibility and practicality in accepting counterfactual arguments similar to the failing firm defence under the influence of Covid-19.

## II. Failing firm-defence in South Korea

In Korea, the failing firm defence is called the "inviable company defence". In Korea, the parties concerned can defend themselves if they meet a three-step test similar to that applied in the EU.[30] Generally speaking, it is not expected that the regulatory authorities' approach to the inviable company defence will be eased. The sharp drop in air transport demand and uncertainty associated with the domestic expansion of Covid-19 will be taken into account by Asiana Airlines' decision of viable (renewable) status. Yet, the strict criteria for the inviable company defence will be difficult to relax and apply.[31]

### *Inviable company criteria*

Article 7(2)(ii) of the Korea Fair Trade Act stipulates the so-called inviable company defence. In other words, where the Fair Trade Commission recognises a business combination as qualifying for inviable company defence, the business combination is an exception. Where such business combination is made with an inviable company, such as a company whose total capital, as presented on its balance sheet, is less than its paid-in capital for a substantial period and satisfies the conditions prescribed by Presidential Decree, it will not ban the business combination. The benefits of failing firm defence include saving administrative costs in bankruptcy proceedings, preserving

30 Korea Fair Trade Comm'n, Guidelines for the Combination of Enterprises Review, § VIII.2.

31 Kang Ji-won/Choi Eun-jin, "Issues and Issues Related to Large Airlines (FSC) M&A - ② Major Issues in Fair Trade Commission's Review of Business Combinations" No. 187 (National Assembly Legislation Research Office, 2021), p. 15.

market resources, allocating production resources to people who have the ability to use them more efficiently, and improving economies of scale or product complement.[32]

According to the Examination Standards for Corporate Consolidation, "An inviable company of the provisions of Article 7 (2) 2 of the Act means a company which is under insolvency because the financial structure of the company is extremely deteriorated or is expected to be under insolvency in the near future" (EXAMINATION STANDARDS FOR CORPORATE CONSOLIDATION, VIII. Determination Standards of Efficiency Promotion Effect and Inviable Company, 2. a.).

In order to be recognised as an exception to a business combination, means satisfying the both of the following conditions:

i/ Where the production equipment, etc. of a company cannot be utilised continuously in the market, if no business combination is conducted;

ii/ Where it is impracticable to conduct other business combination less competition-restrictive than the business combination in question.(Enforcement Decree of the Monopoly Regulation and Fair Trade Act, Article 12-4).

## *A review of the failing-firm defence*

Hyundai Motor's acquisition of Kia Motors

South Korea's auto industry suffered major structural changes in 1997 when the foreign exchange crisis caused a vicious cycle of shrinking domestic demand, reducing production and overfilling facilities. Kia, Korea's second-largest automobile company, remained the seventh largest in the business world, but continued to grow rapidly from the 1980s to the early 1990s. Since the mid-1990s, however, Kia Motors has faced difficulties. Asia's failed investment in large-scale commercial and light commercial vehicles, Kia's independent Sepia and Credos models failed to attract much attention in the market, and Avella, which was developed as a follow-up to Pride, suffered large losses. Along with this, excessive

---

32 Seon Jeong Ho, "Practical Issues in the Review of Business Combinations in the Practice of the Appeal of the Bankruptcy", *Competition Journal*, 205 (Fair Competition Association, 2020), p. 52.

investment in Kia Steel and reckless management, such as guarantee of payment of assets, resulted in a bankruptcy on 15 July 1997.[33]

In 1998, Hyundai acquired 51 % of Kia Motors on the condition that Kia Motors' debt be written off by 7.17 trillion won.[34] The Fair Trade Commission (FTC) is considering the judgment of failing firm defence: i/ The cumulative current account deficit reached 4.59 trillion won due to legal management applications; ii/ Obtain approval for the consolidation plan: iii/ If there is no business combination, Kia Motors' production facilities will exit the related market, and the company admitted that it would be difficult to regenerate themselves.[35]

## *Jeju Air's acquisition of Eastar Jet*

The Fair Trade Commission is accepting the theory of broken companies in at least one case involving the recently depressed aviation sector (Jeju Air/Eastar Jet). which has been sluggish in recent years.[36] Easter Jet was recognised as "an inviable company" under Article 7(2) of the Fair Trade Act, and an exception was granted to the application of the restrictive regulations on competition between companies under Article 7(1).[37] Jeju Air signed a contract on 2 March 2020 to acquire 51.17 % of Eastar Jet shares, and reported the merger of the companies to the FTC on 13 March 2020. In response, the FTC proceeded with the review as quickly as possible, considering the situation in the airline industry which is facing difficulties due to the effects of Covid-19. As a result of the review, Easter Airlines decided that the company could not be revived under the law, and granted exceptions to the restrictions on corporate combinations.

---

33 Jeong Seung-hwa, "Hyundai Motor's Acquisition and Restructuring of Kia Motors", *Management Education Research*, Vol. 8, No. 1 (Korea Society of Management, 2004), p. 36.

34 Park Yong-beom/Choi Seung-jin/Kang Doo-soon, "The best M&A of all time is Hyundai Motor, Kia Motors Acquisition", *Daily Economy*, April 23, 2012. <https://www.mk.co.kr/news/special-edition/view/2012/04/247851/>.

35 Fair Trade Commission Resolution No. 99–43.

36 FTC news, "Jeju Air's acquisition review of Eastar Jet", April 23, 2020. <http://www.ftc.go.kr/www/selectReportUserView.do?key=10&rpttype=1&report_data_no=8536>.

37 Fair Trade Commission, "FTC approved the acquisition of Eastar Jet by Jeju Air", April 23, 2020, p. 1.

According to Eastar Jet's financial situation, its capital was eroded every year from 2013 to 2019 with a total capital of △ 63.2 billion won at the end of 2019. Since there are no candidates for acquisition except Jeju Air, it was judged that it is difficult to use Eastar Jet's assets in the market due to a business combination with fewer competitive restrictions other than the business combination.

## *Korean Air's acquisition of Asiana Airlines*

Recently, Korean Air is promoting the acquisition of Asiana Airlines. As KDB Industrial Bank and Korean Air are considering a joint takeover of Asiana Airlines, there are many speculations from the airline industry, financial sector, investment industry and government. There is a clear consensus that the airline industry should be revived. However, there are many difficulties left in achieving this.

The Fair Trade Commission does not judge competitiveness simply by assessing shares. If the so-called "inviable company defence" is recognised, business combination can be approved. The inviable company defence is a system that aims to continue to utilise the company's assets in the market through approval of business combination rather than withdrawing the inviable company from the market.

Asiana Airlines can only be revived through a business combination with Korean Air. Hyundai Motor's acquisition of Kia Motors in 1999 during the Asian financial crisis revealed the problem of monopolies, but Kia Motors was recognised as an "inviable company" and the acquisition of companies was approved.

*

In conclusion, the Covid-19 crisis is causing economic depression in each country. As a result, numerous companies go bankrupt or face a crisis in their business activities due to difficulties in corporate activities. The challenge is how to enforce competition law during the Covid-19 crisis. However, competition law is to maintain fair and free competition order in the market. It should not especially relax its enforcement during the economic downturn. Competition authorities in each country are taking the same stance.[38]

In Korea, the number of business combination examinations decreased considerably in 2009 from the previous year due to the effects of the real economy recession following the global financial crisis. The total number of screening cases for business combinations was 413, down by 25 % from 550 in 2008.[39] After that, it gradually increased in 2010 and recovered to pre-crisis levels from 2011–2012. There is no indication that the Fair Trade Commission relaxed its review of merger management during that period or would do so to face the current pandemic.

However, it may be a little easier to prove whether or not a failed company can be recognised and that there are no underwriting companies when applying the theory of failing firm defence. The Fair Trade Commission is taking measures to ease the burden on businesses that suffer from the spread of Covid-19 on their normal economic and management activities.[40] Cho Seong-wook, chairman of the Fair Trade Commission, also said, "It is expected that changes will appear at the industry level due to the Coronavirus outbreak. We will promptly review applications for business combination due to restructuring and market restructuring".[41] If the parties involved in the business combination succeed in persuading the FTC to close down by a certain date due to certain considerations related to the Covid-19 epidemic, they can request a prompt review.[42] The same can be thought of in excluded countries such as the United States, the EU, and Japan.

---

38 Ian Conner, "Antitrust review at the FTC: staying the course during uncertain times", Federal Trade Commission, 2020. 4. 6. <https://www.ftc.gov/news-events/blogs/competition-matters/2020/04/antitrust-review-ftc-staying-course-during-uncertain>; Department of Justice/Federal Trade Commission, Joint Antitrust statement Regarding Covid-19, 2020. 3. 24, p. 1.

39 Fair Trade Commission, "Fair Trade White Paper", 2010, p. 142.

40 Fair Trade Commission, "Fair Trade Commission, measures to ease the burden of submitting data for business operators affected by Covid-19 – The deadline for submitting a written opinion of a defendant is also temporarily extended until Covid-19 calms down", 2020. 3. 25.

41 Kim Jin-wook, "Cho Sung-wook" Industry Changes With Covid-19...We will quickly review the corporate combination, NEWSIS, April 1, 2020.

42 O'Melveny Alerts and Publications, Covid-19 Antitrust M&A Considerations, p. 8.

# International experience in regulating grain markets under the World Trade Organisation

Zulfiya Baimagambetova, Assem Akhmetova

One of today's most pressing global challenges is to provide humanity with food. The programmes, decisions and activities of the Food and Agriculture Organisation (FAO) and the World Trade Organisation (WTO) focus on the application of the world trade-liberalisation policy. The grain market, which is the key in the system of the agro-industrial complex of most countries, is thus of great importance in resolving issues of global food problems.

In accordance with the Grains Trade Convention of 1995, "grain" includes barley, maize, millet, oats, rye, sorghum, triticale, wheat and their products, as well as, by decision of the International Grains Council, other grains and products.[1] In 2009, by decision of the International Grains Council, rice and its products are also included in the definition and regulated by this Convention. The most traded grains are wheat, maize and rice, with wheat as leader in global trade.

In the post-war period, the agricultural policy of developed countries was aimed at protecting local farmers, while developing countries were characterised by the use of protectionist measures, including actions aimed at importing agricultural products. This situation has led to the emergence of an imbalance in grain stocks, which, in turn, suggested the use of export subsidies in Europe and the United States. Developing countries have devalued their national currencies in order to protect against imports of agricultural products, including grain.[2]

---

1 See Grains Trade Convention (1995), available at <http://www.igc.int/en/downloads/brochure/gtc1995.pdf> (visited 2 March 2021).

2 See K. Anderson, "Globalization's effects on world agricultural trade, 1960–2050", *Philosophical Transactions of the Royal Society of London*, Series B, *Biological sciences*, 2010, 365, pp. 3007–3021. <https://doi.org/10.1098/rstb.2010.0131>.

According to J.V. Chutcheva and T.S. Makhmudov, countries that produce grain can be categorised into: – countries with developed economies focused on the production of coarse grain; – developing countries focused on rice production for domestic food self-sufficiency; – countries whose economy is focused on the export of wheat.[3]

Today, the main world grain exporters are Australia, Argentina, the European Union, Canada and the USA. The world wheat trade is distributed as follows: countries of the Middle East and North Africa import grain from the European Union; countries of Latin America import from Canada and the USA; countries of Asia importamt from Australia. That said, China and India also occupy leading positions in world grain production, due to their large population, pertain to the importers of grain.

Legal instruments used for regulating the grain market form a system of methods, techniques and tools. These determine a strategy for the development of the global grain market. The latter is formed through the use of trade policy regulation tools: the *protectionism* model and the *liberalism* model. The agricultural sector of the economy use tools of the protectionism model. However, the level of development of the national economy of a country is an essential factor in determining the instruments of legal regulation of the grain trade.

Thus, the indicator determining the vector of development of foreign and domestic trade policy is the economic state of the country. Some scholars[4] note the importance of the grain sector in the agricultural market, emphasising that grain production is considered to be the basis for the functioning of the national agri-food sector, which determines the vector of development of the national economy.

This article examines the experience of legal regulation of grain trade in some countries in terms of their membership and, accordingly, in terms of the obligations assumed when joining the World Trade Organisation.

---

3 J.V. Chutcheva, and T.S. Makhmudov, "Trends in the formation and development of the world grain market" (In Russ.) *Tendenciiformirovaniyairazvitiyamirovogorynkazerna. Modern economics: problems and solutions*, 2015, 3, pp. 138–144.

4 A.M. Anisimov, A.L. Zlochevskij, R.E. Bulavin, E.A. Gan, I.V. Korbut and A.V. Kobuta, "The grain sector. The potential of Eurasian integration and the challenges of economic policy", (In Russ.) "Zernovojsektor. PotencialEvrazijskojintegraciiizadachiekonomicheskojpolitiki", *Journal of Eurasian Economic Integration*, 2015, 3 (28), pp. 18–32.

It probes into the issue of grain trade regulation within the WTO and the legal aspects of the functioning of the grain market at the national and regional levels

## I. Legal regulation of the grain market within the WTO

International trade is the most important and the most ancient form of interaction between countries, determining the nature of international economic relations. Any system of international relations, in turn, requires legal regulation. Today, such a regulator of international trade relations is the World Trade Organisation, coordinating the activities of countries in the field of trade through international agreements.

Modern international trade relations are characterised by the rules adopted by the World Trade Organisation in 1995. The main agreements adopted within the framework of the WTO and regulating grain trade include the following: – the General Agreement on Tariffs and Trade 1947; – the General Agreement on Tariffs and Trade 1994; – the WTO Agreement on Agriculture; – the Agreement on the Application of Sanitary and Phytosanitary Measures; – the Technical Barriers to Trade (TBT) Agreement; – the WTO Agreement on Trade-Related Aspects of Intellectual Property Rights (TRIPS) (when regulating the sale of seeds); – The Agreement on Safeguards.

The direct legal regulator of grain trade within the WTO is the Agreement on Agriculture. This agreement is one of the most controversial agreements adopted within the framework of the WTO. Under this agreement, a state party may provide support measures, which are divided into three types, depending on the degree of trade distortion: "green", "amber" and "blue".

Countries have the right to apply the Green Box measures, which imply support measures that do not have a distorting effect on trade, without restrictions. These include scientific research in the field of grain, phytosanitary measures, crop insurance, computerisation, infrastructure improvement, and others.

The Amber Box refers to measures of state support not included in the Green box but which could distort trade and are discussed during the accession to the organisation. The Amber Box includes price support for grain, interest rates on loans, measures related to compensation for technical equipment, fertilisers, etc. The state is obliged to gradually reduce measures of the Amber Box in accordance with the obligations assumed during accession to the WTO.

According to the Blue Box, states should use subsidy measures that restrict agricultural production. However, such measures are not subject to mandatory reduction if the payments are tied to a certain acreage or a certain crop.

M.V. Cherekaev notes that when defining the grain policy, the WTO member state assume three types of obligations: "access to the market of agricultural and food products / export subsidies / and state support".[5]

## II. Fundamentals of state and legal regulation of grain trade in the US

In the 2019–2020 agricultural year, the US exported 26.2 billion tons of wheat, or 14 % of the wheat trade volume on the world market, making it one of the largest grain exporters for that year. Government regulation of the grain trade in the US is carried out through the Federal Grain Inspection Service, the Agricultural Marketing Service and the Commodity Credit Corporation.

The key regulatory source governing the grain trade in the US is the Special Grain Standards Act of 1916. This sets standards for grain. Thus, the comprehensive legal system regulating grain trade in the US is aimed at establishing trusting relationships among all market participants.

US government programmes are aimed at price support. Thus, according to the Food, Conservation and Energy Act of 2008,[6] support for farmers is provided in the form of cash payments: direct and counter-cyclical payments, commodity loans, the collateral of which is the harvest in the future. Special attention is paid to the issues of grain crop insurance.

---

5 M.V. Cherekaev, "State regulation of foreign trade in grain in developed countries (dissertation for candidate of economic sciences)", (In Russ.) "Gosudarstvennoeregulirovanievneshnejtorgovlizernom v razvityhstranah", Moscow: Russian state Agrarian University – Moscow Timiryazev Agricultural Academy, 2006.

6 See "Food, Conservation, and Energy Act of 2008", available at <https://www.govinfo.gov/content/pkg/BILLS-110hr2419enr/pdf/BILLS-110hr2419enr.pdf> (visited 4 March 2021).

The US Department of Agriculture Risk Management Agency supports grain crop reinsurance. The financing of operations related to the grain trade is carried out through the norms established by the Federal Farm Loan Act. Thus, these Acts are aimed at supporting farmers and are regulated within the framework of the unified state policy of stabilising farmers' incomes.

However, the US system of state support for the development of grain trade is limited by WTO rules. Most of the subsidies are aimed at improving infrastructure, developing scientific activities in the field of grain production.

## III. Fundamentals of state and legal regulation of grain trade in Canada

Today, Canada occupies one of the leading positions among grain exporters. The Canada Grain Act and the Federal Agricultural Stabilisation Act of 1958 are important in the legal regulation of the Canadian grain trade.

The following organisations are the institutional basis for regulating the state agrarian policy: – The Canadian Wheat Board; – Canadian Grain Commission; – The Farm Income Stabilisation Insurance; -Export Development Canada.

The Canadian Wheat Board directly controls the wheat market. Thus, the Canadian Wheat Board sets the basic prices for wheat. It should also be noted that the Farm Income Protection Act provides a number of compensations for fluctuations in grain prices.[7]

The Canadian Wheat Board is a supplier of grain to both domestic and foreign markets. Canada has a state monopoly on grain exports. state support measures are aimed at insuring up to 70 % of the sown area of grain.

Canada is characterised by a single system of state and legal regulation of grain trade.

---

7 See "Farm Income Protection Act, assented to 1991-04-11", available at <https://laws-lois.justice.gc.ca/eng/acts/F-3.3/FullText.html> (visited 16 March 2021).

## IV. Fundamentals of state and legal regulation of grain trade in Japan

Japan is the leading country in terms of government support to farmers. The state actively applies a tax on grain imports, provides leasing for specialised equipment.[8]

Grain trade in Japan is carried out through a policy of strict protectionism. The Basic Plan for Food, Agriculture and Rural Areas is the legal source that determines the policy of grain trade. The Ministry of Agriculture, Forestry and Fisheries is the state body that carries out trade procedures for the export and import of grain.

Nevertheless, as a member of the World Trade Organisation, Japan is a leading state in the application of state subsidies in the agricultural sector.[9] Thus, to assist farmers who produce rice and wheat, the Ministry of Agriculture, Forestry and Fisheries operates in accordance with a special programme aimed at stimulating the production of these grain.[10] This program provides for compensation payments and the implementation of the state function of pricing for grain.

## V. Fundamentals of state and legal regulation of grain trade in Kazakhstan

Kazakhstan is one of the major grain exporters on the world market. Negotiations on the process of the state's accession to the WTO lasted 19 years, from 1996 to 2015. According to some scientists, one of the most controversial factors was the issue of permissible measures of state support for agriculture and the provision of transport subsidies for grain exports.[11]

---

8 See A.A. Kovbasyuk, "Foreign experience of the state support of grain crop production", (In Russ.) "Zarubezhnyjopytgosudarstvennojpodderzhkiproizvodstvazernovyhkultur", *Voprosyupravleniya*, 2016, 1 (19), pp. 148–155.

9 *Ibid.*

10 A.T. Stadnik, D.M. Matveev and Yu.Yu Makarova, "Improving state regulation of the grain market in Russia", (In Russ.) "Sovershenstvovaniegosudarstvennogoregulirovaniyarynkazerna v Rossiiu", *VestnikAltajskogogosudarstvennogoagrarnogouniversiteta*, 2013, 10 (108), pp. 137–142.

11 S.Zh. Aidarbayev, Z.M. Baimagambetova. and A. Umirzakova, "Standards of WTO in the Field of Subsidizing of Agriculture and their Influence on the Agrofood Sector of Kazakhstan", *European Reforms Bulletin*, 2015, 4. 3–5.

The legal regulation of grain trade in Kazakhstan is carried out through the application of the provisions of the Law "On Grain" of 19 January 2001. Oshakbayev notes that before Kazakhstan's membership in the WTO, the state used the purchase of grain for commercial purposes, the provision of direct subsidies to farmers.[12] Thus, the process of accession to the WTO created the need to introduce 39 amendments to this law.

The state Programme for the Development of the Agro-industrial Complex for 2017–2021 regulates measures of state support in the field of agriculture, including grain. The institutional framework for regulating grain trade is the Ministry of Agriculture of the Republic of Kazakhstan.

In all, under the conditions of WTO membership, Kazakhstan has indeed adapted its legislation in accordance with the Agreement on Agriculture, changing the nature of subsidies to the agricultural sector.

## VI. Fundamentals of state and legal regulation of grain trade in the European Union

The Common Agricultural Policy, created in order to ensure regional self-sufficiency in food, regulates the agriculture of the European Union. Under this policy, since 1962, the Union's grain production has been implemented through export subsidies, import duties, direct subsidies, and intervention prices.[13] The price of grain was set by the Council of Ministers of the European Union. It should be noted that the EU policy establishes the licensing of grain exports and imports.

Before joining the World Trade Organisation, the European Union had high tariffs on imported grain. Today, as a member of the WTO, applying the provisions of the Common Agricultural Policy carries out the regulation of the grain industry of the European Union. Thus, the policy is implemented under the principle of unity of multi-level support for

---

12 R. Oshakbayev, "The economy of grain exports in Kazakhstan, Perspectives and analysis of exports of wheat", (In Russ.) Ekonomikaeksportazernovyh v KazahstanePerspektivyianalizeksportapshenicy, *Research on the politics of the transition of agriculture*, 2012, 6, available at <http://www.fao.org/3/CA1815RU/ca1815ru.pdf>.

13 See Common agricultural policy (1962), available at <https://ec.europa.eu/info/food-farming-fisheries/key-policies/committees-and-advisory-councils/civil-dialogue-groups/cap_en> (visited 17 March 2021).

the development of the agricultural sector. Thus, the bill on the Future of Agriculture, Food and Forestry of France contains norms that regulate the principle of compliance with the Common Agricultural Policy.

It should be noted that there is a "double protection" of local farmers: state and cooperative. In France, more than half of the cooperatives are grain producers, which carry out public procurement, buy out grain processing enterprises, organise international cooperative associations and a number of other actions aimed at supporting local farmers. In Germany, the practice of grain crop insurance is actively used, in which the state directly reimburses losses to grain producers.

The management of the agricultural market is carried out through specialised state bodies, whose powers include the development of regulatory documents, state programmes, etc.

Thus, the European Union is characterised by a two-tier system of support for the development of grain trade, which implies assistance to all member countries of the Union in order to maintain the stability of the domestic grain market.

## VII. Fundamentals of state and legal regulation of grain trade in the Eurasian Economic Union

The agricultural sector of the Eurasian Economic Union (EAEU), which includes the grain sector, plays an important role in the international market. The "Unified agricultural policy" operates within the framework of the EAEU.

The legal basis for the formation of a EAEU unified agricultural policy is Articles 94–95 of the Treaty on the EAEU, the Protocol on Measures of state Support for Agriculture (Annex No. 29 to the Treaty on the EAEU) and a number of others. Article 94 of Section XXV of the Treaty on the EAEU provides that the purpose of agricultural policy is to increase the efficiency of production of competitive agricultural products, self-sufficiency, and export promotion.[14]

[14] Treaty on the Eurasian Economic Union (January 2015), available at <https://docs.eaeunion.org/docs/ru-ru/0003610/itia_05062014> (visited 17 March 2021).

Paragraph 2 of Article 95 of the EAEU Treaty[15] stipulates that consultations are organised by the Eurasian Economic Commission at least once a year, which, in our opinion, requires additions and more clarifications.

The EAEU does not have to date a single legal act regulating trade directly in grain, which negatively affects the more efficient functioning of the regional grain market. Nevertheless, within the framework of the EAEU, attempts were made to integrate the mechanism of legal regulation of grain production. Thus, within the framework of the Commonwealth of Independent states (CIS), in 2001 in Dushanbe, the Intergovernmental Council of the Agro-Industrial Complex adopted a Program for the creation and functioning of the CIS grain market for 2001–2010.

In 2011, as a result of the decision of the Customs Union Commission No. 874, Customs Union Technical Regulation on Safety of Grain was approved.[16] This regulation currently has legal force and defines the requirements for grain produced in the territory of the Customs Union and intended for food and feed use. Article 1 of the Regulation establishes that the requirements apply to the processes of production, storage, transportation, sale and disposal of grain.[17]

Within the framework of the EAEU, the Technical Regulations of the Customs Union "On food safety", adopted by the decision of the CU Commission No. 880 of 9 December 2011, and the List of quarantined products (quarantined freights, quarantined materials, quarantined goods) subject to quarantine phytosanitary control (supervision) at the customs border of the Customs Union and in the customs territory of the Customs Union., approved by the decision of the CU Commission No. 318 of June 18, 2010, regulate the requirements for grain.

The next attempt at integration was the creation of a draft agreement on the organisation and functioning of the grain market of the EAEU Member states with the assistance of the Council for Agro-Industrial Policy in 2012.[18] At the same time, within the framework of the EAEU,

---

15 *Ibid.*

16 See Customs Union Technical Regulation on Safety of Grain, adopted 20 August 2012, available at <http://www.eurasiancommission.org/ru/act/texnreg/deptexreg/tr/Documents/TehReg%20TZ%20Zerno.pdf> (visited 18 March 2021).

17 *Ibid.*, article 1.

18 Khan Yu.A. "Priorities of Kazakhstan's grain policy in the context of the Eurasian Economic Union" (In Russ.), "PrioritetyzernovojpolitikiKazahstana v

Concept of an Agreed Agro-industrial Policy of the Customs Union and the Common Economic Space member states was approved, which, however, has now lost its legal force.

Regulation of the grain sector of the EAEU economy is carried out within the framework of the participation of the member states in the World Trade Organisation, which implies the application of the principle of liberalism. Article XXIV of the GATT allows the participation of states in regional economic organisations, subject to compliance with the WTO principles. Thus, on 18 October 2011, CIS member states concluded the Treaty on a Free Trade Area between members of the Commonwealth of Independent states (CIS), entered into force on 20 October 2012 for Belarus, Russia and Ukraine, the first to ratify the treaty. On 25 October 2012, the President of Kazakhstan signed Law No. 46-V on ratification of the Treaty.

The absence of a single sectoral agreement on the settlement of grain trade issues within the EAEU significantly hinders the development of the regional Eurasian grain market. Yu. A. Khan suggests that the creation of a Single grain "holding" will allow structuring the Eurasian grain market, whose policy should be based on the principles of multi-vector and multipolarity.[19]

The regulation of the grain sector of the EAEU is carried out directly by the internal legislation of the member states. This indicates a lack of a single coordinated grain policy within the Union. Thus, the creation of a unified legal system for regulating the grain sector of the EAEU will contribute to the development of the agricultural sector of the Union's economy. The regional legal system for regulating the grain sector should take into account the interests of the member states of the Union in the conditions of their membership in the WTO.

*

In conclusion, the policy that determines the development of the grain sector of the economy of countries, mainly grain exporters, is aimed both at meeting the needs of the domestic market and at stimulating

---

usloviyahEvrazijskogoEkonomicheskogoSoyuza" *Problemyagrorynka* 2015, April-June, 53–64.

19 *Ibid.*

competition in the world market. Grain-producing countries use various instruments to legally regulate grain trade. Factors influencing the use of certain legal instruments include the level of economic development, the historical nature of state support, and WTO membership.

WTO membership requires states to apply only those measures of state support provided for by the Agreement on Agriculture. The laws of the majority of grain exporting countries to date contain the issues of providing state support measures to local farmers. states apply the following types of support: development of research work, determination of the minimum price for grain, provision of subsidies for infrastructure development, crop insurance, and others.

The grain market should also be regulated by an appropriate organisational management system. International experience has shown that the presence of special state bodies, whose powers include the regulation of food markets, provides effective control over the grain market. This is the avenue that must be explored in the coming months and years.

# Retail payments in times of health crisis in the Member states of the European Union[1]

Géraldine Le Labourier-Fleury Le Gros

On 24 September 2020, the European Commission presented its "retail payments strategy" for the European Union. According to the commission, "payments have become strategically significant. They are the lifeblood of the European economy".[2] While the economies of the European states are being severely tested by the health crisis, the study of payments therefore seems essential.

Retail payments are those made by non-financial agents – businesses or individuals – to cover their current expenses. In this area, the Covid-19 pandemic has changed practices, especially in France, as the latest report from the Observatory for the Security of Payment Means reveals.[3] Indeed, the closure of businesses or the health risks associated with their use have increased online purchases and, consequently, the volume of distance payments. At the same time, local shopping has given rise to more contactless payment by bank card or mobile phone. Today, contactless or remote card payment predominates.

While these payment methods undoubtedly contribute to health security, they do not offer the best financial security: the rate of fraudulent transactions is much higher for online and contactless payments than for card payments in contact mode, with typing of the holder's pin code. For the member states of the European Union, the challenge is therefore to find the balance between health security and financial security (I).

---

1 Translated from French by Amandine Cayol and Pierre Chabal.

2 Communication from the Commission to the European Parliament, the Council, the European Economic and social committee of the regions on a Retail Payments Strategy for the EU, COM (2020) 592 final of 24 September 2020.

3 *Rapport annuel de l'Observatoire de la sécurité des moyens de paiements 2019*, p. 7, available on line: <https://www.banque-france.fr>.

But this is not the only issue. Currently, there is no digital payment solution that can be used anywhere in Europe to make any type of retail payment. This situation benefits in particular the major global actors in card payment, such as VISA or Mastercard, based in the United States. Aware of the importance of digital payments in this time of health crisis, the European Commission highlights the need to create an instant European retail payment method, in order to strengthen European sovereignty in the area of payments (II)

## I. The predominance of contactless and remote card payment: The search for a balance between health security and financial security

During the first containment measures, the member states of the European Union wanted to support consumption. To this end, consumers have been encouraged to use payment methods that contribute to health security, such as contactless or remote card payment (A). But these payment methods present a higher risk of fraud which must be taken into account (B). Encouraging contactless or remote card payment therefore supposes maintaining consumer protection and consumer accountability rules (C).

### *A. Encouraging contactless and remote card payment as health security instruments*

Since 2017, Article 11 of the Commission Delegated Regulation supplementing the European Directive on payment services[4] admits the possibility of paying by contactless card within the limit for a single payment of 50 euros, provided that the cumulative amount of previous transactions without contact does not exceed 150 euros or that the number of consecutive contactless transactions does not exceed five operations.

---

[4] Commission Delegated Regulation (EU) 2018/389 of 27 November 2017 supplementing Directive (EU) 2015/2366 of the European Parliament and of the Council with regard to regulatory technical standards for strong customer authentication and common secure open standards for communication.

However, France, like other member states of the European Union, had been cautious in setting the unit payment ceiling at 30 euros. The health crisis has changed the negative perception of contactless payment. Indeed, contactless payment constitutes a barrier gesture against the spread of Covid. By simply presenting their card near a payment terminal, consumers do not touch anything, so that they avoid contamination from touching. In addition, contactless payment reduces checkout times and thereby lengthens queues in which the risk of contamination remains high.

Taking these aspects into account, the European banking authority recommended, in March 2020, to allow contactless payment up to the maximum unit payment limit. Following this recommendation, the French government has therefore raised the unit payment ceiling to 50 euros.[5]

In general, the health crisis has shown the value of using digital payments. The European Commission also wants to continue to encourage it and, if necessary impose, the acceptance of digital payments not only by shopkeepers but also by administrations, hospitals or public transport.[6] However, the health benefits of these payment methods should not obscure a major drawback: the increased risk of fraud.

## B. *The legal and technical consideration of the increased risk of fraud*

To understand the risk of fraud linked to payment by contactless (1) or remote (2) card, they should be studied separately.

### *1. Contactless payment*

In the event of payment by contactless card, payment is initiated by simply presenting the card near the beneficiary's payment terminal. From a technical point of view, this simple gesture can be done by anyone who is in possession of a card.

In France, the fraud rate for contactless card payments is 0.020 % of the total number of transactions and results almost exclusively from the

---

5 Art. 1er, ord. No. 2020-534 du 7 mai 2020 portant diverses dispositions en matière bancaire, *JORF*, 8 mai 2020.

6 COM (2020) 592 final of 24 September 2020, mentioned above.

loss or theft of the card.[7] This low rate is double the fraud rate of card payment at the point of sale. The increase in the unit limit for contactless payments therefore has an impact on fraud. By contributing to increase the volume of these payments and their average amount, it necessarily increases the amount of fraud. How can this risk be limited? At least three solutions can be implemented.

- First, the cardholder can deactivate and reactivate the contactless function of his card, by logging into his personal banking area. Disabling this function when it is not needed helps to limit the risk of fraud.
- Secondly, the use of scoring devices makes it possible to reinforce the security of contactless payments. This is what was decided in France for payments of 30–50 euros.[8] This technique makes it possible to detect unusual transactions, considered risky. This result leads to the refusal of contactless payment and requires cardholder authentication, which further limits the risk of fraud.
- Third, it is possible to combine the contactless function with an authentication system by deploying biometric cards, equipped with a fingerprint reader. Since fingerprints are unique, only cardholders authenticated by their fingerprints can make a contactless payment.[9] But these cards cannot be imposed on the consumer. The General Data Protection Regulation prohibits it.[10] Indeed, according to this regulation, the consumer must consent to the use of his biometric data for authentication purposes to pay by card. This consent must be free, which means leaving a real choice between a biometric payment card and other categories of cards. Biometric cards are therefore not intended to simply replace other types of cards in circulation.

---

7 *Rapport annuel de l'Observatoire de la sécurité des cartes de paiement 2019, op. cit.*, p. 29.

8 *Rapport annuel de l'Observatoire de la sécurité des moyens de paiement 2019, op. cit.*, p. 13.

9 *Rapport annuel de l'Observatoire de sécurité des moyens de paiements 2019, op. cit.*, p. 47.

10 Cf. art. 7 et 9 of Regulation (EU) 2016/679 of the European Parliament and of the Council of 27 April 2016 on the protection of natural persons with regard to the processing of personal data and on the free movement of such data, and repealing Directive 95/46/EC (General Data Protection Regulation), OJEU, 5 May 2016, L119/1.

After studying the risks and measures to combat fraud in the case of contactless card payment, let us consider the risks associated with online card payment.

## 2. Online payment

For online payment, the risk of fraud is even greater because it relies on the communication of the data appearing on the card: the card number, its expiration date and the EMV code on the back. Consequently, it is technically possible for a third party knowing this data to initiate an online payment, without the authorisation of the holder.

In France, the fraud rate for remote payments is 0.170 % of the total number of transactions,[11] a rate 17 times higher than the fraud rate for proximity payments. This higher rate, however, has decreased thanks to the implementation of technical cardholder authentication measures during the online payment process.[12] To further reduce fraud, these measures must now meet the *"strong customer authentication"* requirement imposed by the Directive of 25 November 2015 on payment services in the internal market, known as PSD2.[13]

Strong customer authentication requires compliance with three cumulative conditions:[14]

- First, the use of at least two elements of authentication of the cardholder by means of objects that only he has or data that only he knows or biometric data.

---

11 *Rapport annuel de l'Observatoire de la sécurité des moyens de paiement*, 2019, p. 24.

12 These technical measures include, for example, the 3-D-Secure protocol, whereby the cardholder receives a one-time validation code from his payment service provider, usually sent by SMS. Another example is the marketing of crypto-dynamic payment cards with an electronic ink display showing a temporary EMV code, which is changed, for example, every hour. See on this subject: *Rapport annuel de l'observatoire de la sécurité des moyens de paiement 2019*, *op. cit.*, p. 49.

13 Cf. art. 97 of Directive (EU) 2015/2366 of the European Parliament and of the Council of 25 November 2015 on payment services in the internal market, amending Directives 2002/65/EC, 2009/110/EC and 2013/36/EU and Regulation (EU) No .1093/2010, and repealing Directive 2007/64/EC, OJEU, 23 December 2015, L 337/35.

14 Cf. art. 4 PSD2.

- Then, these means of authentication must be independent of each other so that if one of them is compromised, the others remain reliable.
- Finally, the confidentiality of authentication data must be preserved.

Initially set for 14 September 2019,[15] the implementation of strong customer authentication has been postponed to 31 December 2020, on the advice of the European Banking Authority, to enable online payment actors to meet its technical requirements. And the health crisis has further delayed its deployment. This is now a priority. What will be the result in the fight against fraud? At this stage, it is difficult to assess its impact. According to the European Commission, fraud will decrease but will not disappear. At least two reasons can explain it:

- On the one hand, not all online payments are subject to strong customer authentication requirements: strong authentication is a principle, but several exceptions allow this principle not to be applied. For example, strong authentication is not required in the event of remote payment of a maximum amount of 30 euros, provided that the cumulative amount of previous operations without strong authentication does not exceed 100 euros or that the number of consecutive operations without strong authentication does not exceed five operations.[16]
- On the other hand, even if we can hope that strong customer authentication will reduce the fraud rate, its amount is likely to remain high due to the growing increase in the volume of online payments due, in part, to this health crisis of an exceptional duration.

In short, whether it is contactless or remote card payment, the possibilities to limit fraud exist. However, fraud remains a concern. These payment methods can therefore seem risky for the consumer. Encouraging these payment methods therefore requires maintaining consumer protection and accountability.

---

[15] Cf. art. 38 of Commission Delegated Regulation (EU) 2018/389, mentioned above.

[16] Cf. art. 16 of Regulation (EU) 2016/679, mentioned above.

## C. Maintaining consumer protection and accountability

Since the 2007 Payment Services Directive,[17] one of the objectives of the European Union has been to provide a high level of protection for consumers, victims of unauthorised payment transactions. Currently, article 74 of the PSD2 requires member states of the European Union to adopt the following solutions:

- In the event of a payment for which no strong authentication is required, the consumer does not bear any loss. This solution applies to contactless card payments as well as remote payments made without strong authentication.
- In the event of a payment for which strong authentication has been required, the consumer may be required to bear the losses resulting from the fraudulent use of his lost or stolen payment instrument or from its misappropriation. But, in this case, the maximum limit of losses suffered by the consumer is set at 50 euros. This solution this time concerns remote payments that have been subject to strong customer authentication.

The level of consumer protection is therefore very high. However, this protection should not encourage irresponsibility. Consequently, the consumer bears all losses in the event of fraudulent action on his part or intentional or grossly negligent non-compliance with his obligations.[18]

Among the obligations that raise the most difficulties, the holder of a payment card must take "all reasonable steps to keep its personalised security credentials safe".[19] So what to do if the cardholder who is a victim of phishing discloses this data to a malicious third party? Is he showing gross negligence? In France, the gross negligence of a payment service user who is a victim of phishing is assessed *in abstracto*, based on the behaviour of *"a normally attentive user"*, regardless of whether or not the victim is notified of phishing risks[20] or that the victim is acting

---

17 Directive 2007/64/EC of the European Parliament and of the Council of 13 November 2007 on payment services in the internal market amending Directives 97/7/EC, 2002/65/EC, 2005/60/EC and 2006/48/EC and repealing Directive 97/5/EC, OJEU, 5 December 2007, L. 319/1.

18 Cf. art. 74 PSD2.

19 Cf. art. 69, 2. PSD2.

20 Cass. Com. 28 mars 2018, No. 16-20018 P.

in good faith.[21] This solution may seem harsh, but it is at this price that the holder of a payment card remains generally well protected. This is a kind of balance between the need to protect and the need to hold the cardholder accountable.

In future, one may fear less favourable solutions for the consumer. In its judgment of 11 November 2020, the Court of Justice of the European Union qualifies the contactless function of a payment card as a payment instrument in its own right.[22] This solution makes it a special payment instrument, qualified under PSD2 as a "low value payments instrument".[23] However, for these instruments, the protection regime described above does not apply if the instrument *"is used anonymously"*.[24] And this is the case when a card is used in contactless mode.[25] Indeed, in contactless mode, it is impossible to identify the person who paid and therefore to show that the transaction was authorised by the card holder.[26] The analysis adopted by the CJEU may therefore lead the card holder to bear losses linked to unauthorised contactless transactions, up to a limit of 150 euros since above this limit, this function is blocked. Thus, it is not the faulty behaviour of the cardholder that would justify his liability here, but his simple choice to use the contactless function. Such a solution seems open to criticism this time. In times of health crisis, the use of the contactless function is not really a choice of the consumers but a necessity to ensure their protection and, in general, to contribute to the protection of society.

Since 2007, the harmonisation of payment laws has benefited the consumers. But consumer protection has undoubtedly reached its limits. Above all, harmonisation within the European Union is incomplete. From a technical point of view, card payment depends on national

---

[21] Cass. Com. 1[er] juil. 2020, Bull.civ. IV, No. 319; *D.* 2020, p. 1462. See on this decision: C. Bonnet, "Pas de prise en compte de la bonne foi en cas de négligence grave du porteur d'une carte de paiement", *D. actu.*, 31 août 2020; D. Legeais, "Appréciation de la négligence du titulaire de la carte", *RTD com.* 2020, p. 696. And for an overview of the issue of fraudulent card use after phishing: L.-C. Henry, "L'utilisation frauduleuse de la carte bancaire après hameçonnage: la recherche d'un équilibre", *D.* 2018, p. 2316.

[22] CJUE, 11 nov. 2020 – No. 287/19, available on line: www.curia.europa.eu.

[23] Art. 63, § 1 PSD2.

[24] Art. 63, § 1, b) PSD2.

[25] CJUE, 11 nov. 2020, *op. cit.*, pt 93.

[26] CJUE, 11 nov. 2020, *op. cit.*, pt 88 et 89.

networks which do not allow payment abroad, even within the European Union. The next step is therefore to create a European instant digital payment method.

## II. The creation of a European instant digital retail payment method: strengthening European sovereignty in the area of payments

The creation of a European instant digital payment method is part of the European Commission retail payment strategy. This desire results from the dependence of European card payment players on global payment networks (A). In order to overcome this situation, the SEPA instant credit transfer appears to be the reference instrument for creating a new payment method (B), the chances of success of which will have to be assessed (C).

### *A. Observation of dependence on global card payment networks*

According to the European Central Bank, 10 European countries still have national schemes that do not allow card payments from other EU member states. Payments abroad, within the Union, therefore require going through global networks, such as Visa or Mastercard, all based in the United States. These networks therefore dominate the market for intra-European cross-border payments.

The European Commission makes the same observation: with the exception of solutions offered by global card payment networks (Visa or Mastercard) or by large technology companies (Apple Pay and Google Pay), there is virtually no solution to digital payment, usable across Europe, to make payments in stores and in e-commerce. Several FinTechs operating on a national scale, in the member states of the European Union, consider that this fragmentation hinders their efforts to expand into the Single market. To remedy this situation of dependence, the Commission considers that it is therefore necessary to create a European instant payment method, for the purposes of making any type of retail payment; a different way from the current card payment. On this point, the Commission welcomes in particular the European Payments Initiative – EPI –, launched on 2 July 2020, by 16 European banks.

The EPI offers a solution to pay a beneficiary anywhere in Europe, seven days a week, instantly. The objective is to carry out all types of transactions: local payment – at a point of sale –, online payment in the context of electronic commerce and payment among individuals. This ambitious project is based on an existing payment instrument: the SEPA instant credit transfer.

## B. SEPA instant credit transfer as a benchmark instrument for the creation of a new European instant digital payment method

The bank transfer enables one to transfer a sum of money from one account to another, with a simple scripture. This instrument is mainly used to make payments of a large amount (for example, paying the rent, wages or tuition fees). In France, the bank transfer is the instrument with the lowest fraud rate.

Due to the advancement of e-commerce and the digitalisation of the economy, the European Payments Council in 2017 created the SEPA instant credit transfer. This makes it possible a transfer, in 10 seconds, to any other account in the SEPA area, 24 hours a day, 7 days a week. This therefore makes it a particularly interesting tool to inspire the project led by the EPI. To better understand this, we can compare the SEPA instant credit transfer with payment by card. This comparison will thus make it possible to highlight its advantages (1) and its disadvantages (2)

### *1. The advantages of SEPA instant credit transfer*

When it comes to the benefits of SEPA instant credit transfer there are many. We will mention three.

- First, the processing time is 10 seconds, after accepting the debit from the payer's account. From this point of view, it has nothing to envy to payment by card.
- Second, the SEPA instant credit transfer allows for very large payments, and even between individuals, which is not possible with card payments. Originally at a maximum amount of 15,000 euros per transaction, it was increased to 100,000 euros on 1 July 2020 by the European Payments Council. It is therefore possible to pay for a car by means of a SEPA instant credit transfer while such a

payment is not possible with a card that has a significantly lower limit on the amount of use.

- Finally, the SEPA instant credit transfer offers a certain security to the payer and to the beneficiary. First, payment security for the payee, since the payor's account balance is checked before the debit is accepted, contrary to what can happen in the case of payment by card. For this reason, the amount transferred to the beneficiary's account is immediately available. Secondly, a more secure instrument in terms of fraud than remote card payments, because the SEPA instant credit transfer avoids the communication of data appearing on a payment card. Given the risk of online card payment fraud, mentioned above, the SEPA instant credit transfer appears to be a less risky instrument in terms of fraud.

However, instant transfer has its drawbacks.

## 2. *The disadvantages of SEPA instant credit transfer*

There are at least two disadvantages to note:

- First, the payer must designate the beneficiary's account, in particular by means of his IBAN identifier. This can give rise to difficulties in the event of an error in the designation of the beneficiary's account because the instant transfer is irrevocable. Above all, the IBAN is sensitive data that should be protected from any fraudulent use. The latest report from the Observatory for the Security of Payment Means shows that the IBAN is data liable to be misused for the purpose of carrying out fraudulent direct debits.[27] Thus, the beneficiary of a SEPA instant credit transfer may fear, when communicating his IBAN, that malicious third parties will intercept this data and use the IBAN to debit his bank account, without his authorisation. In addition, to make a SEPA instant credit transfer, the payer must connect to his personal banking area, via the website of his bank or a mobile application. Access to this banking area requires the use of customer identification data, generally an identifier and a confidential code. Again, this is sensitive data as it provides access to a webpage containing banking information and payment features. The payer must therefore be vigilant to preserve the security of this data, by keeping it secret.

---

[27] *Rapport annuel de l'observatoire de la sécurité des moyens de paiement 2019*, *op. cit.*, p. 41.

– Secondly, the SEPA instant credit transfer is chargeable. The most common cost is 1 euro per transaction, while the cost of using a payment card is significantly lower. The average cost of a traditional payment card is 40 euros per year, regardless of the number of transactions carried out.

So, in light of this quick comparison, what are we to think of the future European instant payment method?

## C. The chances of success for European Payments Initiative – EPI

As with any payment instrument, the success of European Payments Initiative will depend not only on its flexibility of use, on its cost but above all on its security.

With regard to flexibility of use, EPI specifically wants to provide consumers with a single payment solution allowing all types of transactions to be carried out. Currently, the use of payment instruments is fragmented: consumers have several instruments serving very distinct uses: i/ the payment card is used to make local purchases or distance purchases, within the framework of electronic commerce; ii/ the bank transfer is used to pay rent or tuition fees; iii/ the direct debit is used to pay for telephone or electricity subscription.

The EPI wishes to offer a single payment solution allowing all types of transactions to be carried out, even between individuals. From this point of view, this payment method will probably seem more flexible in use.

On the cost side, the EPI project will only be successful if the cost of this new payment method remains reasonable. The European Commission believes that the fees for Instant Payments should be the same as regular bank transfers, otherwise Instant Payments will remain a niche product. It seems to us that the cost should be similar to that of a payment card since it is currently the most widely used payment instrument, and therefore the most successful instrument.

Finally, the success of the EPI project will depend on consumer confidence in this new payment method. To attract consumers, the European Commission advocates placing the new European instant payment method on an equal footing with other instruments, such as cards. This can be easily achieved since the SEPA instant credit transfer, on which the EPI is based, is governed like payment by card. In the event of an unauthorised payment transaction, the consumer is therefore well protected.

One will have to wait until the Summer of 2022, as the period announced for the operational launch of the EPI.

# Short-selling regulations and regulatory improvements in Korea since Covid-19

Hye-Hwal Seong

"Short sale" or "short selling" refers to the sale of securities that an investor does not own. There are two ways to make it possible to sell for someone who does not own any securities. One is called "covered short selling" in which an investor sells stocks borrowed from others through lending transactions. The *Financial Services and Capital Market Act* (FSCMA) treats the sale of borrowed stocks differently from the sale of one's own stocks and applies complex short selling regulations such as marking an order as a short selling order and limiting selling prices.

The other is called "naked short selling", where one sells when one does not have any own stocks nor has any borrowed stocks. The reason why naked short selling is possible is that the consignment margin in a stock account serves as a collateral. The securities firms can complete a transaction by the settlement date (the "T+2" system) after allowing the sale of the stock based on the consignment margin by counter-selling or receiving the stock.

Prior to 2000, both institutions and individual investors could make naked short selling on the stock exchange. This is now prohibited since 2000 in Korea yet naked short selling is technically possible for institutional investors and foreign investors. Even if do not have stocks in their accounts, they can place selling orders providing they confirm that they can fill their accounts with the stocks by the settlement date. Individual investors are not allowed to submit selling orders if they do not have stocks in their accounts, making it technically impossible to make naked short selling. The FSCMA strictly prohibits naked short selling, and violations are subject to almost the same level of penalties as insider trading and market manipulation. Even, monetary penalty by the *Financial Supervisory Commission* is imposed for the violation.

Although short selling itself is not an unfair trading, it is closely related to unfair trading because it is possible to manipulate the market price by artificially lowering the price and let a person with bad information make unfair profits through short selling. In addition, since it can cause settlement defaults and stock price decline in a crisis, most countries regulate short selling in various ways while, still, allowing it.

Short selling has been a much debated issue in the Korean stock market over the past twenty years. Foreigners and institutional investors account for almost all short selling while individual investors account for only 1 % of short selling, leading to controversy over the unfairly inclined playground to individual investors. As the public opinion of around 70 % appears to be negative for short selling, most individual investors attack short selling as an 'axis of evil' and even insist on a complete ban, while financial authorities and market experts say that such attacks are too much of a 'witch hunting' and has been putting an emphasis on gradual improvement of the short sale regulation.

If short selling, which has been banned since March last year due to the Covid-19 outbreak, resumes later in 2021, it is expected that individual investors' campaign against short selling will take place again. This article examines the history of short-selling regulation and regulatory changes since Covid-19 and suggests desirable improvement direction of the short selling regulation in Korea.

## I. The history of short selling regulation

The first short selling regulation in the history of the world occurred in 1610 for the shares of the East India Company on the Amsterdam Stock Market in Netherlands, the beginning of the modern stock market.

Isaac Le Maire, who was once a director of the East India Company and now having a dispute with the company, had pushed the company's stock price down through naked short selling and spreading false and misleading rumors. Accordingly, the directors of the East India Company at the time urged the Dutch Republic Parliament to ban short selling, saying that short selling "causes unmeasurable damage to naive investors such as orphans and widows" and the Parliament passed a bill banning short selling on 27 February 1610. However, the world's first ban on short selling was ineffective, and in 1689 it was finally changed to taxing the profits from short selling instead of a total ban.

In the UK, the South Sea company bubble burst in 1720 and caused great losses to even Isaac Newton. Criticism had been heavily poured out on short selling and in 1734 eventually short selling was banned by law. However, the law was not enforced properly and was repealed in 1860.

In France, short selling was prohibited by an emperor's decree in 1724. Furthermore, in 1802, Napoleon 1$^{st}$ mandated the receipt of real securities in all securities transactions and made short selling a crime. However, this law was also weakly enforced and abolished in 1885.

In the USA, Congress banned the short sale of gold traded on the New York Stock Exchange in June 1864, but it was discarded after only two weeks due to rising prices. In addition, when the stock market collapsed in 1929, short selling was criticised as the main cause of the stock price crash, and restrictions on short selling of securities began in earnest. Since the Securities and Exchange Commission enacted the "uptick rule" in 1938, the short sale regulation has been revised several times since then and is currently regulated under the "Regulation SHO".

In Korea, the history of short selling regulation began in 1996 with the introduction of a securities lending system that allowed inter-institutional lending for listed stocks. Short selling was possible even before the introduction of this system because the 'future trading' system then was abolished, and the current ordinary trading system was adopted in 1969 in which short sellers could borrow stocks to sell from securities firm. The need for regulation for short selling, however, was weak as it was difficult to achieve large-scale short selling due to small amounts of stocks open to be lent by securities firms and credit regulations on them. Whereas the new inter-institutional lending system might trigger a large volume of short selling.

Accordingly, in order to prevent the risk of a plunge in the stock price due to short selling and to stabilise investors' anxiety, the stock exchange introduced the "uptick rule" in September 1996 which prohibited submission of orders with the selling price below the previous transaction price.

The history of short selling regulation in Korea then eventually began.

In November 1997, inter-institutional stock lending was allowed for KOSDAQ stocks and foreign investors too could participate in inter-institutional lending system in 1998 leading to a far more activated short selling.

Until May 2000, short selling had been widely carried out as a plausible investment strategy sometimes crossing over price manipulation since there was no rule banning short selling in principle except for the uptick rule and this price regulation was not so effective. Therefore, it is not an exaggeration to say that short selling was almost unlimited at the time.

In 2000, due to a naked short sale accident by Woopoong Savings Bank, naked short selling came to be completely banned. In March, Woopoong Savings Bank sold 350,000 shares of Seongdo ENG (a KOSDAQ-listed company) and faced a sharp rise in the stock price leading to failure of delivery of the shares to buyers by settlement date (two days after the transaction). After the accident, the government in June 2000 let the exchange's rules be changed to prohibit naked short selling and to indicate whether to sell short when placing an order.

Since then, the short selling regulation had remained unchanged until 2008.

The global financial crisis in 2008 and the European fiscal crisis in 2011 brought shock waves to the stock market, leading to total bans on short selling in many countries around the world. The Korean financial authority, Financial Supervisory Commission, banned short selling for all listed stocks on Korea Exchange including KOSDAQ market for eight months (1 October 2008 to 31 May 2009). In 2011 again, from 10 August to 9 November, short selling was banned for 3 months.

In 2016, the covered short selling net position reporting and the disclosure system were introduced into the FSCMA, which had been regulated until then by the rules of Financial Investment Business Association. And on 16 March 2020, right after the Covid-19, it was decided to ban short selling for all listed stocks for the third time. However, short selling was exceptionally allowed for market makers[1] who supply liquidity to the market even during the period. Accordingly, the balance of short selling position has been steadily maintained even though the total ban on short selling.

Currently, short selling regulations exist in various ways in the FSCMA and rules and regulations of the Korea Exchange. The law stipulates the prohibition of naked short selling, the concept and scope of

---

1 A market maker refers to a securities company that plays a role in activating trading by submitting bidirectional orders for stocks that do not trade much. It is often called a liquidity provider.

short selling, the obligation to report and disclose the net balance of short selling, restrictions on the acquisition of IPO shares by short sellers, and criminal penalties and government's monetary penalties for illegal short selling.

The exchange's rules stipulate the method of placing short selling orders, price limitation for covered short selling (uptick rule), follow-up management of short selling orders, and exceptions to market makers.

## II. Changes after Covid-19

### *(a) Temporary short selling ban and resumption*

The Financial Supervisory Commission implemented a temporary ban on short selling of all listed stocks on the Korean stock market based on the FSCMA for six months from 16 March 2020 to 15 September 2020, fearing rapid market volatility caused by Covid-19. Six months later, the ban was extended for another six months to 15 March 2021 as Covid-19 re-spread ahead of the end of the ban and market volatility expanded again. However, individual investors' opposition to the short sale was intensified and they contended for even a permanent ban on short selling.

Given the conflicting situation, the government decided to extend the ban on short selling again to 2 May 2021 and proceed supplement actions for resuming short selling. Short selling resumed on 3 May 2021 on medium and large sized stocks (KOSPI 200 and KOSDAQ 150 index stocks) while the ban on short selling will be extended without a deadline for the time being.

### *(b) The increase of individual investors and stock market booming since Covid-19*

Since Covid-19, individual investors have increased sharply in the Korean stock market, and accordingly, various indicators of the stock market such as deposit money for stock trading and trading value have increased significantly.

As of the end of 2020, each indicator is as follows.

- The number of individual investors surged from 6.12 million at the end of 2019 to 9.14 million at the end of 2020, the largest increase rate in history: 49 %. Among them, 32.8 % of 9.14 million individual investors started stock trading in 2020. In particular, the number of individual investors of young people under 30 increased by 103 % (1.6 million) compared with the previous year in 2020. The number of women stockholders increased 61 % from 2.41 million to 3.89 million while that of men increased 41 % from 3.73 million in 2019 to 5.25 million in 2020.

As of the end of April 2021, the number of individual investors is estimated to exceed 10 million.

- The amount of stocks held per individual investor was 77.45 million won, almost twice the GDP per capita (37.17 million won). The number of active accounts[2] for stock trading exceeded 40 million for the first time in history. Considering that the number of residents registered in Korea at the end of 2020 was about 52 million, and 43 million people were over 20, almost all of them had one personal account.

The number of accounts has consistently increased since Covid-19.

- In 2020, individual investors bought a net 47.49 trillion KRW in the KOSPI market. They bought a net 16.32 trillion KRW in the KOSDAQ market (13.6 billion US dollars). At that time, the institutional investors net sold 25.54 trillion KRW in the KOSPI market and 10.45 trillion KRW in the KOSDAQ market. Foreign investors net sold 24.65 trillion KRW in the KOSPI market and 147.6 billion KRW in the KOSDAQ market in 2020.
- Deposited money for stock trading by individual investors increased 140 % from 27 trillion KRW at the end of 2019 to 65 trillion KRW at the end of 2020, and credit loans borrowed from securities firms by individual investors increased by 100 % from 9 trillion KRW at the end of 2019 to 19 trillion KRW at the end of 2020.
- The KOSPI index, Korea's leading index, rose 30 % from 2197.67 point on 30 December 2019 to 2837.47 point at the end of 2020, while the average daily trading volume of the entire stock market (KOSPI+ KOSDAQ) stood at 22.9 trillion KRW, up 100 % from a record high of 11.5 trillion KRW in 2018 and up 150 % from 9.3 trillion KRW in 2019.

---

2 An active account refers to a stock account that has more than 100,000 won in the account and has been traded at least once in 6 months.

## (c) Individual investors' strong arguments against short selling

Individual investors, who have increased rapidly since Covid-19, have argued against short selling more systematically, with an individual investors' organisation at the core. In October 2019, to protect the rights and interests of individual investors, an organisation called the Korea Investors Association was established as a non-profit organisation. It has been actively engaged in activities for investor protection as individual investors have rapidly increased since the spread of Covid-19 in 2020. As of the end of April 2021, the number of members was around 45,000.

Recently, in the USA, there was a case of short squeeze of hedge funds that sold short GameStop stock by WallstreetBets, an Internet forum for individual investors. The Korea Investors Association is using WallstreetBets as its role model for KstreetBets to rally up the power of individual investors.

Throughout the past year in Korea, the Association has consistently raised the following arguments against short selling. It opposes the full resumption of short selling which has been temporarily prohibited; The Hong Kong-style short selling system,[3] which allows short selling only to large-cap stocks, should be introduced; For illegal short selling such as naked short selling, the level of criminal penalties must be raised and a punitive damage compensation introduced. In addition, it is argued that a system that is fully computerised and can monitor naked short selling in real time is necessary for strict prohibition and effective monitoring of naked short selling.

The government and the National Assembly have accepted many of these arguments. In other words, short selling was partially resumed from 3 May 2021 and it is decided to allow only mid and large-cap stocks like Hong Kong. In addition, the FSCMA was revised to punish criminal with penalties for illegal short selling severely almost at the same level as unfair trading such as insider trading and price manipulation. However, the real-time monitoring system to prevent naked short selling was not

---

3 Hong Kong style short selling is a system that allows short selling only in stocks with a market capitalization of more than 3 billion Hong Kong dollars and a 12-month turnover rate (the rate at which stockholders change) is 60 % or more. This is a system that restricts short selling to large stocks rather than prohibiting all stocks.

accepted because it is excessive: not all cars are equipped with an alcohol detection device to prevent drunk driving.

Currently, individual investors are still pressing for the introduction of a real-time monitoring system for naked short selling and even demanding that short selling be banned permanently.

### (d) Revision of the law and changes of regulatory system

The revised bill of the FSCMA, which significantly strengthened the short selling regulation, passed the National Assembly in December 2020 and went into effect in April 2021. The contents are as follows.

First, the level of criminal punishment has been significantly increased. Previously, it was limited to a fine of 100 million KRW or less, but now illegal short selling will be punished by imprisonment for one year or more, or a fine of three times to five times the illegal profits which is almost the same level as insider trading and price manipulation. However, while for insider trading and price manipulation, if illegal profits exceed 500 million KRW, three years or more is aggravated by imprisonment, but there is no aggravated punishment clause for violations of the short selling regulation.

Next, by introducing a regulation similar to Regulation M of the USA, a person who sold short after the announcement of the capital increase plan of a listed corporation is prohibited from participating in the capital increase. Exceptions to this regulation are allowed when there is no harm to the fairness of the public offering price. In case of violating this provision, a monetary penalty is imposed by the Financial Supervisory Commission, and the limit of the penalty is not more than 5 million KRW. If the amount of 1.5 times illegal profits exceeds 5 million KRW, then the penalty will be 1.5 times illegal profits.

In addition, in order to secure the truthfulness of covered short selling, information on the stock lending-borrowing transaction for the purpose of short-selling (contract date and time, counterparty, item/quantity, lending commission rate, lending period, etc.) is kept for five years. A person who is obligated to store lending transaction information shall submit such data without delay if requested by the Financial Supervisory Commission or the Korea Exchange. Violation of this obligation to store and submit lending transaction information is subject to a fine of 60 million KRW for corporations and up to 30 million KRW for non-corporations.

Next, the legitimacy of the measure of prohibition of short selling was reinforced by directly stipulating in the law the ground for the government's measure which was stipulated in Presidential Decree in the past.

Apart from the revision of the law and the Presidential Decree, the following system was introduced to supplement the short selling system.

First, by introducing a new individual lending system, the amount of short selling by individual investors has been expanded by more than 100 times than in the past. The new lending system is aimed to dispel controversy over the unfair playing fields by drastically expanding short selling opportunities for individual investors, which account for only 1 % of short selling.

Next, from 16 March 2021, in order to reduce excessive short selling by market makers, it hardens the regulation for the market makers such as i/ prohibiting the stock market short selling by the market makers of the Mini KOSPI200, ii/ the unexceptional application of the uptick rule to market makers. In addition, the Commission plans to shorten the detection cycle of naked short selling (6 months → 1 month) and to strengthen post detection and surveillance of illegal short selling through advanced detection techniques.

## III. The positive function of short selling and the need to maintain it

Although a lot of controversy has been raised and even an argument for a permanent ban is raised, the short selling system needs to be maintained considering the positive functions and international coherence of regulations as follows.

First, short selling greatly contributes to fair and reasonable pricing, yet it is strange that it exists. Except the short sellers, all market participants – like investors, companies and the government – dislike short selling. So why has short selling existed through a long history? Because it plays a large role in contributing to fair and rational pricing by detecting and dismissing false information such as fraudulent accounting and stock price manipulation, and by establishing a counterbalance with credit buying (buying with borrowed money) to balance the market. A fair and reasonable price is a stock price that fits into the intrinsic value of a company. The prices of individual stocks are collected as a stock index, and the stock index becomes i/ a representative economic indicator and ii/ the basic data for economic activities of all people in a country. Accordingly, the stock market efficiently performs the resource allocation function in the national economy. The investor's trust that should be protected is also given to the assumption that stock prices are fair and reasonable. Therefore, the most fundamental protective value that precedes all values in the stock market that the price of individual stocks is formed in accordance with the intrinsic values of companies.

Second, as discussed above, the short selling system has passed the verification of time since its role or function was sufficiently recognised in the history of the global stock market during already 420 years.

Third, short selling is an internationally practiced system. Short selling is allowed in almost all countries that have a stock market. Even in this Covid-19 outbreak, most countries did not ban short selling, and even if they banned it, only Korea and Indonesia have maintained short selling ban for such long periods of time.

Fourth, if short selling is not allowed, foreign investors can leave. Foreign investors have a significant impact on the Korean economy and the stock market. The government has long made great efforts to join the FTSE and MSCI indices, which are keys in attracting foreign investment. However, if there is a Galapagos regulation such as a short selling ban that is not in major countries, the Korea discount may increase due to the departure of foreign investors.

Fifth and foremost, Korea is the most stringent country in the world that regulates short selling. In September 2020, the government and the National Assembly decided to extend the ban for six months on condition of the improvement of the short selling problem. Accordingly, the FSCMA which greatly strengthened penalties for short selling violations was passed. Now, short-selling violations can be punished by severe criminal and administrative penalties and this is stricter than the enforcement against unfair trading such as insider trading given the administrative penalty which is not applied to unfair trading. Under the current law, short selling using non-public material information is punished by insider trading, and short selling for stock price manipulation is punished by price manipulation.

Therefore, the punishment for illegal short selling can be said too harsh compared to the blamableness of the act since the new short sale penalty provision will be applied to simple short selling orders coming from errors.

Compared with foreign countries, in the case of criminal penalties, only Hong Kong punishes with imprisonment for naked short selling and the imprisonment penalty is two years and less. Japan has a 300,000 yen monetary penalty for illegal short selling. There is a misunderstanding for the case of the USA (20 years or less imprisonment), often used as a representative basis for the claim to strengthen criminal penalties for illegal short selling. The imprisonment clause of 20 years or less in Section 32 of the US Securities Exchange Act of 1934 is a comprehensive rule that sets limits on penalties for all violations of this law and should not be viewed as a basis for penalising short selling violations specifically.

In fact, there has been no case of criminal punishment for illegal short selling ever. Moreover, the USA has abolished the uptick rule, yet an important device to prevent price decline due to short selling orders, unlike Korea.

*

Concluding on the desirable future regulatory direction, this paper argues for the positive function of short selling and the need to resume short selling but … the backlash of individual investors against short selling should also be understood.

The hostility of individual investors over short selling comes from the fear of falling prices but there are also great dissatisfaction with the inequality of opportunity such as 1 % versus 99 % and the allegations of insider trading by institutional and foreign investors using material non-public information. Therefore, the government should make special efforts to restore the trust of individual investors by expanding the opportunities for short selling by individual investors as much as possible, and clarify whether there is insider trading by institutional and foreign investors through rigorous investigation of large-scale short selling right before an important corporate disclosure.

The government has taken measures to significantly expand short selling opportunities for individual investors ahead of the resuming of short selling for medium and large-cap stocks (constituents of KOSPI200 and

KOSDAQ150) from 3 May 2021. In other words, in order to resolve the unfairness of the playground, which is positively inclined to institutions and foreign investors, the new individual lending system will provide about 100 times the amount available for short sale than the amount available in the previous lending system. On the other hand, measures such as preliminary training, simulation transactions, and restrictions on the number of lendable stocks are introduced to protect individual investors from the risk of short selling which may cause infinite losses.

Given all the measures taken by the government, this is a reasonable level of regulation. Therefore, it is desirable to watch the enforcement of the revised law and the operation of the new individual lending system for the time being and consider whether to supplement it in the future.

# The principle of separation of patrimonies in France put to the test of the 2020 *Solidarity Fund*[1]

Pierre Fleury Le Gros

The first half of 2020 was marked by the onset of the Covid crisis and its profound impact on French economic activity. Some statistics produced by INSEE enable us to measure its impact:[2] more than 4 companies out of 5 believe they have suffered a drop in their activity. For a third of them, this drop represents between 10 and 50 % of turnover compared to the same period in 2019. For another third, this drop represents more than 50 %. Some activities have been more affected than others: in the cultural activities sector, losses of more than 50 % concern 7 companies out of 10…

In an attempt to curb the impact of the crisis, the French Government has put in place various aids including i/ loans guaranteed by the state, ii/ deferral of social charges and iii/ the *solidarity fund*. The latter, intended for companies particularly affected by the economic consequences of the spread of the epidemic, was established by ordinance No. 2020-317 of 25 March 2020. Its article 1 provides that the *solidarity fund* has the purpose of the payment of financial aid to natural and legal persons governed by private law who exercise an economic activity particularly affected. At the heart of the concerns of this Ordinance, we find, on the one hand, the economic, financial and social consequences of the spread of Covid-19, and on the other hand, the measures taken to limit its spread, such as closures imposed on businesses considered to be "non-essential".

The possibility of benefiting from the payment of aid is subject to conditions, which are specified by decree. Since the start of the crisis,

---

1 Translated from the French by Amandine Cayol and Pierre Chabal.

2 See the French National Statistics Institute: <https://www.insee.fr/fr/statistiques/4994488#titre-bloc-6>.

no less than four successive decrees have been adopted,[3] the conditions imposed having partially changed.

This chapter analyses one of these conditions, the one the application of which gives rise to various objections. The seriousness of these objections is assessed on several levels. These objections range from i/ a simple lack of opportunity to ii/ questioning the distinction made in French law between the patrimony of a legal person and the patrimony of its managers, as natural persons. In its initial version, article 1–6 ° of the decree specified that the system was applicable on the condition that *natural persons or, for legal persons, their majority manager, (1) are not holders, on 1 March 2020, of a full-time employment contract or an old-age pension and (2) did not benefit, during the period between 1 March 2020 and 31 March 2020, from daily social security allowances of an amount greater than 800 euros.* Over the course of the decrees, the text has been revised and the conditions have changed slightly. But the general principle of the exclusion operated by the decree (due to the existence of an employment contract) remains the same. However, it is precisely this principle that is the source of questions.

The aid can be paid to two categories of companies hit by the crisis: on the one hand, single-family enterprises or "business in its own name", on the other hand, enterprises with legal personality. Although the text places them on the same level, a distinction must be made.

With regard to individual enterprises, the restriction enacted by the decree can be criticized for a simple lack of expediency, without this restriction calling into question the principle of distinction between the patrimony of the legal person and that of its manager. This concerns individual entrepreneurs who operate their activity using their own assets. The dangers inherent in this mode of exploitation have often been analysed.[4] In French law, the attribution of legal personality results from birth. The consequence of this birth is to assign the natural person who has just been born a *patrimony*, that is to say a single container intended to house his assets and liabilities. This container will last until his death, the end of the existence of legal personality immediately resulting in the

---

3 Decrees No. 2020-314 of 25 March 2020, No. 2020-873 of 16 July 2020, No. 2020-1200 of 30 September 2020 and No. 2020-1328 of 2 November 2020.

4 D. Legeais, *Droit commercial et des affaires*, 22e éd., Sirey, No. 291, p. 143; S. Piedelièvre, *Droit commercial*, Cours Dalloz, No. 126, p. 122; M. Cozian, A. Viandier and F. Deboissy, *Droit des sociétés*, 32e éd., Lexis Nexis No. 44, p. 18.

disappearance of the patrimony. Every natural person therefore has a patrimony and only one, in which his debts and receivables are intended to go, the mass of assets being intended to meet all the liabilities. In this unique patrimony, there is no partitioning between personal assets and liabilities, and professional assets and liabilities. In other words, the natural person must answer for all of her debts, professional or not, with all of her assets, whether these are for professional or purely private use.[5] Only the creation of an EIRL allows the creation of a patrimony allocated to the exercise of the activity, thus authorising the manager to confine the risks to the assets that it involves.[6] This unicity of the patrimony then explains the restriction operated by article 1–6 ° of the decree. Partially at least.

In such a situation, the aid beneficiary is indeed the natural person, manager of the company. Since there are not two distinct patrimonies, the financial aid will necessarily be paid into the assets of his personal patrimony. However, the aim of the legislator is to reserve this aid for the most deprived people, in order to limit the effects of the crisis, which may have the consequence of suppressing any financial return into the assets of the patrimony and to aggravate the liabilities. Reserving this aid for the most deprived leads the legislator, logically, to choose to limit its payment to people whose only source of income is that affected by the crisis. It then logically excludes from the scope of this aid people who have a full-time employment contract in parallel of this activity and this activity becomes somewhat "secondary". The exclusion is understandable, because the full-time employment contract necessarily consists of a "main" activity; the salary received must be the main source; and the second activity, that impacted by Covid, provides more of an additional income. Consequently, the fact of not being able to exercise his second activity exercised under the regime of the sole proprietorship will certainly cause a, sometimes, consequent reduction in income, but

---

5 The Economic Initiative Act of 2 August 2013 reduced the scope of this risk by introducing a system of "declaration of unseizability" designed to protect the main residence. The risk to assets was thus reduced, without however making it disappear completely. The Macron Act of 2015, which instituted de jure unseizability of this residence, increased this protection by making it automatic, but it does not solve the problem in its entirety for the rest of the assets, which remain subject to the risk.

6 F. Terré, "La personne et ses patrimoines ou l'EIRL", *JCP* E 2011, 1011; B. Dondero, "L'EIRL ou l'entrepreneur fractionné", *JCP* 2010, act. 379.

not a total deprivation of resources. He is therefore not one of the most deprived people, if we refer to the spirit of the law.

It will be objected, however, that depending on the social system chosen by the manager, this manager risks having to dispense with the minimum contributions inherent in his status (in particular "retirement" contributions and "sickness" contributions), which may mean several thousand euros per year, even though this activity may be completely stopped due to the Covid-19 crisis. Deprived of aid, the manager will then have to assume the costs of this parallel activity with the income derived from another activity, which seems unfair. In other words, it would have been logical for him to receive the aid so as to prevent him from being forced to pay liabilities, even though state restrictions prevent him from carrying out the activity which can justify their payment. Whether we approve of this solution or not, this solution does not, however, infringe the principle of separation of patrimonies. It is at the same time the consequence of the principle. As regards activities carried out by means of the creation of a legal person, however, the situation is different.

The text leads to excluding, from the benefit of the aid, legal persons whose majority manager holds a full-time employment contract. The question then arises of the interpretation of the text: does it refer to the case of an employment contract binding the manager to his company, or the case of an employment contract binding him to another entity than the company that he manages?

*A priori*, one might be tempted to think that the text targets both hypotheses, on the basis that where the law does not distinguish, there is no need to distinguish. Indeed, Article 1–6° does not make a distinction as to whether the employment contract was concluded in the company managed, or in another company. Moreover, it is in this sense that the DGFIP (directorate general of public finances) interprets the text. However, this interpretation is subject to criticism: the application of the text with regard to managers who have entered into an employment contract outside the company that they manage violates the principle of separation of patrimonies. Consequently, compliance with this principle should lead the DGFIP to confining this limitation only to persons who have concluded a contract in the company that they manage. We will find, however, that this would inevitably have the consequence of considerably reducing the scope of the text. And it is then the question of the advisability of its creation and its drafting as it is that should be asked. It will therefore be necessary to distinguish, on the one hand, the hypothesis of the contract concluded in the managed company (part I), and on the other hand, the hypothesis of the contract concluded with another company than that which is managed (part II).

## I. The majority manager with a contract in the company he manages

French law does not prohibit a director of a company from also being an employee of that company. But this possibility is subject to many restrictions which do not always allow such a combination for the majority manager. An overview of some of the main forms of legal persons will therefore make it possible to ensure that the majority manager holding a contract in his company can be one of the targets of the prohibition caused by article 1–6 ° of the decree.

In certain forms of companies, the majority manager cannot also be an employee of the legal person that he manages. This is particularly the case in limited liability company. If the combination of managerial functions and employee status is permitted, this is on a three-fold condition.

First of all, the employment contract must correspond to actual work, that is, to actual employment.

Then, the functions performed by the employee must be distinct from the general management functions that he performs as manager.

Finally, there must be a relationship of subordination between the employee and the manager. It is this 3rd condition that poses a problem when the manager has a majority since the control he holds in the company seems to be exclusive of any relationship of subordination.

When he is a minority share-holder, the manager is already in a delicate position. It is indeed difficult to prove the existence of the relationship of subordination, even though he finds himself in a situation where, as a manager, he must give himself orders in the context of his salaried job. This situation is delicate but not incompatible with the status of employee: the fact of being in the minority makes it possible to consider that a form of subordination with regard to the legal person remains, since the manager can be dismissed by a decision of the majority that he does not control.[7]

---

[7] However, this approach has been criticised for conflating the two statuses of the person concerned.: M. Deslandes, "Réflexion sur le cumul d'un mandat social et d'un contrat de travail", *D.* 1982. Chron. 19.

When he is a majority shar-holder, this residual form of subordination no longer exists at all, even though it constitutes an essential criterion of the employment contract. The Court of Cassation thus excludes the possibility that the majority manager of the limited liability company is also an employee (since a *Cavois* judgment of 7 February 1979). This exclusion is not unique to the french "S.A.R.L" (a kind of limited liability company). It is also found in the french "S.A" (another kind of limited liability company), for example for its managing director.[8]

In other forms of company, such as the French S.N.C (general partnership), this exclusion is not obvious. This issue gives rise to a hesitant doctrine[9] on the interpretation to be given to a case law which sometimes seems contradictory.[10] The same is true for the French S.A.S. (simplified join stock company) in which case-law does not seem to exclude this possibility, as well as for the French S.A.S.U (single-member simplified join stock company). The whole problem lies in the existence of the link of subordination which may be lacking. Some authors refer to a case-law position consisting in deducting this subordination from the sole keeping of a distinct technical function prior to the corporate mandate.[11]

It is therefore possible to believe that article 1–6° of the decree applies to cases in which the majority manager of a legal person is also an employee of the latter.

In this case, it is understandable that the leader is excluded from benefiting from the aid provided for by the decree. Indeed, the slowdown in activity caused by the Covid crisis may result in forcing the legal person to place its manager on part-unemployment. Unemployment insurance then covers the salary he receives in return for his function as an employee, which is clearly distinct from his

8 Cass. Soc. 29 June 2017, No. 16–15.814: Dr. Sociétés 2017, No. 189, obs. J. Heinrich.

9 M. Cozian, A. Viandier, F. Deboissy, *op. cit.*, No. 1640, p. 660.

10 Cass.nsoc, 14 October 2015, No. 14-10960: BJS 2015, p. 646, note A. Couret. *Comp*, Cass. Com, 29 Sept. 2009, No. 08-19.777, *Rev. Sociétés* 2010, p. 314, note A. Lecourt.

11 G. Auzero and N. Ferrier, "Cumul d'un contrat de travail et d'un mandat social", in *Répertoire de droit des sociétés*, Dalloz, No. 27. For example, Cass. Com, 16 Mai 1990, No. 86-42.681. It should be noted, however, that in this decision the manager did not have a majority, so that there is some doubt as to the real scope of the solution adopted.

managerial function.[12] Thus, the legal person will already receive the aid since it no longer has to ensure the payment of wages and contributions from its own resources. It is therefore understandable that the legislator decides not to grant additional assistance from the *solidarity fund* when the majority manager holds an employment contract in the company he heads.

However, one may be surprised at the solution adopted when the manager is not a majority share-holder. In this case, the legal person can again request assistance from the solidarity fund. The legal person is then doubly assisted, on the one hand by the payment of the salary through unemployment insurance, and on the other hand by a payment from the *Covid fund*. How to explain this difference in treatment? How should the manager's greater or lesser participation in the capital of the company have an impact on the company's ability to benefit from the aid from the guarantee fund? The extent of this participation certainly conditions the control capacity that the manager can exercise. But it has no impact i/ neither on the specific and exceptional needs of this company in the context of the Codiv 19 crisis ii/ nor on the resources of this company. We can only be surprised to see that the restriction edited by article 1–6° disappears when the leader is no longer in the majority. This is a difference in treatment that nothing seems to justify.

From the foregoing, it can be concluded that the main target of article 1–6° is perhaps not the group of majority managers holding an employment contract within the company they manage. Indeed, we were able to observe that this group is quite small, without being non-existent. In cases where this group is concerned, however, there is no explanation for the decision to treat their situation differently from those of non-majority leaders. It is therefore necessary to analyse the second possibility which falls within the foreseeability of the text: the case of the majority manager holding an employment contract concluded with another company. Can this second group of recipients, which could be more numerous, really be the main target of article 1–6°? It is possible to doubt it, except if we should consider that the legislator was able to create a text whose implementation deeply calls into question the principle of the separation of patrimonies.

12 This does not give entitlement to any unemployment benefit, as the manager is not covered by the employee scheme but by the self-employed scheme.

## II. The majority manager with a contract in a company other than the one he manages

We assume this time that the manager has an employment contract with a different entity from the one he heads. Like in the previous case, the legislator suggests distinguishing the case of the majority leader from the case of the leader who is not in the majority. Once again, the benefit of the application of the text is ruled out only to the detriment of the company, of which the manager is both in the majority and the holder of this employment contract. On the contrary, the fact that the manager is in the minority once again allows the company to be eligible for the *Covid fund*.

First, the doubts raised in Part I as to the advisability of operating an exclusion based on the majority situation or non-majority situation of the leader can be raised again here. Regardless of the lack of timeliness of this difference in treatment, Article I-6° this time raises a much more important problem linked to the non-respect of the principle of separation of patrimonies.

For at least two reasons, the fact that the manager holds an employment contract outside the company he manages should not be considered in determining the latter's eligibility for employment. payment of aid.

First, aid from the guarantee fund goes to the business, not to its manager. The sums are paid into the bank account of the legal person, and therefore become part of its personal assets, not that of its manager. Whether or not the manager has income from another activity is therefore an element outside the debate on the question of the payment of aid to the company he manages. Indeed, in the same way that this assistance integrates the assets of the company, and not his own assets, the income derived from this external activity integrates his personal assets, and not that of the legal person. The latter can therefore in no case claim the benefit of these sums. By comparison in a very different area, the French social system provides for the payment of a back-to-school allowance to help families who are most in need. The payment of this allowance is conditioned by the parents' income, that is to say the sums which integrate their personal assets. But assuming that one or the other of these parents also manages a legal person, at no time will the services in charge of this payment go to question the potential beneficiaries of the aid about the turnover achieved by the legal person managed: these distinct resources are not those of the household in question, but those of a legal person with its own patrimony. The evidence of this fact dispenses with any further reasoning. Consequently, only the resources of the legal person should be taken into consideration to condition the payment of the aid, not those of its manager, except if one were to confuse the assets of the patrimony of the manager with the assets of the patrimony of the legal person that he manages.

Second, and correlatively, the legal person must face its own costs with its own resources: it must therefore be able to free itself in particular from the payment of social contributions, insurance, the rental of professional premises, payment of land taxes for the buildings which it owns, professional tax, accountant's fees or even, sometimes, the repayment of bank loans. To do this, it can only rely on its own resources, not on those of its manager, however large. Conversely, the manager's resources are only intended to enable him to assume the charges that appear as liabilities of his personal assets, and not those inherent in the liabilities of another legal or natural person. For this second reason, it is therefore incongruous to base the payment of aid in the light of an income which can in no way benefit the legal person and enable it to meet its expenses.

Therefore, either it should be understood that this text only covers the case of the majority manager holding an employment contract in the company he manages, or it should be considered, as the DGFIP (directorate general of public finances) does, that the text also covers the case of a manager with an employment contract, outside the company he manages.

In the first case, the solution does not infringe the principle of the separation of patrimonies, but its field of application is limited given the fact that the group of majority managers authorised to be employees of the company they direct is restricted.

In the second case, it would have to be concluded that the legislator knowingly drafted a text whose application amounts to denying an essential principle: the separation of patrimonies. More seriously still, this interpretation of the text is a form of implicit incitement to a practice which can prove to be dangerous. It can indeed push the leader who has the necessary resources to help the company he manages, to help it meet his expenses. In application of the principle of separation of patrimonies, such a practice can only occur within a strict framework, because it is obviously totally excluded that the manager directly settles the company's debts. To do this, the manager can make an *"advance"* or a *"associate's current account contribution"* to provide the legal person with liquidity which, once integrated into its assets, can be used to meet the liabilities. This technique, the fallacious nature of which has been pointed out,[13] is in reality a "credit operation" which can be carried out by a partner whom the law "authorises to infringe as an exception to the banking monopoly".[14]

The manager behaves in fact like a credit organisation supporting the legal person he is managing. The problem lies in the fact that such a practice is not without risk, because in doing so, the manager may, first, conceal the state of insolvency of his company; secondly and consequently, the manager can enable his company to continue to carry on an activity by letting third parties believe that the company is in good financial health; thirdly, thereby generating a much larger liability susceptible to harm creditors in the event of the opening of insolvency proceedings. Thus, in a judgment of 1 July 2020, the Commercial Chamber of the Court of Cassation decided that "the current account contribution" may constitute "abnormal financing" intended to artificially support the company's cash flow concealing the persistence of its state of suspension of payments.

Such artificial support of business activity is i/ risky for the company and its potential creditors but ii/ risky for the manager as well. The case law is clear:[15] the liability of credit organisations can be sought when it is demonstrated that improper support has been provided and has led to a worsening of the liabilities of the legal person. Even if article 650-1 of the Commercial Code (resulting from Law 2005-845 of 26 July 2005) largely limited this possibility by instituting a principle of civil irresponsibility of the creditor, the calling into question of the creditor remains possible in the cases provided for by law.[16] However, this responsibility can also be sought among *de jure* or *de facto* managers when difficulties lead to placing the company in compulsory liquidation.

---

[13] M. Cozian, A. Viandier and F. Deboissy, *op. cit.*, No. 568, p. 249.

[14] H. Hovasse, *Comptes courants d'associés et monopole des banques*, *JCP* E 2010, 1284.

[15] Cass. Com., 16 octobre 2007, *Gaz.proc.coll.*, 2008-1, p. 59, note R. Routier; Cass. Com., 7 février 2012, *JCP E*, 2012, 1373, No. 15, obs L. Dumoulin.

[16] M. Mignot, J. Lassere Capdeville, M. Storck, N. Eréséo, J.-P. Kovar, *Droit bancaire*, Dalloz, 2e édition 2019, No. 1869 et s., p. 163 et s.

In the first place, a liability action for insufficient assets may be brought in application of Article L. 651-2 of the Commercial Code at the request of the liquidator if the liquidation procedure reveals a lack of assets. Such an action then assumes that the court reports the existence of a mismanagement that contributed to this lack of assets, this fault then can very well consist of abusive credit support to the company. However, the omission of the declaration of cessation of payments within the legal period may constitute a management fault.[17] Consequently, the contribution to the associate's current account intended to avoid the suspension of payments could be considered as a management error capable of justifying the extension of the procedure. And this even if the state of insolvency has not been established. When the debtor establishes that credit reserves enable him to meet the liabilities, liquidities provided by the manager may be taken into account.[18] Thus, depending on whether the judge considers that the contribution to the current account constitutes i/ a management fault or ii/ a salvation act intended to avoid the cessation of payments, the manager risks being condemned to bear all or part of the liabilities, this time on his own patrimony.

Second, the manager may also be exposed to criminal sanctions under the same conditions, and thus be prohibited from running a business.

For these two reasons, we express great reservations about the advisability that the manager would support the legal person he manages when the benefit of the guarantee fund is not granted to it. This violation of the principle of the separation of patrimonies is a legal anomaly. We asked the government a written question to challenge it on this issue (written question No. 20264 to the Ministry of the Economy on 28 January 2021). On 1 April 1 2021, the Ministry provided a puzzling response.

In the first place, the Ministry confirms that the main purpose of the decree is to exclude majority managers who have a full-time employment contract with a person other than those they manage: "except in specific circumstances, a majority manager cannot, in principle, conclude an employment contract with the legal person he manages because of the absence of a relationship of subordination. The amended decree n° 2020-371 thus aims to exclude majority managers who have a full-time employment contract with a person other than those they manage".

---

17 Cass. Com., 4 nov. 2014, No. 13–23.070 P, *D.* 2014. 2238, obs. A. Lienhard.

18 Cass. Com., 24 mars 2004, No. 01–10.927 P, *D.* 2004. 1022, obs. A. Lienhard.

But the Ministry had been questioned to explain, in this case, the problem linked to the non-respect of the principle of separation of patrimonies. The answer given completely ignores this aspect. More seriously, the Ministry's response seems to persist in the idea that if the disbursement of aid were allowed while the leader had other resources, there would be "overcompensation". The Ministry says: it is only when the company concerned employs at least one employee that this overcompensation can be avoided: "The evolutions of the solidarity fund have increased its field of action, and it is thus possible since the reinforced aids from late. September [2020], for companies whose majority manager has a full-time employment contract, to benefit from the solidarity fund when the salaried workforce is greater than or equal to one. This development makes eligible a wider spectrum of companies while avoiding overcompensation".

This position of the Ministry is regrettable, on the one hand, because the fact that at least one employee is responsible for the company is once again a given independent of the level of personal resources of the manager, on the other hand, because even in the absence of this one employee, there could be no overcompensation, the manager not being able to claim in a personal capacity for the benefit of the aid of the *Covid fund* due to the separation of patrimonies…

# Part II

# Regional and interregional issues

# Introduction

Yesbol Omirzhanov

It is known that the basis of all foreign policy relations is the economic dynamic among states. This part of the book is devoted to the issues of contemporary economic relations among miscellaneous countries. It is the lengthier one in the book, with up to nine chapters by noted participants, thus vouching to this key substance of, notably, post-cold war renewals given that such renewals emerge as largely consequences of the Cocid-19 pandemics.

In the chapter bearing upon tax regulation principles in the European Union and in the Eurasian Economic Union, Ilya Lifshits considers the legal instruments for solving the problems of double taxation in the European Union and the Eurasian Economic Union. The author reviews the tax competences of the European Union and those of the Eurasian Economic Union, then analyses regulation of indirect and direct taxation, as well as the question of other issues regarding the tax cooperation of Member-states of these two Unions.

The next chapter, written by Sagyngaliy Aidarbayev, Aizat Bekzhan and Bakhyt Uderbayeva, dwelling on implementing WTO standards in public procurement: the experience of the EU and of the situation in the EAEU, presents the general characteristics and the peculiarities of legal regulation of public procurement in the European Union (EU) and the Eurasian Economic Union (EAEU). They also analyse the impact of the Agreement on Government Procurement (AGP), in force within the World Trade Organisation (WTO), on the establishment and development of the public procurement sector in these two integration unions.

In the chapter on Brexit and European private international law regulations in the field of judicial cooperation in civil and commercial matters, Catherine Golhen focuses on the analysis of the main legal documents regulating new trade relations between the European Union and the United Kingdom. It analyses documents applicable to the contractual relationship between France and the United Kingdom.

The author also considers the law applicable to contracts, the competent court and the recognition of judgments in Franco-British relations from 1 January 2021.

Guillermo Palao Moreno, looking at Brexit and international commercial litigation in Europe in times of Covid-19, analyses the dramatic consequences derived, from the point of view of the legal management of international commercial litigation, in a geographical space where economic activity will continue to be intense. He also reflects upon those issues connected to litigation derived from the thriving cross-border commercial activity between businesses established on both sides of the English Channel (excluding personal, family or inheritance matters).

In the chapter on the the legal issues of personal data transfers after the Brexit, Fanny Rogue investigates the framework for personal data transfers outside the EU under the General Data Protection Regulation (GDPR). In this chapter, specific examples of the interpretation of the European regulation Court of Justice of the European Union (CJEU) are also given. Here the author furthers in many way her analyses published in the previous book in the same series.

Tackling the human and commercial challenges of the single European market and of the Asian market, Michel Bruno looks at the development of the European market and of the Asian states, pointing out two factors restraining European countries. i/ At home, Member states are not in the same position in the face of the globalisation of trade and, therefore, of numerous trade agreements concluded by the EU with third states, in particular Asia. ii/ European trade is hindered by trade agreements with Asian countries, which emphasise the de-industrialisation of the EU at the expense of the benefits of multinationals. Moreover as these damage labour laws and workers' rights in most Asian countries and in the EU.

In the chapter bearing upon Covid-19 challenges for China and Central Asia cooperation within the Belt and Road Initiative, Kuralay Baizakova and Fatima Kukeeva aptly demonstrate the main factors influencing cooperation between the People's Republic of China and Central Asia and Central Asian states within the framework of the Belt and Road Initiative. The authors conduct their analysis in the direction of cooperation between Central Asian countries with China on different projects and made their own dialectical conclusion.

In his chapter on the GATT principles during Covid-19: focusing on export restrictions of face-masks, Chan-Mo Chung devotes his analysis of the challenges facing GATT principles by examining their application to restrictions imposed on the export of face-masks. Making the analysis quite specific, provisions applicable to export prohibitions/restrictions of face-masks during the Covid-19 pandemic in regard of the General Agreement on Tariffs and Trade (GATT), the author gives his critique of the system.

Culminating at the close of Part II, a chapter on the US military presence in Korea and the operational control over the South Korean army, gives Tai-Uk Chung an opportunity to comprehensively detail and account for the history of the development of relations between South Korea and the United States and to express concerns about the current situation between China and the United States.

In all, these chapters contribute to the construction of a critical global analysis.

# Tax regulation principles in the European Union and in the Eurasian Economic Union

Ilya LIFSHITS

Tax revenues are the principal source of income for almost any state and form the bedrock of its financial sovereignty. This is why states are extremely reluctant to accept and assume obligations in the area of taxation. International tax treaties are thus largely limited to double taxation avoidance agreements and mutual administrative assistance in tax matters. However, the creation of a single market in a regional integration association implies the harmonisation of tax laws, as well as the creation of a non-discrimination regime for persons originating from the Member states of such an association.

This chapter analyses the legal instruments for the accomplishment of these tasks in the European Union and the Eurasian Economic Union, by first reviewing the tax competences of these associations, then analysing regulation of indirect and direct taxation, as well as an analysis of other issues regarding the tax cooperation of these unions' Member states. Its conclusion strives to determine the specific aspects of tax regulation in these inter-state associations.

## I. Tax competence of the EU and the EAEU. Direct and indirect taxation

The EU as an integration association has not been vested with the powers to impose various types of taxes or to define an object of taxation, a tax base, a tax rate, tax periods, or other elements of taxation, as stated in the introduction to the website article presenting the tax policy of the EU: "The EU does not have a direct role in collecting taxes or setting tax rates".[1]

---

[1] Taxation: Towards fair, efficient and growth-friendly taxes; available at: <https://europa.eu/european-union/topics/taxation_en> (accessed on 31.03.2021).

Tax-related issues are set forth in art. 110 – 113 of the TFEU, in a number of directives and regulations. art. 110 prohibits Member states from imposing "*directly or indirectly*, on the products of other Member states *any* internal taxation of *any* kind in excess of that imposed *directly or indirectly* on *similar* domestic products" (italics mine). Part 2 of art. 110 relates to the purpose of internal taxation: "no Member state shall impose on the products of other Member states any internal taxation of such a nature as to afford indirect protection to other products".

The wording of this article, in particular, the words "directly or indirectly" and "any", used twice in one sentence, clearly demonstrates the intention of the authors of the TFEU to exclude the possibility of any compulsory payment, including direct and indirect taxes, to discriminate against the products of other Member states. There is an evident reflection of the approach used in art. III of the GATT-47, which states that "internal taxes and other internal charges … should not be applied to imported or domestic products so as to afford protection to domestic production".[2] It is noteworthy that the GATT-47 wordings are broader, since they cover not only the imposition but also the application of taxes and the taxation of not only imported but also domestic products. It must also be noted that the purpose of the imposition of taxation rules in the TFEU is to create an internal (single, common) market in the territory of the European integration entity. That is why the respective rules should also be considered within the framework of the EU internal market law.

The Treaty on the Eurasian Economic Union (the TEAEU)[3] contains three articles (71–73), providing for the principles of the tax interaction of the Member states, indirect tax collection and personal income taxation. Protocol No. 18 enclosed to the Treaty deals with the procedure of indirect tax collection. As opposed to the case of the EU, goods imported from the territory of one Member state to the territory of another Member state of the EAEU are subject to indirect taxes based on the principle of the country of destination (clause 1 of article 71 of the TEAEU). This

---

2 Available at <https://www.wto.org/english/docs_e/legal_e/gatt47_01_e.htm> (accessed on 31.03.2021).

3 Entered into force on January 1, 2015. English text of the TEAEU is available at <https://docs.eaeunion.org/en-us> (accessed on 31.03.2021). The Eurasian Economic Union includes 5 member states: Republic of Armenia, Republic of Belarus, Republic of Kazakhstan, Kyrgyz Republic and the Russian Federation.

means that the sale of goods to another Member state of the Union is exempt from VAT and excise duties as regards the seller (a zero VAT rate is applied), while the buyer is obliged to pay VAT and excise duties to the budget of his state upon receipt of the goods. In addition, as a general rule, a national treatment regime is established for the sale of like products of other Member states under the same circumstances.

As regards personal income taxation, the Treaty establishes the rule of the direct effect, such that a Member state is entitled to tax the income of residents of another Member state in connection with their employment at a tax rate applicable to tax residents of the first Member state, starting from the first day of employment. For example, in the Russian Federation, the rate for individual income tax is 13 % for residents (and 15 % for income exceeding 5 million rubbles) and 30 % for non-residents.[4] However, by virtue of the above rule of the Treaty, for residents of the EAEU Member states employed in the Russian Federation, a rate of 13 %, rather than 30 %, is applied from the first day of employment.

Art. 113 of the Treaty on the Functioning of the European Union allows the Council, by unanimous decision, to harmonise turnover taxes, excise duties and other forms of *indirect taxation*, but it sets limits for such harmonisation: "to the extent that such harmonisation is necessary to ensure the establishment and the functioning of the internal market and to avoid distortion of competition". Thus, the EU's right to harmonise (i.e., issue directives) is expressly provided for in respect of the legislation of the Member states on indirect taxation. This right was embodied in several directives, in particular in Council Directive 2006/112/EC on the common system of value added tax.[5] The European Council may adopt a decision authorising the Council to act in this case by a qualified majority on the basis of the rule of art. 48 (7) of the Treaty on the European Union, which constitutes a so-called *passerelle clause.* A possibility to use this regulatory provision in the area of taxation was emphasised by the President of the Commission in 2018.[6]

---

4 Article 224 of the Russian Tax Code, English text is available at <https://www.ey.com/en_ru/tax/tax-code-of-the-russian-federation> (accessed on 31.03.2021).

5 Council Directive 2006/112/EC of 28 November 2006 on the common system of value added tax. OJ L 347, 11.12.2006, p. 1–118.

6 State of the Union 2018 Address, p. 15 Available at <https://ec.europa.eu/info/sites/info/files/soteu2018-brochure_en.pdf> (accessed on 31.03.2021).

By contrast, the Treaty of Eurasian Economic Union does not describe the competences of the bodies of the Union in the area of taxation, although the need to harmonise legislation affecting mutual trade with respect to taxes is explicitly emphasised in the Treaty (clause 2, Article 71).

*Direct taxation* in the EU continues to be carried out mainly at the level of the Member states. However, to the extent to which direct taxation affects the efficient functioning of the internal market, the EU has secured the right to pass legislation in the respective areas in the form of directives, of which there are currently three:

(1) Taxation of transactions between parent companies and subsidiaries (Directive 2011/96/EU as amended on 2014);[7]
(2) Taxation of mergers and divisions (Directive 2009/133/EU as amended on 2013);[8]
(3) Taxation applicable to interest and royalty payments made between associated companies (Directive 2003/49/EU).[9]

The purpose of the first directive is to exempt from taxation dividends distributed from subsidiaries to parent companies and to eliminate double taxation at the parent company level, and the purpose of the second and third directives is to clear obstacles to the free flow of capital.

Special attention should be given to the issues of the cooperation of tax authorities in conducting administrative enquiries in the EU (Regulation 904/2010),[10] in the exchange of information (Directive

---

7 Council Directive 2011/96/EU of 30 November 2011 on the common system of taxation applicable in the case of parent companies and subsidiaries of different Member states. OJ L 345, 29.12.2011 p. 8–16.

8 Council Directive 2009/133/EC of 19 October 2009 on the common system of taxation applicable to mergers, divisions, partial divisions, transfers of assets and exchanges of shares concerning companies of different Member states and to the transfer of the registered office of an SE or SCE between Member states. OJ L 310, 25.11.2009, p. 34–46.

9 Council Directive 2003/49/EC of 3 June 2003 on a common system of taxation applicable to interest and royalty payments made between associated companies of different Member states. OJ L 157, 26.6.2003. pp. 49–54.

10 Council Regulation (EU) No. 904/2010 of 7 October 2010 on administrative cooperation and combating fraud in the field of value added tax. OJ L 268, 12.10.2010, pp. 1–18.

2011/16/EU as amended in 2016),[11] and in the recovery of claims relating to taxes (Directive 2010/24/EU).[12] The Directive on the exchange of information was intended to ensure uniform participation of EU Member states in the exchange of information provided for by the OECD Multilateral Convention on mutual administrative assistance in tax matters.[13]

## II. The issue of double taxation

In the area of avoidance of double taxation, there is no EU legal act or a multilateral treaty that would impose a general obligation on Member states to eliminate double taxation. Moreover, a corresponding proposal of the Commission in 1976 was not adopted.[14] Neither was a common convention for the EU analogue of the OECD Model Convention on taxes on income and capital adopted, although the Commission made appropriate efforts noting the differing provisions of conventions and the harm that they cause to the functioning of the internal market, as well as the conflict of the provisions of these conventions with the law of the Union.[15] In 2005, the experts of the Commission counted 277 conventions in force.[16]

---

11 Council Directive 2011/16/EU of 15 February 2011 on administrative cooperation in the field of taxation and repealing Directive 77/799/EEC. OJ L 64, 11.3.2011, pp. 1–12.

12 Council Directive 2010/24/EU of 16 March 2010 concerning mutual assistance for the recovery of claims relating to taxes, duties and other measures. OJ L 84, 31.3.2010, pp. 1–12.

13 Available at <http://www.oecd.org/tax/exchange-of-tax-information/convention-on-mutual-administrative-assistance-in-tax-matters.htm> (accessed on 31.03.2021).

14 See the relevant information at the website of the Commission <https://ec.europa.eu/taxation_customs/business/company-tax/transfer-pricing-eu-context/transfer-pricing-arbitration-convention_en> (accessed on 31.03.2021).

15 Communication from the Commission to the Council, the European Parliament and the European Economic and Social Committee 'Removing cross-border tax obstacles for EU citizens'. COM(2010) 824. Available at <https://ec.europa.eu/taxation_customs/sites/taxation/files/resources/documents/taxation/gen_info/tax_policy/com%282010%29769_en.pdf> (accessed on 31.03.2021).

16 Report on the meeting of experts entitled "EU Law and Tax Treaties" – EC Law and Tax Treaties. Workshop of experts. Working document. July, 5, 2005.

The interaction of double taxation agreements (DTAs) and the EU law has been repeatedly examined by the Commission and the Court of Justice of the European Union. On the one hand, DTAs apply to direct taxation, the potential harmonisation of which is not directly assigned to EU institutions. On the other hand, the different taxation regimes depending on the citizenship or residence of nationals represent an obvious barrier to the functioning of the internal market.[17] The solution to this basic problem of double taxation in the EU was partially resolved by the Court with reference to the obligation of the Member states to exercise their powers in accordance with Community law.[18] In cases where the principles of the treaties are violated as a result of the application of the DTAs or the national laws implementing them, such DTAs and laws shall be amended.[19]

It must be admitted that in the field of direct taxation, a supranational legal order has not yet been created, the relevant issues are regulated at the level of the Member states, and the elimination of double taxation in the EU is regulated by bilateral conventions, which are supplemented by the Tax Arbitration Convention of 1990,[20] signed by all EU Members and enacted in 1995. It sets forth the procedure for the settlement of disputes between the tax authorities of the Member states regarding the taxation of profits of associated companies. The application of this Convention is expounded by a special document entitled the

---

Ref.: TAXUD E1/FR DOC(05)2306. Available at <https://ec.europa.eu/taxation_customs/sites/taxation/files/resources/documents/taxation/personal_tax/double_tax_conventions/eclawtaxtreaties_en.pdf> (accessed on 31.03.2021).

17 EC Law and Tax Treaties. Workshop of experts. Working document. July, 5, 2005. See note 166 *supra*, p. 3.

18 The Report (note 166 above) quotes the following Judgments of the Court: Judgment of the Court of 14 February 1995, Case C-279/93 (Schumacker), point 21; Judgment of 11 August 1995, Case C-80/94 (Wielockx), point 16; Judgment of 27 June 1996, Case C-107/94; (Asscher), point 36; Judgment of 15 May 1997, Case C-250/95 (Futura), point 19; Judgment of 28 April 1998, Case C-118/96 (Safir), point 21; Judgment of 16 July 1998, Case C-264/96 (I.C.I.), point 19.

19 The report (note 16 above) quotes the following Judgments of the Court: Judgment of 23 September 2003, Case C-58/01 (Océ Van der Grinten), point 54; Judgment of 12 December 2002, Case C-385/00 (F.W.L. de Groot v. Staatssecretaris van Financiën), points 84, 94, 99 et. seq; Judgment of 8 March 2001, Case C-397/98 (Metallgesellschaft), points 71 et seq; Judgment of 18 November 1999, Case C-200/98 (X AB et Y AB), points 10 and 31.

20 Convention on the elimination of double taxation in connection with the adjustment of the profits of associated enterprises (90/463/EEC). OJ L 225, 20.8.1990, p. 10.

Code of Conduct[21] (Code of conduct 2006/C 176/02), enacted jointly by the Council and representatives of Member states[22] and revised in 2009.[23] The Convention stipulates that if the tax authorities of different Member states have not reached an agreement on the procedure for taxation of the income of a company that has branches in these states, then the decision shall be made by the Advisory Commission, consisting of the chairman, two representatives of the dissenting tax authorities and an equal number of independent Members.

For the uniform application of the Tax Arbitration Convention, the Directive 2017/1852 of 10 October 2017, "On tax dispute resolution mechanisms in the European Union", was adopted,[24] which entered into force on 1 July 2019. This directive establishes a mechanism for dispute resolution between Member states on the interpretation and application of agreements and conventions for the elimination of the double taxation of income and capital. The dispute resolution procedure can be initiated by a taxpayer himself, and the scope of application of the directive is wider than that of the Tax Arbitration Convention, since the latter deals only with transfer pricing and distribution of taxable income between affiliated branches in different countries, and the directive applies to all cases of the elimination of the double taxation of income and capital. It is anticipated that more than 2000 disputes will be considered within the framework of the tax dispute resolution mechanism (*mutual agreement – MAP*), of which 900 have been pending for more than two years.[25]

---

21 Code of conduct for the effective implementation of the Convention on the elimination of double taxation in connection with the adjustment of the profits of associated enterprises. OJ C 176, 28.7.2006, pp. 8–12.

22 OJ 28.07.2006 (C 176/8).

23 Revised Code of Conduct for the effective implementation of the Convention on the elimination of double taxation in connection with the adjustment of the profits of associated enterprises. OJ C 322, 30.12.2009, p. 1–10.

24 Council Directive (EU) 2017/1852 of 10 October 2017 on tax dispute resolution mechanisms in the European Union. OJ L 265, 14.10.2017, p. 1–14.

25 Press Release of the European Commission of July 2019 Available at <https://ec.europa.eu/commission/presscorner/detail/en/IP_19_3377> (accessed on 31.03.2021).

## III. Addressing tax avoidance

Separate mention should be made of the EU tax competence regarding the combat of the use of legal tax avoidance schemes. For such actions, the term "tax avoidance" is used, while the illegal reduction of the income tax base or an amount of tax is described by the term "tax evasion". The field of *tax avoidance* is governed by the Council Directive 2016/1164 of 12.07.2016 "On laying down rules against tax avoidance practices that directly affect the functioning of the internal market"[26] (as amended by the Directive 2017/952).[27] The reference to the internal market in the title of the directive is not accidental. The legal base for its adoption was not the tax provisions of the TFEU but the general Article 115 on the approximation of laws, vesting the Council with the right to adopt directives precisely to ensure the creation and functioning of the internal market.

Interestingly, the preamble of the directive begins with the designation of a certain modern "trend", idea or principle in the area of taxation: "The current political priorities in international taxation highlight the need for ensuring that tax is paid where profits and value are generated". This idea became the focus of the OECD initiative, expressed in the adoption of 15 recommendations preventing the erosion of the tax base and profit shifting (*Addressing BEPS*),[28] which are also referred to in the preamble. The text of the directive specifies the main tax requirements that should be introduced into the legislation of the Member states to implement the recommendations of the OECD: limiting the deductibility of interest from taxable earnings, taxation upon change of tax jurisdiction (so-called exit taxation), general rules on counteracting tax abuse (the so-called GAAR – *General anti-abuse rules*), rules on controlled foreign companies (CFCs) and hybrid schemes (hybrid mismatch), allowing the double counting of expenses.

---

26 Council Directive (EU) 2016/1164 of 12 July 2016, laying down rules against tax avoidance practices that directly affect the functioning of the internal market. OJ L 193, 19.7.2016, p. 1–14.

27 Council Directive (EU) 2017/952 of 29 May 2017 amending Directive (EU) 2016/1164 as regards hybrid mismatches with third countries. OJ L 144, 7.6.2017, p. 1–11.

28 Available at <http://www.oecd.org/tax/beps/> (accessed on: 31.03.2021).

Direct taxation in the EAEU is fully within the competence of the Member states. There are several bilateral double taxation agreements among the Member states that operate outside the legal system of the Union, for instance, between Armenia and Russia of 28 December 1996, between Kazakhstan and Russia of 18 October 1996,[29] or between Kazakhstan and Belarus of 11 April 1997.[30]

## IV. Financial transaction tax

A compelling project that should be considered in the broader context of the EU financial industry regulation reform necessitated by the global financial crisis is an attempt to impose a *financial transaction tax*. The tax, the idea of which is associated with the names of the economists of repute, such as John Keynes and James Tobin, received the catchy nickname of a "Robin Hood tax" for its noble goal.[31] It was intended to limit speculation on the stock market and at the same time to replenish the state budget. In 2011, the European Commission proposed a draft directive that would oblige all EU Member states to impose tax on financial transactions and harmonise the main elements of taxation, e.g., a taxpayer, a tax base, or a tax rate. For the adoption of the relevant EU directive in accordance with art. 113 of TFEU, it was required to ensure a unanimous vote of Member states in the Council. However, soon enough, one had to admit that it would not be possible to achieve unanimity: most of the EU states doubted both the economic expediency of the tax imposition and the legal impeccability of such a measure.

In 2012, following an inquiry from 11 states (Belgium, Germany, Estonia, Greece, Spain, France, Italy, Austria, Portugal, Slovenia and Slovakia), the Commission submitted to the Council a proposal for the establishment of enhanced cooperation in the area of financial transactions tax, which was soon approved by the Council and the European

---

29 Available at <https://www.nalog.ru/rn77/about_fts/inttax/mpa/dn/> (accessed on 31.03.2021).

30 Available at <http://nalog.gov.by/ru/kazahstan/> (accessed on 31.03.2021).

31 Huber, J., Kirchler, M., Daniel Kleinlercher, D. and Sutterhttps, M. Market versus residence principle: experimental evidence on the effects of a financial transaction tax, *The Economic Journal*, 127 (October), F610-F631. Doi: 10.1111/ecoj.12339 2017; see also: www.euractiv.com/section/economy-jobs/news/belgium-told-to-get-off-the-fence-stop-blocking-ftt/.

Parliament (in 2016, Estonia announced that it did not intend to participate any further). In the beginning of 2013, the Commission proposed a draft of the directive, accompanied by an explanatory note.[32]

According to the plan, the directive on financial transaction tax was to enter into force in 2013, and the legislation of the Member states adopted in accordance with the directive was to be applied from 1 January 2014. However, this did not happen, mainly because of disputes on the composition of transactions constituting the tax base and on the composition of taxpayers. Nevertheless, the Commission remains optimistic and includes the financial transaction tax among enhanced cooperation projects, which Jean-Claude Juncker describes with a catch phrase: "Those who want more do more".[33]

*

In conclusion, the overview of the EU tax law, the abundant references to the OECD recommendations and the formulation of "new" principles of fair and efficient taxation help the EU to substantiate its own competence and adherence to the principles of subsidiarity and proportionality in regulating a new area of financial competence – harmonisation of the *direct taxes* of the Member states with the aim to prevent tax evasion.

In the area of direct taxation as material part of the sovereign powers of states, until recently, a significant part of the competence has been reserved to the Member states, which regulate issues regarding the elimination of double taxation on the basis of bilateral conventions. However, the EU's attempt in 2017 to pass legislation in the double taxation area was successful: a directive aimed at creating a mechanism for resolving disputes on the application of double taxation treaties was adopted. Thus, the development of the communitarisation of the double taxation issue can be acknowledged, replacing international treaties with legal acts of the Union.

---

32 Proposal for a Council Directive implementing enhanced cooperation in the area of financial transaction tax. Brussels, 14.2.2013 COM (2013) 71 final.

33 Scenario 3 of the White Paper on the Future of Europe: Those Who Want More Do More (2019), available at <https://ec.europa.eu/info/sites/info/files/enhanced-cooperation-factsheet-tallinn_en.pdf> (accessed on: 31.03.2021).

In general, the EU tax law is characterised by a significant penetration of the advisory acts of the Organisation for Economic Cooperation and Development, with the adoption of approaches and principles developed under the aegis of this organisation. By contrast, the volume of legislation of the EAEU in the tax field is rather modest at present. The regulation at the union level is limited by the principles of indirect taxation in trade in goods and services between Member states. The avoidance of double taxation is achieved fairly in all aspects by legal instruments outside the legal framework of the union.

However, the logic of the integration and the functioning of the single market will inevitably lead to greater use of tax regulation at the central level in both unions. Overall, the associations of the states are in a better position to implement a single or harmonised tax regime since such associations are established on the basis of international agreement and have their own budget and common bodies. Therefore, the intensity of tax regulation will increase in line with the development of integration in the European Union and in the Eurasian Economic Union.

# Implementing WTO standards in public procurement: EU experience and situation in the EAEU

Sagyngaliy Aidarbayev, Bakhyt Uderbayeva,
Aizat Bekzhan

This chapter presents the general characteristics and the peculiarities of legal regulation of public procurement in the European Union (EU) and the Eurasian Economic Union (EAEU). Il also analyses the impact of the Agreement on Government Procurement (AGP), in force within the World Trade Organisation (WTO), on the establishment and development of the public procurement sector in these two integration unions.

International trade is the most important motor of economic development in the global community. One of the dynamically developing sectors of world trade is international government procurement markets. The WTO is the only international organisation, which regulates as well as coordinates the activities of states in the sphere of international trade, sets the rules of trade between them. Its basis is the WTO agreements adopted and signed by the majority of foreign trade Member states.

The WTO emerged as the successor to the General Agreement on Tariffs and Trade (GATT) as a result of the Uruguay Round of multilateral trade negotiations in 1986–1994, which were held under the auspices of GATT. The Uruguay Round concluded on 15 April 1994 with the Marrakesh Protocol, which opened for signature the Agreement Establishing the WTO.[1] This agreement is a comprehensive document, to which many other agreements are appended, regulating a wide range

1 Marrakesh Agreement Establishing the World Trade Organization, 1994 [online] Available at: <https://www.wto.org/english/docs_e/legal_e/04-wto_e.htm> (accessed: February 10, 2021).

of issues concerning trade in goods and services, as well as trade-related aspects of intellectual property rights.

The multilateral agreements that make up the WTO contain legal rules to guide governments in mutual trade in goods and services. As such, they supersede more than 30000 bilateral agreements and create the legal framework for modern international trade. Their basic principles are most-favoured-nation treatment.[2]

Each state acceding to the WTO accepts a package of binding documents, which include the multilateral WTO agreements. However, there are so-called "plurilateral" (i.e., non-binding) WTO agreements, which means that states determine for themselves whether or not to accede to such agreements. One such agreement is the WTO Agreement on Government Procurement (GPA), concluded in 1994 and now in force as of 30 March 2012, which is a very significant international instrument in the field of government procurement.

## I. Relevance of the research area

Government procurement is a serious tool of state regulation of a country's economy, occupying an important place in the state's economy. Government procurement is an important segment of the economy, estimated at 10–15 % of GDP in both developed and developing countries, and forms a significant segment of international trade.

The increased role of government procurement in international trade has led to government procurement being included in many regional trade agreements along with liberalisation of goods, services, capital and labour markets.

In today's economy, public procurement is an indispensable element of public finance management and other resources of the public sector of economy and is designed to fulfil not only the functions of meeting public needs, but also those of government regulation of the economy.

Legal regulation of government procurement is a complex and continuous process of adoption, adjustment and application by the state of legal norms that regulate the sphere of public procurement by establishing

---

2 Дюмулен И.И. Всемирная торговая организация. – М.: Экономика, 2003. С. 271.

unified rules, rights and obligations of its subjects. Public procurement as an object of international and national legal regulation is also a complex, continuous process of meeting public needs by attracting external performers on a reimbursable basis and consists of a set of interrelated and sequential stages: forecasting, planning, formation, placement, execution and monitoring.

## II. Methodology pursued in the study

The methodological and empirical basis of the research consists in applying general methods of scientific knowledge: history, comparisons, analysis, synthesis, classification; special methods: formal-legal, structural-functional, comparative-legal. The application of the above methods has led to a deep, qualitative analysis of the normative acts of foreign and domestic law concerning the legal regulation of public procurement.

In particular, the study of the genesis and subsequent evolution of the acts of harmonisation of the WTO in the field of public procurement on the basis of historical and legal method of knowledge.

## III. Discussion and results

As noted above, prior to 1979, the area of government procurement was not covered by the GATT legal framework. During the 1979 Tokyo Round of multilateral trade negotiations, the WTO Agreement on Government Procurement emerged. Under this agreement, members were required to grant national treatment and most-favoured-nation (MFN) treatment in government procurement. After the Uruguay Round in 1994, the GPA was revised and modernised. Such areas as specific national procurement organisations, types of goods, types of services, threshold value of contracts were defined, in which each WTO member was negotiating accession to the agreement.[3]

The updated WTO Agreement on Government Procurement, which came into force in 2014, simplifies and modernises the previous text. It

---

3 Всемирная торговая организация. Экономика, политика, право: монография. – 3-е изд., дополн. / И.И. Дюмулен; ВАВТ Минэкономразвития России. – М.: ВАВТ, 2012. С. 169.

now adequately takes into account the widespread use of electronic procurement tools, expands the list of national procurement organisations, and expands the list of goods and services covered by the agreement. The revised agreement includes "new, simpler rules to discourage corruption and protectionism",[4] as well as improved transitional measures designed to facilitate accession to the WTO GPA by developing and least-developed countries.[5]

In addition to classical international organisations and bodies, there are a number of integration associations that pay quite a lot of attention to the problem of public procurement regulation. The European Union, as well as the Eurasian Economic Union can certainly be attributed to the latter.

Sphere of public procurement in the EU countries is regulated by three levels of legislative regulation: international, regional and national. The main source of EU law in the field of public procurement is the Treaty on the Establishment of the EEC of 1957[6] and the EU Directives.

In 2014 The Council of the European Union and the European Parliament adopted two directives aimed at simplifying public procurement procedures and making them more flexible. EU countries had until April 2016 to transpose the new rules into national law (with the exception of e-procurement, where the deadline was October 2018).[7] By that date, EU Member states had to adopt national legislation compliant with the norms of the new directives.

The old directives (Directive 2004/18/EC – "classic public sector directive" and Directive 2004/17/EC – "public utilities directive") were replaced by the following: i/ Directive 2014/24/EC on public

---

4 ВТО: пересмотренное Соглашение по правительственным закупкам вступит в силу 6 апреля [электронный ресурс] Доступно: <http://www.ictsd.org/bridges-news/мосты/news/вто-пересмотренное-соглашение-по-правительственным-закупкам-вступит-в-силу-6> [Дата обращения: 10 февраля, 2021].

5 Revised WTO Agreement on Government Procurement to come into force on 6 April 2014. [online] Available at: <https://www.wto.org/english/news_e/news14_e/gpro_11mar14_e.htm> (accessed: February 10, 2021).

6 Treaty establishing the European Economic Community, 1957 [online] Available at: <https://ab.gov.tr/files/ardb/evt/1_avrupa_birligi/1_3_antlasmalar/1_3_1_kurucu_antlasmalar/1957_treaty_establishing_eec.pdf> (accessed: January 31, 2021).

7 EU Public Procurement Directives [online] Available at: <https://ec.europa.eu/environment/gpp/eu_public_directives_en.htm> (accessed: January 18, 2021).

procurement,[8] and ii/ Directive 2014/25/EC on procurement by organisations operating in the water, energy, transport and postal services sectors.[9]

The new rules are designed to ensure greater inclusion of shared societal goals in the procurement process. These goals include environmental protection, social responsibility, innovation, climate change, employment, health and other social and environmental considerations.[10] The main achievements of the new directives, in particular, are: extensive use of electronic communications, support for small and medium-sized businesses, reduction of formal requirements for the composition of applications and for participants, the possibility of applying new, simplified procedures in all of the areas mentioned.

It is worth noting that the directives do not impose a new general regulatory regime on Member states in public procurement. Member states may apply their national procedures adapted to the directives.

The directives limit their scope to those measures required to coordinate the impact of the directives and allow Member states to make substantive changes to the procedural rules in public procurement, which must not conflict with the rules of the 2007 Treaty on the Functioning of the European Union[11] (TFEU). EU Member states remain free to regulate the practicalities of public procurement themselves.

---

8 Directive 2014/24/EU of the European Parliament and of the Council of 26 February 2014 on public procurement and repealing Directive 2004/18/EC Text with EEA relevance [online] Available at: <https://eur-lex.europa.eu/legal-content/EN/TXT/?uri=celex:32014L0024> (accessed: January 5, 2021).

9 Directive 2014/25/EU of the European Parliament and of the Council of 26 February 2014 on procurement by entities operating in the water, energy, transport and postal services sectors and repealing Directive 2004/17/EC Text with EEA relevance [online] Available at: <https://eur-lex.europa.eu/legal-content/EN/TXT/?uri=celex:32014L0025> (accessed: January 5, 2021).

10 EU Public Procurement Directives [online] Available at: <https://ec.europa.eu/environment/gpp/eu_public_directives_en.htm> (accessed: January 18, 2021).

11 Договор о функционировании Европейского союза (новая редакция), 2007 [электронный ресурс] Доступно: <https://eulaw.ru/treaties/tfeu/> (Дата обращения: 19 марта, 2021).

According to Article 33 of the 1947 General Agreement on Tariffs and Trade[12] (GATT), participants of GATT/WTO can be not only states, but also individual customs territories with full autonomy in the implementation of their foreign trade relations and in other matters provided by GATT. The European Union has been an independent member of the WTO since the latter was established on 1 January 1995, however the 28 Member-states of the EU (as of today 27 Member-states, the UK has not been a member of the EU since 31 January 2020) continue to be independent members of the organisation, since not all the issues to be discussed within the WTO fall within the exclusive competence of the EU.[13]

At the same time, according to Articles 207 and 218 of the TFEU, the European Union has the relevant competence to negotiate and conclude agreements with third countries or international organisations as part of a common trade policy, and here it is primarily the EU participation in GATT/WTO and the norms and agreements adopted within their framework.[14] Moreover, as the Court of Justice of the EU has repeatedly pointed out, the competence of the Union to conduct a common trade policy is exclusive, even if this does not follow explicitly from the provisions of Article 207 or any other article of the Treaty, and any other decision could jeopardise the effective protection of the common interests of the Union.[15]

It should be noted that the international obligation of the EU to participate in the WTO GPA was reflected in paragraph 17 of the preamble of Directive No. 2014/24/EC: "…customers are obliged to apply the provisions of this directive to business entities from third countries that are signatories to the WTO GPA".[16]

---

[12] Генеральное соглашение по тарифам и торговле, 1947 [электронный ресурс] Доступно:<https://www.hse.ru/data/2011/11/15/1272897051/%D0%93%D0%90%D0%A2%D0%A2-47%20%28rus%29.pdf> (Дата обращения: 25 марта, 2021).

[13] Камалян А.М. Правовое регулирование государственных закупок в Европейском Союзе: дисс. … канд. юрид. наук. – Москва, 2018. – С. 136.

[14] Pingel I. "De Rome à Lisbonne. Commentaire article par article des Traités UE et CE"; Paris, 2010. p. 1018.

[15] Opinion 1/75, pp. 1363–1364 [ECLI:EU:C:1975:145]; Case C-70/94 *Werner v Bundesrepublik Deutschland*, para 8–9, 12 [ECLI:EU:C:1995:328]; Case C-83/94 *Leifer and Others*, para 8–9, 12 [ECLI:EU:C:1995:329].

[16] Directive 2014/24/EU of the European Parliament and of the Council of 26 February 2014 on public procurement and repealing Directive 2004/18/EC

As A.M. Kamalian notes, the main provisions of the GPA are almost identical to the European directives adopted in 2004, which is not surprising since the European Union is a signatory to the Agreement. In accordance with European Union Council Decision 94/800 of 22 December 1994,[17] the Agreement applies within the EU, being binding both on the Union itself and on EU Member states.[18]

Nevertheless, there are two important differences in the regulation of public procurement in the WTO and in the EU. First, the general principle of non-discrimination in the EU applies not only to contracts whose value exceeds established thresholds (as in the WTO), but to all contracts, even if due to their low value they are not covered by directives. Secondly, the European Union has extended the principle of non-discrimination to all parties to the Agreement, although the latter, by virtue of its legal nature as a multilateral trade agreement, is largely dependent on the principle of reciprocity.

Thus, the regulation of public procurement under GATT/WTO has been of great importance in the development of European Union public procurement law, including in view of the binding nature of the agreements for the EU as a direct party to them. Nevertheless, the fact that the total number of participants in the Agreement on Government Procurement is quite small, with the main share being developed countries, raises many questions. Today, the European public procurement sector is the most open and liberalised in the world, with highly competitive external companies. This sector is also growing rapidly and is in demand in emerging economies, where European companies are very competitive.

The Eurasian Economic Union (EAEU), an integration association operating on the basis of the Treaty on the Eurasian Economic Union[19] (EAEU Treaty), signed in Astana on 29 May 2014, has been operating in the Eurasian space since 2015. This document regulates all the main areas of integration, including the sphere of public procurement,

---

Text with EEA relevance [online] Available at: <https://eur-lex.europa.eu/legal-content/EN/TXT/?uri=celex:32014L0024> (accessed: January 5, 2021).

17 Council Decision concerning the conclusion on behalf of the European Community, as regards matters within its competence, of the agreements reached in the Uruguay Round multilateral negotiations (1986–1994) (OJ L 336, 23.12.1994, pp. 1–2).

18 Камалян А.М. Указ.соч. С. 141.

19 Договор о Евразийском экономическом союзе, 2014 [электронный ресурс] Доступно: <https://online.zakon.kz/document/?doc_id=31565247#pos=116;-50> (Дата обращения: 19 марта, 2021).

to which Article 88 of the EAEU Treaty and Annex No. 25 to it are dedicated. To date, the five Member states of this integration association are the Republic of Armenia, the Republic of Belarus, the Republic of Kazakhstan, the Kyrgyz Republic and the Russian Federation.

The main text of the Treaty on the EAEU in relation to public procurement contains only one article, article 88, which enshrines the most general provisions. Thus, the Treaty contains a general exemption for procurement, information about which constitutes a state secret. Article 88 also provides special treatment for national banks of the Member states. They are not subject to the Treaty, but are procured in accordance with their internal procurement rules, which must be consistent with the general principles and objectives set out in the Treaty. Among other things, Article 88 establishes the basic principles of Eurasian Economic Union law on public procurement. As in the European Union, the EAEU Treaty proclaims openness and transparency of procurement, as well as non-discrimination (granting national treatment) with respect to participants in public procurement.[20]

As for Annex No. 25, it contains a number of norms that harmonise the legislation of the Member states in the field of public procurement.[21]

Particular attention should be paid to the Agreement on Government Procurement, which operates within the framework of the World Trade Organisation. The fact is that EAEU members have very different attitudes to this document and, accordingly, to the obligations enshrined in it: Armenia is a full party to the agreement; Russia, Kyrgyzstan and Kazakhstan are observers (while Russia, Kyrgyzstan and Kazakhstan are negotiating accession); and Belarus is not a WTO member. This situation creates a number of uncertainties, since Armenia in its state procurement should be guided not only by the law of the EAEU, but also by the WTO, which means to admit to its market in accordance with the national regime, for example, potential suppliers from the USA, Japan and the European Union. The latter, incidentally, is a party to the WTO Agreement on Government Procurement as a customs territory covering all its Member states.[22]

---

[20] Камалян А.М. Указ. соч. С. 172.

[21] Интеграционное право: учебник / отв. ред. Кашкин С.Ю., М., Проспект, 2017. С 353.

[22] Камалян А.М. Указ. соч. С. 175.

Thus, the regulation of public procurement at the level of the Eurasian Economic Union should be considered very conditional, since the main burden is borne by the national legislation and bodies of the Member states. In this regard, there is a huge scope for borrowing and rational adaptation to their specifics of the provisions of the European Union directives in this area. However, one should not forget that borrowing should be competent and expedient, since it is necessary to prepare an appropriate basis, both legal and technical.

*

In conclusion, governments in most countries are the biggest buyers of a wide variety of goods, from commodities to high-tech equipment. At the same time, political pressure in favour of domestic suppliers over their foreign competitors can be very strong. The WTO Agreement on Government Procurement sought to make laws, regulations, various procedures and practices relating to government procurement more transparent and ensure that they did not protect goods produced by domestic producers or domestic suppliers or discriminate against foreign goods or suppliers. Its purpose was to open, as far as possible, this field of commerce to international competition.

The WTO provides an arena for the settlement of disputes and the creation of principles and norms to regulate the trade activities of states through the negotiation process. Each agreement is subject to ratification by the state which has undertaken the obligations under the agreement.

WTO agreements are a form of lawful intervention in the internal affairs of states, since each state, by joining this organisation, voluntarily accepts legal obligations under the agreements to which it becomes a party. The norms and rules of the WTO are enshrined in the agreements negotiated by the Member states of the organisation to liberalise world trade in general.

The European Union, being one of the initiators of the GPA, has extensive experience in its application, as well as in bringing its own legal norms into conformity with its requirements. In this regard, the study of the EU experience in reforming the system of public procurement becomes a necessity in today's realities.

It is also necessary to note the practical importance of this issue for the development of the integration process within the EAEU. In this regard, the study of many years of EU experience in creating a system of supranational norms governing public procurement can provide a theoretical basis for the improvement of the public procurement system in the EAEU and, possibly, help to accelerate the integration process in this area.

# Brexit and European private international law regulations in the field of judicial cooperation in civil and commercial matters

Catherine Golhen

London is certainly a privileged city for the resolution of commercial disputes. But the question arises as to the part played in this success by the place that the United Kingdom occupied in Europe. Linked to this are the questions of the access to harmonised rules of jurisdiction in the European Union, of the rules facilitating the circulation of the decisions within the European Union, and of the access to rules harmonising the law applicable to the contracts within the European Union.[1] For economic actors, the United Kingdom's membership in the European Union was seen as a guarantee of predictability for economic actors.[2] This includes predictability on the rules of jurisdiction in the event of litigation, predictability of the rules of recognition and enforcement of decisions given in the United Kingdom on the territory of the European Union and vice versa, and predictability as to the law which will be declared applicable, whatever the court seized.

The UK officially left the European Union at midnight on 31 January 2020. The Withdrawal Agreement made the UK a third country of the European Union. However, the EU law was to continue to apply until the end of the transition period, i.e. until 31 December 2020, in exchange for the UK to access to the internal market and the customs union. From 1 1 January 2021 onwards, EU law no longer applies to the

1 Report on the implications of Brexit in the field of judicial cooperation in civil and commercial matters by the High Legal Committee of the Paris Financial Centre, 30 January 2017.

2 Report on the implications of Brexit in the field of judicial cooperation in civil and commercial matters by the High Legal Committee of the Paris Financial Centre, 30 January 2017.

UK, but in return the UK no longer has access to the internal market and to the customs union.

The European Union and the United Kingdom signed a *Trade and Cooperation Agreement* on 30 December 2020. This agreement entered in force on 1 January 2021. It defines the modalities of cooperation between the EU and the UK in a number of areas: trade, fisheries, transport, social security coordination, police and judicial cooperation, the participation of the UK in EU programmes, etc.[3] The agreement has not yet been ratified, but has been provisionally applied since 1 January 2021. The agreement provides for rules on judicial cooperation in criminal matters but it does not provide for mechanisms of judicial cooperation in civil and commercial matters. This chapter focuses on this this judicial cooperation in civil and commercial matters. In this respect, the existence of several reports on the implications of BREXIT drafted by the High Legal Committee of the Paris Financial Centre must be mentioned. In particular, on 30 January 2017, a report was issued on judicial cooperation in civil and commercial matters.

Thus, from 1 January 2021, Regulation 593/2008 of 17 June 2008 on the law applicable to contractual obligations, known as the Rome I Regulation, the purpose of which is to designate the law applicable to an international contract, is no longer binding on the UK. The same applies to Regulation 1215/2012 of 12 December 2012 on jurisdiction and the recognition and enforcement of judgments in civil and commercial matters, known as the Brussels-I-bis Regulation. The purpose of this last text is to indicate which court has jurisdiction to decide an international dispute, as well as to set out the procedures for the recognition of a judgment from one Member state to another Member state. These texts are based on a principle of mutual trust between Member states: trust in their judicial institutions and in the correct application of the regulations they make.

What effect will this inapplicability of European texts have on the relations with the United Kingdom? This chapter will focus on these two texts applicable to contractual relations between France and the United Kingdom. We will voluntarily go beyond the scope of this study to include other European regulations in the field of judicial cooperation, in particular those relating to the taking of evidence, the notification

---

3 Brexit.gouv.fr

and service of procedural documents, the European order for payment, etc. The Rome-I Regulation and the Brussels-I-bis Regulation thus harmonised three elements of judicial cooperation: the law applicable to contracts, the rules of jurisdiction and the rules of recognition and enforcement of decisions. We will therefore consider successively the law applicable to contracts (I), the competent court (II) and the recognition of judgments in Franco-British relations since 1 January 2021 (III).

## I. The law applicable to contracts

The law applicable to contracts in civil and commercial matters was previously determined from the point of view of both France and the United Kingdom by the Rome-I Regulation of 17 June 2008. This regulation provides for a principle of free choice of the law applicable to the contract and sets out, in the absence of a choice, an objective connecting rules to designate an applicable law. Thus, a contract for the sale of goods is subject to the law of the seller's habitual residence, a contract for the provision of services is subject to the law of the service provider's habitual residence, etc. The interpretation of this regulation is entrusted to the Court of Justice of the European Union. The uniformity of the rules between France and the United Kingdom, as well as the unity of interpretation, allowed a total similarity of the solutions applicable in the United Kingdom and in France. The harmonisation of solutions is in this respect a means of combating forum shopping and reducing litigation. There was no point in bringing a case before a French court more than before an English court, since the courts applied the same rule and interpret it in the same way.

What is the influence of the Brexit in this respect?

From the EU perspective,[4] the so-called "universal nature" of the Rome-I Regulation considerably limits the impact of Brexit.[5] The applicable law is that designated by the Regulation, even if it is not that of a Member state. France will therefore continue to designate the law applicable to a contract by application of the Rome-I Regulation, despite the

---

4 *Adde* the reports of the High Legal Committee of the Paris Financial Centre (HCJP) on Brexit.

5 M. Audit, S. Bollée and P. Callé, Droit du commerce international et des investissements étrangers, LGDJ, Domat droit privé, 3rd ed. 2019, No. 161.

UK's exit from the EU. If the parties to a contract designate the UK law, then this one is fully applicable and this choice is binding on the French judge as before Brexit. If the parties have not chosen the applicable law, a French judge may still be led to apply UK law if it is designated by the conflict rule of the Rome-I Regulation.

From the British perspective, the situation is more complex. From now on, the conflict rules specific to the British legal system will apply. In order to limit the impact of Brexit, the United Kingdom chose, on 29 March 2019, to incorporate the provisions of the Rome-I Regulation into the English national law. This is what the Financial Markets Law Committee (FLMC) had recommended to the UK. Initially, the harmonisation of solutions between France and the UK will remain. However, the provisions of British national law incorporating the Rome-I Regulation will no longer be interpreted by the Court of Justice of the European Union, but by the British courts. In the long run, these differences in interpretation could lead to different solutions.

However, the question arises as to the impact of Brexit on previous contracts in which English law was designated. As has been pointed out in the literature,[6] it is possible that the parties will challenge their choice of UK law to govern their contract. The Brexit could be considered as a change of circumstances justifying a form of revision for unforeseen circumstances, if the incorporation of EU law into UK law had been a determining factor in the choice of UK law at the time of conclusion of the contract. It is true that, in principle, the parties are expected to accept future changes in the chosen law if they are intended to apply to current contracts. But this solution could be discussed in the case of a change as radical as the disappearance of EU law.

Apart from this issue, concerning the law applicable to the contract, Brexit will therefore have a limited impact. The harmonisation of the solutions between France and the United Kingdom will, to a large extent, be ensured. It could even be fully ensured if the UK courts chose to base their interpretation of the UK rules incorporating the Rome-I Regulation on the interpretation of the Court of Justice of the European Union. In that case, no disharmony of solutions would exist and, as a consequence, no forum shopping would develop.

---

6 M. Audit, S. Bollée and P. Callé, *Droit du commerce international et des investissements étrangers*, LGDJ, Domat droit privé, 3rd edn, 2019, No. 161.

What about the competent court?

## II. The competent court

Until 1 January 2021, the competent court was determined by application of Regulation No. 1215/2012 of 12 December 2012, known as the Brussels-I-bis Regulation. The applicability of this regulation assumed in principle, and still assumes from the French point of view, that the defendant is domiciled in a Member state. When the defendant is domiciled in France, i.e. in the European Union, the jurisdiction of the French courts is determined by the Brussels-I-bis Regulation. In contractual matters, this regulation offers a choice of jurisdiction between the court of the Member state of the defendant's domicile and the court of the place of performance of the obligation which serves as the basis for the claim. Let us take the example of the sales of goods: this is the place where, under the contract, the goods were or should have been delivered. For the provision of services, it is the place where, under the contract, the services were or should have been provided.

If the defendant is domiciled in France, i.e. in the European Union, the Brussels-I-bis Regulation will always apply to determine the jurisdiction of the French courts. The jurisdiction of the French courts will then be guaranteed by the application of Article 4 giving jurisdiction to the courts of the Member state of the defendant's domicile. In other words, if the defendant is domiciled in France, the French courts will have jurisdiction, even if the claimant is British or domiciled in the UK. However, as the UK is no longer bound by the Brussels I bis Regulation, their courts could take jurisdiction on the basis of other criteria. The possibility of parallel proceedings in France and the UK for the same dispute will therefore be multiplied, with the risk of contradictory decisions.

In the case of a jurisdiction clause, namely a clause designating the courts of a Member state, i.e. the French courts, the Regulation applies regardless of the domicile of the parties. Such clauses may therefore give jurisdiction to the French courts, even if none of the parties was domiciled in France.

Since 1 January 2021, if the defendant is domiciled in the United Kingdom and unless there is a choice of court clause designating the courts of a Member state, the Brussels-I-bis Regulation no longer applies to determine the jurisdiction of the French courts.[7] Jurisdiction is determined in France by the rules of ordinary law. The French court system has jurisdiction if the defendant is domiciled in France. But it has jurisdiction if one of the parties has French nationality, whether a natural person or a legal entity, by application of Articles 14 and 15 of the Civil Code, which establish a privilege of jurisdiction on the basis of the French nationality of the parties. The jurisdiction of the French courts should therefore be broader in Franco-British disputes than it was before 2021,[8] since the application of these nationality privileges is currently excluded in the European judicial area when the Brussels-I-bis Regulation is applicable.

This wider jurisdiction of the French courts could come up against British injunctions. It is well known that the United Kingdom has a developed system of injunctions to regulate proceedings. In particular, there are anti-suit injunctions, whereby a British court prohibits a party, under threat of heavy penalties including criminal penalties, from initiating or pursuing legal proceedings before a foreign court. Such an injunction can therefore be used to stop proceedings commenced abroad if the UK courts consider themselves best placed to deal with them. The Court of Justice of the European Union condemned anti-suit injunctions. They were left out when the Brussels-I or Brussels-I-bis Regulation was applicable. With the Brexit, the British courts are free to issue such injunctions and prohibit, for example, the referral of a case to a French court.

As has been pointed out in the literature, it is certainly not impossible that recognition of such injunctions will be refused in the EU Member states. But this refusal of recognition does not necessarily deprive the injunction of its effectiveness,[9] as long as the party is liable to heavy penalties in the United Kingdom. It is the threat of the penalty in the United Kingdom that compels the party who has received an injunction to comply with it even if the injunction is never recognised in France.

---

7 M. Audit, S. Bollée and P. Callé, *Droit du commerce international et des investissements étrangers*, LGDJ, Domat droit privé, 3rd ed. 2019, No. 678.

8 M. Audit, S. Bollée and P. Callé, *Droit du commerce international et des investissements étrangers*, LGDJ, Domat droit privé, 3rd ed. 2019, No. 678.

9 M. Audit, S. Bollée and P. Callé, *Droit du commerce international et des investissements étrangers*, LGDJ, Domat droit privé, 3rd ed. 2019, No. 678.

It is time to turn to the question of recognition and enforcement of foreign judgments

## III. Recognition and judgments enforcement

Regulation 1215/2012 of 12 December 2012 also aimed to harmonise and liberalise the recognition of judgments between France and the UK. A French judgment could thus be recognised and enforced in the United Kingdom without any particular procedure in the state of enforcement, and vice versa. The so-called *exequatur* procedure had thus been abolished. It was sufficient when the judgment was accompanied by a standard form issued in the state of origin and translated into the language of the country of enforcement. This liberal regime for the free movement of judgments emanating from a European Union state is no longer applicable to British judgments to be recognised in France or to French judgments to be recognised in the United Kingdom. They are treated as any judgment emanating from a third state, in the absence of a bilateral convention binding the states.[10] The procedure for recognising a French judgment in the United Kingdom or a British judgment in France is therefore longer and more costly, since the mechanism for abolishing *exequatur* has ceased to apply. The procedure is now contentious and falls within the competence of the French court, which will check the conformity of the decision with the French international public policy before inserting the French executory clause. It is likely that most UK decisions will receive *exequatur* and can be enforced in France, but this will necessarily take much longer than before, since a judicial procedure has to be followed.

As for a French judgment that should be enforced in the UK, it must now follow the UK procedure. Strictly speaking, there is no *exequatur* procedure in the United Kingdom, but the beneficiary of a foreign judgment ordering payment of a sum of money must apply for enforcement of the foreign judgment as a debt instrument.[11] This is technically a new

---

10 M. Audit, S. Bollée and P. Callé, *Droit du commerce international et des investissements étrangers*, LGDJ, Domat droit privé, 3rd ed. 2019, No. 741.

11 Report on the implications of Brexit in the field of judicial cooperation in civil and commercial matters by the High Legal Committee of the Paris Financial Centre, 30 January 2017.

action with the foreign judgment as evidence. Again, this is a cumbersome and costly procedure.

To remedy this difficulty, the UK has applied for membership to the Lugano Convention of 30 October 2007. The Brussels-I-bis Regulation states that it does not affect the Lugano Convention.[12] Therefore, the termination of the Brussels-I-bis Regulation between France and the United Kingdom is not an obstacle to the possible application of the Lugano Convention. This Convention extends the system of judicial cooperation in civil and commercial matters as it results from the old Brussels-I Regulation to the Member states of the Economic Free Trade Association (EFTA). The Convention thus organises a simplified regime of recognition of judgments between the states of the European Union and Denmark, Iceland, Norway and Switzerland. This convention, originally binding the European Union and the EFTA states, is now open for signature by states outside the European Union and EFTA. It would not be a question of the United Kingdom joining the EFTA, which would mean that the United Kingdom would be linked to the European Union for its economic and commercial relations under the same conditions as the other EFTA states. This seems unthinkable given the conditions of the UK's exit from the EU. It would simply be a matter of the UK acceding to the Lugano Convention while remaining a third country to the EU and EFTA.

The application for accession to the Lugano Convention was made on 8 April 2020 by the UK, but it requires the unanimous consent of the parties, and therefore specifically the consent of the EU. While Iceland, Norway and Switzerland have given their consent, the EU has not done so. The deadline expired on 14 April 2021. From then on, the application for membership expired.

Another possible way forward is for the United Kingdom to accede to the Hague Convention of 30 June 2005 on Choice of Court Agreements. This Convention has been in force in the EU since 1 October 2015. The United Kingdom applied for accession on 28 September 2020, with effect from 1 January 2021. Unlike the Lugano Convention, it is not necessary to obtain the agreement of the other contracting parties. This Convention facilitates the recognition of judgments given between states parties to the Convention, but only for the judgments given on the basis

---

12 Art. 73 of the Regulation of 12 December 2012.

of a choice of court agreement, i.e. on the basis of a jurisdiction clause. It will therefore improve the movements of judgments between France and the United Kingdom where the contract in issue contained a choice of court clause. However, it does not provide any solution for judgments given without a choice of court clause.

In this respect, transitional provisions would be welcome to deal with the case of judgments given before the date of termination of the Brussels-I-bis Regulation, but whose recognition is sought after that date. The question arises as to their recognition regime. "Should we consider that they are intended to have effect, namely in a sense of binding, in the other Member states as soon as they are delivered. They could continue to benefit from the liberal regime of the Regulation. Or should we consider that only the date on which a party intends to use a decision in another state should be considered relevant for the applicability of the Regulation?"[13] To date, the question remains open.

*

In conclusion, as far as judicial cooperation in civil matters is concerned, Brexit is a source of uncertainty and complexity. The division of jurisdiction between the courts likely to be seized of a dispute no longer exists. The recognition and enforcement of French judgments in the United Kingdom or vice versa have become more complex. The United Kingdom also loses access to a harmonised system, since British judgments are now confronted with a large number of regimes depending on the Member states. However, via the injunctions, English judges are able to indirectly obtain an effect that is equivalent to enforcement without having to go through the exequatur.

---

[13] M. Audit, S. Bollée and P. Callé, *Droit du commerce international et des investissements étrangers*, LGDJ, Domat droit privé, 3rd ed. 2019, No. 741.

# BREXIT and international commercial litigation in Europe in times of COVID-19: Quiet dawn or perfect storm?

Guillermo PALAO MORENO

2020 has been a completely unusual year, with significant implications also in the field of international Commercial Litigation. As regards the European continent, 2020 has a unique and complex meaning. To the crisis due to COVID-19, the full culmination of BREXIT, after years of negotiation between the United Kingdom of Great Britain and Northern Ireland (UK) and the European Union (EU), must be considered. The resulting legal panorama after a full BREXIT is not at all promising, despite the publication of the *Trade and Cooperation Agreement between the EU and the European Atomic Energy Community, of the one part, and the UK of Great Britain and Northern Ireland, of the other part* (thereafter the *Trade and Cooperation Agreement*).[1]

Of particular note is the perspective of cross-border Commercial disputes, which may arise between business which are established in a Member state of the EU and in the UK. After more than three decades of sharing significant legal instruments, which have provided an enviable legal certainty to business, a new period has been opened for Europe, characterised by the reduction of the level of the existing legal certainty in this area.

This chapter analyses the dramatic consequences derived, from the point of view of the legal management of international Commercial litigation, in a geographical space where economic activity will continue to be intense.

---

1 OJ L 444/14, 31.12.2020.

## Brexit: State of affairs

With the publication of the *Agreement on the withdrawal of the UK of Great Britain and Northern Ireland from the European Union and the European Atomic Energy Community* (thereafter the *Agreement on the withdrawal*),[2] the most long and fruitful period of intra-European Commercial collaboration between both sides of the English Channel came to an end.

This legal turnout did not take place immediately, since upon signing the Agreement on the withdrawal there was a transitory stage of reflection – during which European Regulations continued to be applicable, in accordance to art. 127 of the Agreement on the withdrawal –, which was designed for the parties to negotiate the redefinition of their future relationships; something which implied a delay of the legal consequences resulting from its full application as of 31 December 2020.[3]

Nevertheless, it was not until the last moment that the awaited Trade and Cooperation Agreement was published, with the intention of overcoming the mentioned uncertainties. However, the desired results were not produced, nor was the appropriate extension of the transitional period requested in the terms set to such an end in art. 132 of the Agreement on the withdrawal (1 July 2020). An analysis of the Trade and Cooperation Agreement shows that not a single provision such Agreement has been committed to the legal issues related to the cross-border Commercial disputes that are presumably going to take place between business established in the UK and in the member states of the EU. Thus, despite the expectations generated, the *status quo* existing in the transitional period remains intact and all the legal consequences arising from Brexit are fully displayed.[4]

---

2 OJ L 29, 31.1.2020.

3 Recommendation for a Council Decision authorising the opening of negotiations for a new partnership with the United Kingdom of Great Britain and Northern Ireland (COM (2020) 35 final).

4 "Notice to stakeholders", published by the European Commission: "Withdrawal of the United Kingdom and EU rules in the field of Civil Justice and Private International Law".

## Different scenarios and implications for International Commercial litigation

The derivations that result from BREXIT are expected to occur in relation to a great range of issues. This chapter seeks to provide some reflections in relation to those connected to litigation derived from the intense cross-border Commercial activity between business established on both sides of the English Channel (excluding, personal, family or inheritance matters). In relation to this, since the moment of its foundation, the EU was intended to become a large internal market, which has effectively favoured an exponential multiplication of Commercial relations vis-à-vis its Member states. A Commercial reality to which a complex regulatory framework generated from the European Policy of Judicial Cooperation in Civil matters was likewise developed, to serve the objectives of the internal market and to provide an estimable level of legal certainty to those business established within the borders of this market. A regulatory framework that, just like the rest of the EU acquis, will cease to support citizens and business respect to their disputes.

In spite of the publication of a Trade and Cooperation Agreement, an uncertain stage opens on future relations between the UK and the EU, which may adversely affect the legal certainty that business need for the management of their Commercial disputes.[5] Thus, it is of great practical significance to refer to the regulatory framework which, in times of full BREXIT, will result to be applicable for the management of International Commercial disputes that may arise in this new scenario. A legislative framework that, from January 2021, runs in parallel and alone for the UK.[6]

---

5 C. Górriz López, "Brexit: pasado, presente y futuro", *CDT*, 2021, v. 13, 1, pp. 298–341, p. 326.

6 In this respect, the post of Professor Andrew Dickinson: "Walking Solo – A New Path for the Conflict of Laws in England", at the blog Conflict of Laws (at: <https://conflictoflaws.net>).

## I. International commercial litigation before national courts

The development of an area of Freedom, Security and Justice has derived in a complex regulatory framework in constant growth and revision that offers a positive level of efficiency, legal certainty and predictability to business within the single market. This sophisticated system is mainly ruled by the so-called "Brussels's System", whose two main instruments are the Regulation (EU) No. 1215/2012, on jurisdiction and the recognition and enforcement of judgments in Civil and Commercial matters (Brussels I bis Regulation);[7] and – for the relationships of the Member states of the EU vis-à-vis the members of the European Free Trade Agreements (EFTA) –, the "parallel" Lugano Convention of 2007 (Lugano Convention II).[8]

These two instruments concentrate the fundamental elements relating to the regulation of cross-border Civil and Commercial disputes related to the internal market. Nevertheless, the European institutions have also designed other instruments in order to frame specialised procedures and to serve the needs of particular Civil and Commercial matters within the EU.[9] All this provide a significant service to legal certainty in the internal market, and have been accompanied by a significant number of European Regulations and Directives which constitute a dense network.

Therefore, at present we should question where the replacement regulatory solution for Commercial litigation between business established in the UK and those who are established in one of the 27 Member states of the EU, should be found – once the transitional period has ended without the development of replacement rules for the ancient regime. A legitimate concern that, from the UK's perspective, has led to an intense legislative effort which has been carried out against the clock.

---

7 OJ L 351, 20.12.2012.

8 OJ L 339, 21.12.2007.

9 Regulation No. 805/2004 (OJ L 143, 30.4.2004); Regulation (EC) No. 1896/2006 (OJ L 399, 30.12.2006); Regulation (EC) No. 861/2007 (OJ L 199, 31.7.2007); Regulation (EU) No. 2015/848 (OJ L 141, 5.6.2015).

## A. International jurisdiction

According to art. 67.1 Agreement on the withdrawal, the jurisdiction rules of the Brussels-I-bis Regulation will cease to be applicable after the transitional period. This is the case, except to those legal proceedings which were initiated before the end of the transitional period and with respect to those proceedings or actions that are related to such legal proceedings, in accordance with the rules on *lis pendens* and connected actions – arts. 29, 30 and 31 Brussels Ibis Regulation.

As a consequence, in 2021 the UK has become a full "third state" for the purposes of the application of these European Regulations. This change has obvious negative consequences regarding questions such as the effectiveness of the submission agreements in favour of the British courts; as long as art. 25 Brussels-I-bis Regulation is no longer of application, and rules of International jurisdiction of the Member states are fully applicable.[10]

This new situation implies, for instance, that the Spanish courts would be competent, with regard to any litigation of a Commercial nature between companies domiciled in Spain with their British partners, in accordance with art. 22 Organic Act of the Judiciary Power of 1985 (as modified in 2015). Similarly, and in relation to Great Britain, this scenario would derive into the application of the Civil Jurisdiction and Judgments Act of 1982.

Nevertheless, it must be affirmed that such circumstances could give rise to similar solutions to those provided by the Brussels-I-bis Regulation, this for two reasons. First, the strong influence of this Regulation for the Spanish legislator when drawing up art. 22 Organic Act of the Judiciary Power should be considered. Second, the attempt to "mirror" the former legal framework, that has guided the British legislator when drafting the different legislative instruments known as the EU Exit Regulations, should also be taken into account.[11]

---

10 I. Lorente Martínez, "Brexit y cláusulas de sumisión en los contratos internacionales", *CDT*, 2017, v. 9, 2, pp. 408–418; A. Mukarrum, "Brexit and English Jurisdiction Agreements: The Post-Referendum Legal Landscape", at: SSRN: <https://ssrn.com/abstract=2839342>, pp. 1–10.

11 Civil Jurisdiction and Judgments (Amendment) (EU Exit) Regulations 2019 (SI 2019/479), which was amended by Jurisdiction, Judgments and Applicable Law (Amendment) (EU Exit) Regulations 2020 (SI 2020/1574); Law Applicable to Contractual Obligations and Non-Contractual Obligations (Amendment etc) (EU

Those difficulties will continue, despite this parallelism with the pre-Brexit situation. On the one hand, in both cases the new solutions consist of national rules which will not benefit from the interpretation of the Court of Justice of the EU (ECJ). On the other hand, it should also be mentioned the will of the UK to recover its own flexible Common Law institutions, which were rejected by the ECJ, as for instance doctrines like *forum non conveniens.*[12] A "devolution" process which also affects to issues like the face-to-face notification modes traditionally used on the Island.[13]

Litigants in Europe now face a "back to the past" effect, which the UK intends to avoid by mimicking its Regulations with those provided for in the European instruments, and through an active Conventional policy, to alleviate the void and the legal uncertainty left by the non-application of European instruments,[14] in order to enter into a bilateral Agreement with the EU in this area based on the European acquis,[15] as opposed to the impossibility of considering the application of neither the ancient Brussels Convention of 1968, nor the Lugano Convention of 1988 (Lugano Convention I).[16]

As a consequence, the UK has taken the necessary steps to – as a member of The Hague Conference on PIL – become party (again, in its own right) of The Hague Convention of 2005.[17] Additionally, the UK has expressed its willingness to adhere to the Lugano Convention II.

---

Exit) Regulations 2019 (SI 2019/834) which was also amended by SI 2020/1574; European Enforcement Order, European Order for Payment and European Small Claims Procedure (Amendment etc.) (EU Exit) Regulations 2018 (SI 2018/1311).

12 Judgement ECJ 1.3.2005, Case C-281/02, *Owusu, Rec.*, 2005, p. I-1383.

13 Regulation (EC) No. 1206/2001 (OJ L 174, 27.6.2001) and Regulation (EC) No. 1393/2007 (OJ L 324, 10.12.2007), which will be respectively replaced by Regulation (EU) 2020/1783, and Regulation (EU) 2020/1784 (both at: OJ L 405, 2.12.2020).

14 Private International Law (Implementation of Agreements) Act 2020.

15 B. Cortese, "Brexit e diritto internazionale privato tra Roma, Bruxelles e Lugano: 'How can i just let you walk away?' ", *CDT*, 2021, v. 13, 1, pp. 153–179, p. 178; G. Rühl, "Private International Law Post-Brexit: Between Plague and Cholera", available at SSRN: <https://ssrn.com/abstract=3553768>, pp. 1–10, pp. 3–6.

16 P. Bertoli, "La "Brexit" e il diritto internazionale privato e processuale", *Riv. dir. int. pr. proc.*, 2017, 3, pp. 599–632, pp. 605–612.

17 Civil Jurisdiction and Judgments (Hague Convention on Choice of Court Agreements 2005) (EU Exit) Regulations 2018. Communication "Getting ready for changes Communication on readiness at the end of the transition period between the European Union and the United Kingdom" (COM/2020/324 final).

Something that, however, seems to pose legal complexities and will not lead to the same result as it pretends to alleviate.[18] In any case, it will be necessary to pay attention to the future steps that the different actors involved (the UK, the EU, The Hague Conference or the EFTA), will take in this area in the future.

## B. Recognition and enforcement of foreign decisions

The end of the transitional period has also implied that the judicial authorities must end the bilateral application of the rules provided by in the Brussels-I-bis Regulation, to proceed with the recognition and the enforcement of the decisions. Nevertheless, this effect will emerge gradually – in accordance to art. 67.2, (a) Agreement on the withdrawal –, as this EU instrument will be still of application to the recognition and to the enforcement of decisions issued in judicial proceedings initiated before the end of the transitional period, as well as to public documents formalised or officially registered and court settlements approved or concluded before this moment.

Once the Cooperation and Trade Agreement has been approved, the national PIL rules of each country must be followed,[19] which are based on the tradition principle of reciprocity. As a result, besides a fragmented legal environment, this will give rise to an increase of litigation. This will be the case even if national legislations adopt those instruments as a model. In the case of Spain, Title V (arts. 41–61) Spanish Act of International Legal Cooperation in Civil Matters will be of application;[20] while in the case of Great Britain the legal answer will be found again, in the Civil Jurisdiction and Judgments Act of 1982.

---

18 "Assessment on the application of the United Kingdom of Great Britain and Northern Ireland to accede to the 2007 Lugano Convention" (COM (2021) 222 final); R. Arenas García, "El Reino Unido y el Convenio de Lugano", *La Ley UE*, 2020, 83, pp. 1–12; B. Hess, "The unsuitability of the Lugano Convention (2007) to Serve as a Bridge between the UK and the EU after Brexit", *MPILux Research Paper*, 2018, 2.

19 C. Tuo, "The Consequences of Brexit for Recognition and Enforcement of Judgments in Civil and Commercial Matters: Some Remarks", *Riv. dir. int. pr. proc.*, 2019, pp. 302–318.

20 OJ *(Spain)* 182, 31.7.2015.

## II. Alternative Dispute Resolution

During the last decades there has been an increase in the use of Alternative Dispute Resolution (ADR) mechanisms in Europe, to deal with International Commercial disputes. This increase, fostered by the use of new technologies, has also been favoured by Covid-19. The reasons which underline and support this rise exceeds the objectives of this Chapter, but it is an incontestable reality today.[21] The current intensive use of ADR mechanisms requires analyzing the consequences that Brexit will imply for them.

### A. *International Mediation in commercial matters*

In accordance with art. 69.1, (b) Agreement on the withdrawal, Directive 2008/52/EC,[22] applied in some situations during that period. However, once this moment has elapsed, business must refer for its regulation to the binding international Conventions and the internal legislation of each country involved. While in Spain the Act 5/2012 will be of application,[23] in the UK the relevant instrument also results from the transposition of Directive 2008/52/EC, whose provisions have been adapted to a full Brexit. In this respect, both the Civil Procedure Amendment Rules 2011 and the Cross-Border Mediation (EU Directive) Regulations 2011, should be considered; in Scotland the Cross-Border Mediation (EU Directive) Regulations 2011 will apply.[24] In any case, the aforementioned national rules will continue to be fully in force.

However, certain differences derived from the process of the national incorporation of the Directive 2008/52/EC should be considered. The Spanish legislator opted for a wide territorial scope of application and, as a result, the Spanish 5/2012 Act is of application also regarding those situations involving business domiciled in the UK and in another third countries (*ex* its art. 3.1).

---

21 S. Barona Vilar, *Nociones y principios de las ADR (solución extrajurisdiccional de conflictos)*, Valencia, Tirant lo Blanch, 2018, pp. 20–26.

22 OJ L 136, 24.5.2008.

23 OJ *(Spain)* 162, 7.6.2012. Also Royal Decree 980/2013 (OJ *(Spain)* 310, 27.12.2013).

24 E.B. Crawford and J.M. Carruthers, "United Kingdom", in C. Esplugues, J.L. Iglesias and G. Palao (Eds.), *Civil and Commercial Mediation in Europe. National Mediation Rules and Procedures*, Cambridge, Intersentia, 2013, v. I., pp. 515–539.

However, in the UK a stricter incorporation of the Directive 2008/52/EC was accepted, limiting the scope of application of their national legislation to only intra-community disputes. A geographical restraint that has been alleviated in the UK, by adopting the appropriate modifications to its Regulations for Brexit reasons; thus, expanding the cross-border situations which they cover (and including the UK, together with the current Member states of the EU).[25] This led to the effects that national law will continue to regulate cross-border Mediation procedures also in the UK. However, the interpretation and the uniformity which the ECJ provides will not be applicable to the new UK legislative framework.

As for the near future, the importance of the United Nations Convention on International Settlement Agreements Resulting from Mediation (the "Singapore Convention on Mediation") should also be underlined.[26] A multilateral instrument which was published simultaneously with the UNCITRAL Model Law on International Commercial Mediation and International Settlement Agreements Resulting from Mediation, 2018.[27] The Singapore Convention is a significant instrument, highly inspired by the well-known Convention on the Recognition and Enforcement of Foreign Arbitral Awards of 1958 (the "New York Convention"), which has not been signed or ratified yet, neither by the UK, nor by any Member state of the EU.

At the current stage both the EU and the UK must take their own strategic decisions in this regard, once the latter is no longer affected by the *ad extra* competence of the EU.[28] Therefore, once the Singapore Convention has entered into force – on 12 September 2020 –, its ratification by the UK may prove to be useful for this country, in accordance with the importance of London as a venue for international Commercial Mediations. Anyway, at present it is difficult to ascertain whether the Singapore Convention could also be used to facilitate the circulation of Mediation settlement agreements issued on both sides of the English Channel.[29]

---

25 The effect of the Cross-Border Mediation (EU Directive) (EU Exit) Regulations 2019.

26 GA Resolution 20.12.2018 (A/RES/73/198).

27 GA Resolution 20.12.2018 (A/RES/73/199).

28 Opinion ECJ 1/13, 14.10.2014 (ECLI:EU:C:2014:2303).

29 C. Esplugues Mota, "La Convención de Singapur de 2018 sobre mediación y la creación de un título deslocalizado dotado de fuerza ejecutiva: una apuesta novedosa, y un mal resultado", *REDI*, 2020, v. 72, 1, pp. 53–80; Th. Schnabel,

## B. International Commercial Arbitration

The international Commercial Arbitration sector will, in principle, suffer less impact due to Brexit. The fact that Arbitration in Commercial matters has been systematically excluded from the scope of application of the various European instruments – i.e. art. 1.2, (d) Brussels-I-bis Regulation[30] –, a not excessively traumatic transition to the new post-Brexit scenario should take place. In addition to a continued application of the different and significant international Conventions that bind the UK and the current 27 Member states of the EU, which facilitate the cross-border circulation of awards between the UK and the EU Member states – i.e. the New York Convention of 1958,[31] or the European Convention on International Commercial Arbitration of 1961[32] –, the respective national Arbitration Acts form the affected countries will continue to apply. National legislation which is based on the Model Law on International Commercial Arbitration of 1985 (modified in 2006).[33] In this respect, the Spanish Arbitration Act 60/2003,[34] and the Arbitration Acts in Great Britain (English of 1996 or Scottish of 2010).

Nonetheless, the end of the transitional period will derive in some changes which should be taken into account. Although European Regulations have pursued to maintain a certain position of neutrality regarding the ruling of international Commercial Arbitration, the ECJ has adopted a more active position regarding certain elements and with some Common Law institutions, after their interpretation in relation to the objectives of European instruments.[35]

---

"The Singapore Convention on Mediation: A Framework for the Cross-Border Recognition and Enforcement of Mediated Settlements", *Pepp. Disp. Resol. L.J.*, 1 2019, v. 19, 1, pp. 1–60. *Vide*: Singapore Mediation Convention Reference Book, Cardozo JCR, 2019, v. 20, 4, pp. 1001–1267.

30 F. Ferrari (Ed.), *The impact of EU Law on International Commercial Arbitration*, Huntington, Juris, 2017, pp. 31–62; L.H. Wilhelmsen, *International Commercial Arbitration and the Brussels I Regulation*, Cheltenham. Edward Elgar, 2018.

31 United Nations, *Treaty Series*, v. 330, 4739.

32 United Nations, *Treaty Series*, v. 484, 7041.

33 United Nations A/40/17, Annex I, Supplement 17.

34 OJ *(Spain)* 309, 26.12.2003.

35 Judgements ECJ, 25.7.1991, Case C-190/89, *Marc Rich* (ECLI:EU:C:1991:319); 17.11.1998, Case C-391/95, *Van Uden* (ECLI:EU:C:1998:543); 10.2.2009, Case C-185/07, *Allianz/West Tankers Inc.* (ECLI:EU:C:2009:69); and 13.5.2015, Case C-536/13, *Gazprom OAO* (ECLI:EU:C:2015:316).

Therefore, British judicial and arbitral authorities – mainly English, due to the importance of London as an international seat for international Commercial Arbitrations –, are entitled to make use of Common Law institutions such as anti-suit Injunctions, in relation to litigation related to persons domiciled in the Member states of the EU. In addition to this, British legal judicial authorities will no longer be obliged by the delimitation that the ECJ has made of the concept of public order present in art. V New York Convention of 1958.[36]

*

In conclusion, this Chapter has analysed the current regulatory framework governing Commercial disputes which may arise between business established in the UK and in the 27 Member states of the EU after Brexit. Something which has derived into a complex scenario, because the Trade and Cooperation Agreement has provided no legal solution to the end of the transitional period of the Agreement on the withdrawal. A panorama that appears to become even more complicated due to the effect of Covid-19. It can be affirmed that a new period begins not exempt from a negative level of legal uncertainty, which steps back on the outstanding achievements made during the last three decades in the EU. Particularly, when the good level of efficiency and legal certainty guaranteed previously for traders in intra-European disputes is considered.

Nothing prevents the construction of a new and future common regulatory framework between the UK and the EU, which might offer greater legal certainty to the parties in this specific area. Moreover, it may even occur that this legal lacuna could be alleviated from the British perspective, through unilateral initiatives or even by gaining ground in the international arena and updating the British Conventional system in the field of cross-border Commercial disputes.[37] Nevertheless, as far as international Commercial litigation in Europe is concerned, nothing will ever be the same again.

---

[36] M. Molfa and R. Monico, "The impact of Brexit in international Arbitration", *Riv. dir. int. pr. proc.*, 2019, 4, pp. 856–874, pp. 859–867.

[37] B. Cortese, *op. cit.*, pp. 177–178.

Therefore, business will have to be vigilant and should rapidly adapt to this new and complex regulatory scenario. Let us trust that this new dawn of relations between the UK and the EU will give rise to a luminous sky for all and that the storm clouds that lurk them will be avoided.

# The legal issues of personal data transfers after Brexit

Fanny Rogue

In a previous publication in this Kazakh-French-Korean law series, we discussed the legal challenges of personal data protection.[1] On that occasion, we wondered about the notion of personal data and the legal issues involved in applying the general principles of personal data protection. In that first (2019) contribution, we were not able to address the major issue of the free flow of personal data in a globalised environment. It is therefore quite natural for this chapter to choose this theme for this new (2021) publication.

It should first be remembered that personal data is "information relating to an identified or identifiable natural person (…) by reference to an identifier".[2] This information is related to the private life and individual freedom of a natural person and cannot be used, modified, given or transferred freely. Since the Directive 95/46 of 24 October 1995,[3] the European legislation strictly regulates the processing of personal data, and in particular data transfers. The General Data Protection Regulation (GDPR),[4] adopted on 25 April 2016 and applicable since 222 May 2018, repealed this directive, while retaining its own philosophy. The European legislator maintains a balance between two objectives that may at first

---

1 F. Rogue, "The legal challenges of personal data protection", in A. Cayol, Z. Sairambaeva and P. Chabal (Eds.), *The challenge of change for the legal and political systems of Eurasia*, Brussels, Peter Lang, 2020, p. 263.

2 GDPR, art. 4, 1°.

3 Directive 95/46/EC of the European Parliament and of the Council of 24 October 1995 on the protection of individuals with regard to the processing of personal data and on the free movement of such data, OJEC November 23, 1995.

4 Regulation (EU) 2016/679 of the European Parliament and of the council of 27 April 2016 on the protection of natural persons with regard to the processing of personal data and on the free movement of such data, and repealing Directive 95/46/EC (General Data Protection Regulation), OJUE May 4, 2016.

appear contradictory: i/ to ensure a high level of protection of personal data, and ii/ to promote the free flow of such data within the European Union.[5]

Thus, Article 1 of the GDPR states that the Regulation "protects fundamental rights and freedoms of natural persons, and in particular their right to the protection of personal data", but also that "the free movement of personal data within the Union shall be neither restricted nor prohibited for reasons connected with the protection of natural persons with regard to the processing of personal data".

The legal framework created by the GDPR (and, before that, of Directive 95/46) facilitates the flow of personal data within the EU. Of course, the data controller[6] and its processor[7] will have to comply with the general principles[8] and obligations under the Regulation,[9] but they will not have to obtain any other formality or authorisation. It should be noted that the GDPR applies to any processing of personal data that is carried out in the course of the activities of an establishment of a controller or processor on the territory of the EU,[10] but also, when the controller or processor is not established on the European territory, when their activities are relate either to the offering of goods and services to persons located within the EU or to the monitoring of the behaviour of natural persons, when this behaviour is located within the EU.[11] In this respect, the power of attraction of the GDPR is very important, as the legislation applies to controllers or processors located outside the EU, as long as the data processing they carry out is directly relevant to individuals residing or living in the EU.

On the contrary, as soon as personal data is transferred outside the European territory, the GDPR framework becomes stricter. In principle, data transfers outside the EU[12] are not

5 TFUE, art. 16, § 1. OJUE June 7, 2016.

6 The one who determines the purposes and means of data processing (GDPR, art. 4, 7).

7 The person who processes the data on behalf of the controller (GDPR, art. 4, 8).

8 GDPR, art. 5 and s.

9 GDPR, art. 24 and s.

10 GDPR, art. 3, 1.

11 GDPR, art. 3, 2.

12 And the European Economic Area (EEA). Member countries are therefore not considered as third parties and the flow of personal data is facilitated with these countries (Norway, Iceland and Liechtenstein).

allowed.[13] It is only under certain limited conditions that a controller or processor may export personal data it processes to a third country.

This chapter investigates the framework for personal data transfers outside the EU under the GDPR (I), before discussing the strict interpretation of the Regulation by the CJEU on this issue (II).

## I. The GDPR framework for personal data transfers outside the EU

Surprisingly, the GDPR (like Directive 95/46 before it) does not define what a transfer of personal data outside the EU is.[14] Let's take a general approach and define the transfer of personal data as the operation whereby such data leaves the European territory, to a third country that does not apply European data protection legislation. A transfer can take place by any means (communication, copy, flow of personal data) and any medium (hard disk, flash drive, cloud, internet or intranet...). The assessment of the transfer operation is therefore very broad, but does not go so far as to consider that making personal data available on a website accessible to everyone can be qualified as a personal data transfer outside the EU.[15] The transfer of data may be carried out by a controller or by a processor, as data exporter. In general, the data exporter is located within the EU. The data may be sent to a third party (data importer) or transmitted "intra-company" (transfer between several entities of the same controller or processor).

Thus, as the CJEU recently pointed out, "the operation of having personal data transferred from a Member state to a third country constitutes, in itself, processing of personal data".[16]

Transfers of data outside the EU are in principle prohibited by Article 44 of the GDPR: "Any transfer of personal data which are undergoing processing or are intended for processing after transfer to a third

---

13 GDPR, art. 44.

14 Even though it defines cross-border processing (GDPR, art. 4, 23), which take place within the EU and which condition the use of the "one-stop shop" mechanism of the lead supervisory authority (GDPR, art. 56 and seq.).

15 ECJ, 6 November 2003, C101/01, Lindqvist.

16 CJEU, July 16, 2020, *Data Protection Commissioner C/ Facebook Ireland Ltd & M. Schrems* (so-called Schrems II judgment), C311-18, § 83.

country or to an international organisation shall take place only if (...)". This prohibition principle is justified in view of the risks incurred by the persons whose data are transferred. In particular, they can avoid this by exercising their right to data protection.[17] However, the prohibition can be lifted if certain conditions are met by the controller or the processor. The strict supervision of data transfers outside the EU is justified by the need to respect a high level of protection of the individuals whose data are processed.[18] The European legislator is being pragmatic: under the present globalised economy, it would have been illusory to impose an absolute ban on personal data exports to third countries.[19] However, taking globalisation into account must not be done at the expense of the protection of individuals.

Thus, a controller or processor must make sure that the transfer of personal data that it intends to set up towards a third country comply with Articles 45–49 of the GDPR. The Regulation organises a complex system of diverse and hierarchical grounds that may justify the implementation of a personal data transfer to a third country. First, it will be necessary to verify whether the European Commission has issued an adequacy decision attesting that the third country (or, more restrictively, a territory or sector of activity of that country) ensures an adequate level of protection of personal data.[20] In other words, the third country ensures, through its legislation or case law, a protection of personal data equivalent to the GDPR. If such a decision exists, the personal data transfer can be implemented, without authorisation.

To date, few third countries[21] have been subject to an adequacy decision. Neither China, Kazakhstan nor Russia have been granted an adequacy decision, despite the existence of domestic data protection legislation. An adequacy decision is currently being negotiated with South Korea. As for the situation of the United Kingdom after Brexit, a

---

17 GDPR, Recital 116.

18 GDPR, art. 44 *in fine*.

19 GDPR, Recital 101: *"Flows of personal data to and from countries outside the Union and international organisations are necessary for the expansion of international trade and international cooperation"*.

20 GDPR, art. 45.

21 Andorra, Argentina, Canada (*Personal Information Protection and Electronic Documentation Act*), Faroe Islands, Guernsey, Israel, Isle of Man, Japan, Jersey, New Zealand, Switzerland, and Uruguay.

transitional phase of six months[22] has been adopted following the cooperation agreement with the EU of 24 December 2020. During this transitional period, the GDPR remains in force in the UK. At the end of this period, any transmission of personal data to the UK will be considered as a transfer of data outside the EU, subject to the strict framework mentioned here. There is currently a negotiation about an adequacy decision between the UE and the UK.

In the absence of an adequacy decision, the controller or processor must provide "appropriate safeguards".[23] In this respect, they may adopt Binding Corporate Rules (BCR). These are internal rules on personal data protection that apply within a group of companies. The aim is to define a code of conduct within the group that ensures a high level of protection for personal data transfers. All the entities of the group, whether or not they are located in the EU, undertake to comply with these rules, guaranteeing internal compliance with the European data protection standard. These BCRs are subject to approval by the supervisory authority.[24] Once approved, intra-group data transfers will be allowed, provided that the BCRs are respected. The disadvantage of these BCRs is that they only govern transfers of personal data within the same group. As soon as the transfer is made to an external importer, another guarantee must be implemented to legitimise the transfer. In this respect, the data controller or processor may conclude standard data protection clauses (SCC) with the non-EU importer of the personal data. These are standard contracts that will bind the exporter and the importer of personal data to ensure a high level of data protection.

These SCCs can be adopted by the European Commission or by a national supervisory authority.[25] The European Commission has adopted SCCs (SCC Decisions) on the basis of Directive 95/46, which remains in force pending the drafting of new SCCs in application of the GDPR and the recent case law of the CJEU. Thus, there are SCCs regulating the transfers of personal data between two controllers[26] and between

---

22 Until July 1, 2021.

23 GDPR, art. 46.

24 In France, the CNIL.

25 In this case, the SCCs adopted by the national authority must be approved by the European Commission.

26 Commission Decision 2001/497/EC, July 15, 2001 on standard contractual clauses for the transfer of personal data to third countries (amended by Decision 2004/915/

a controller and a processor.[27] In addition to these measures, it is also possible to justify the transfer of personal data outside the European territory with regard to a Code of Conduct or a certification process. Such mechanisms are currently not used or are barely used, as they were recently introduced by the GDPR and require a prior approval process by the national supervisory authority or the European Commission.

Alternatively, between public authorities, a legally binding and enforceable instrument may be adopted, such as an international agreement on cooperation in the fight against financial fraud. Other *"appropriate safeguards"* are covered by Article 46 of the GDPR but are intended to be subsidiary, as they are subject to prior approval by the national supervisory authority: *ad hoc* contractual clauses and non-binding administrative arrangements between public authorities.

Exceptionally, and despite the absence of a declaration of adequacy adopted by the European Commission and of appropriate safeguards, it is nevertheless possible to transfer personal data outside the EU, in certain situations referred to in Article 49 of the GDPR and in particular if the controller has obtained the explicit consent of the person whose data is being processed. These special derogations therefore allow personal data to be transferred to a third country that does not provide a level of protection that is equivalent to that of the GDPR and regarding which the exporter and importer cannot implement safeguards to achieve a high level of protection of personal data.

There is therefore a potential infringement of individual freedoms, including privacy. For this reason, these exemptions are to be interpreted strictly[28] and must be implemented for a one-time, not repetitive transfer of personal data outside the European territory.[29]

It is the responsibility of the data controller, the exporter of data, to ensure that the legal framework for data transfers outside European territory is properly respected. This is particularly the case when the

---

EC of December 27, 2004 and by Implementing Decision 2016/2297 of December 16, 2016).

27 Commission Decision 2010/87, February 5, 2010 on standard contractual clauses for the transfer of personal data to processors established in third countries under (amended by Implementing Decision 2016/2297 of December 16, 2016).

28 EDPB, Guidelines 2/2018, May 25, 2018, *on derogations of Article 49 under Regulation 2016/679.*

29 GDPR, art. 49, 1 and 2.

controller deals with a processor who carries out all or part of the processing operations and who is not located on European territory. In this respect, the choice of the processor is subject to the latter presenting appropriate technical and organisational measures.[30] A written contract must be concluded between the controller and the processor specifying the rights and obligations of each. In particular, the processor may only process personal data on documented instructions from the controller, including with respect to data transfers outside the EU. The controller, when choosing its processor, must take into account the national legislation applicable to the latter, in order to ensure that a transfer of personal data to this processor is possible and in order to determine, if necessary, the appropriate safeguards that must be implemented, in the absence of a national legislation equivalent to the GDPR.

The same vigilance is required from the processor, when he himself resorts to subcontracting and is led to transfer the data to his processor located outside the European territory. In this respect, he cannot engage another processor without having first obtained the written authorisation of the controller.[31] He must also conclude a written contract with his own processor and ensure that the latter presents sufficient guarantees in terms of data protection. Specifically, if a data controller in France wishes to outsource a processing operation (for example, data storage on a server) to a processor located in South Korea, it will need to use BCRs (if the processor is a member of the group), SCCs or any other appropriate safeguards within the meaning of Article 46 GDPR.

The same applies if the controller is located in France, outsources a processing operation to a processor in Germany who in turn decides to store the data on a server in Kazakhstan. Appropriate safeguards (BCRs, SCCs or others) will have to be adopted by the German processor, under the supervision of the French controller.

Both the controller and the processor must be particularly vigilant: a violation of the GDPR with respect to data transfers outside the European territory is punishable by an administrative fine, imposed by a supervisory authority, of up to €20 million or 4 % of the total worldwide annual turnover of the preceding financial year (whichever is higher)[32] and by

[30] GDPR, art. 28.

[31] GDPR, art. 28, 2.

[32] GDPR, art. 83, 5, b.

criminal sanctions in France.[33] In addition, the supervisory authority may also suspend data flows outside the EU or ban the processing of personal data.[34] To enable data subjects to achieve such remedies, the controller must inform them of its intention to transfer data to a third country, of the existence or absence of an adequacy decision, and of the appropriate safeguards it adopts to ensure a high level of protection of personal data.[35]

The risk of sanctions is even greater today, given the strict interpretation of the GDPR by the CJEU regarding transfers of personal data outside the EU.

## II. The strict interpretation of the European regulation by the CJEU: The Schrems II ruling and its consequences

In a recent case, the CJEU provided useful clarification on the legal framework restricting transfers of personal data outside the European territory. Let us set the scene first.

An Austrian citizen, Maximillian Schrems, a user of the social network Facebook since 2008. In 2013, filed a complaint with the Irish Data Protection Commissioner, because of the transfer of his data by Facebook to its headquarters in the United States. At the time, Edward Snowden revealed the NSA and FBI's surveillance of the personal data of European social networks users, in particular under the PRISM and UPSTREAM surveillance programs.[36] Mr. Schrems requested that his personal data should not be exported to the U.S., to avoid being incidentally subject to surveillance by U.S. government agencies. Facebook is defending itself by invoking its adherence to Safe Harbor, an agreement between the United States and the EU which justified that companies declared to the Department of Commerce ensure a high level of

---

33 C. pén., art. 226-22-1.

34 GDPR, art. 58, 2 (f et j).

35 GDPR, art. 13 et 14.

36 Section 702 of the FISA (*Foreign Intelligence Surveillance Act, Amendments Act, Public Law n°110–261, July 10, 2008*) and E.O. 12333.

protection of personal data (through a self-certification mechanism). The Safe Harbor was subject to an adequacy decision by the Commission.[37]

The Commissioner having rejected his complaint, Mr. Schrems appealed to the Irish High Court, which referred several questions to the CJEU for a preliminary ruling. In a first ruling on this case, the CJEU invalidated the Safe Harbor adequacy decision[38] because this agreement did not provide sufficient protection of personal data, in particular because European citizens could not claim a right to an effective remedy against the collection and processing of data by the U.S. authorities, in the context of their surveillance activities.

Following this decision of the CJEU, the U.S. government and the European Commission negotiated a new agreement, adopted by a decision of the European Commission on 12 July 2016,[39] the "EU-US Privacy Shield Framework Principles". This agreement was supposed to remedy the shortcomings of Safe Harbor in terms of privacy and personal data protection and the right to a fair trial. In this respect, the American government had instituted an ombudsman, the Privacy Shield Ombudsperson, which was supposed to fill the gap in the ability of Europeans to have an effective remedy against American government agencies.

Despite the adequacy decision, scholars and practitioners quickly agreed on the weaknesses of this decision. This concern about the real adequacy of the Privacy Shield increased further following the adoption by the U.S. federal government of the Cloud Act,[40] which allows U.S. authorities to obtain from providers of electronic communications services or remote computing services (Cloud) the disclosure of the personal data they hold, regardless of where the data are located, in the context of criminal investigations.

It is in this context that the Schrems case spread.

---

37 Commission decision 2000/520/EC, 26 July 2000 pursuant to Directive 95/46/EC of the European Parliament and of the Council on the adequacy of the protection provided by the Safe Harbour privacy principles and related frequently asked questions issued by the US Department of Commerce.

38 CJEU, Oct. 6, 2015, Case C-362/14, *Schrems v. Data Protection Commissioner.*

39 European Commission Implementing Decision No. 2016/1250/EU, 12 July 2016.

40 "Clarifying Lawful Overseas Use of Data Act or Cloud Act (H.R. 4943)", March 23, 2018.

Following the invalidation of Safe Harbor, the complaint was referred to the Commissioner. Facebook argued that the majority of its data transfers to the United States were covered by SCCs, ensuring a sufficient level of protection of personal data with respect to the requirements of European law. Mr. Schrems reformulated his complaint in the light of this new argument, and the Commissioner then referred it directly to the High Court, which again referred new questions to the CJEU for a preliminary ruling.

In a second decision on the Schrems case, the CJEU will invalidate the Privacy Shield agreement and strictly regulate the use of the SCCs.[41] The Privacy Shield adequacy decision is invalidated because the Privacy Shield does not provide a level of protection that is equivalent to the GDPR. The surveillance system of the US governmental agencies violates the privacy and the protection of personal data of European citizens. It does not support any limitation and persons concerned do not have a real possibility to defend their rights before the courts, the recourse to the Ombudsperson appearing insufficient. This surveillance system does not respect the principle of proportionality of any processing of personal data with regard to the rights and freedoms of individuals.

As for the SCCs, they are valid, given their contractual nature. The decision of the Commission establishing these SCCs is not binding on third countries and is therefore not subject to invalidation. Nevertheless, the level of protection of the individuals whose personal data are processed cannot be compromised. For this reason, the CJEU considers that it is up to the exporter of the data (Controller or processor subject to the GDPR) and the importer of the data, located in a third country, to verify that the legislation of the third country allows the importer of the data to comply with its obligations as set out in the SCCs, and this before any transfer of personal data.

In other words, it is up to them to verify, *in concreto*, that the legislation of the third country respects a level of protection of privacy and personal data equivalent to the European legislation. If this is not the case, the supervisory authority may suspend or prohibit the transfer of data. In this case, the validation *in abstracto* of the SCC decision does not legitimise the transfer of personal data to the United States, since it

---

[41] CJEU, 16 July 2020, Case C-311/18, *Data Protection Commissioner v. Facebook Ireland Ltd, Maximillian Schrems.*

has been established that the US legislation does not ensure a level of data protection equivalent to that established by the GDPR. Therefore, in order to legitimise the transfer of data to the U.S., the exporter and importer of personal data will have to adopt, in addition to the SCCs, additional safeguards to ensure a high level of data protection, such as pseudonymisation and encryption of the transmitted data. However, it is not clear whether this is sufficient. For this reason, in France, a decree has been adopted to stop all transfers of health data to the United States. This also calls into question the hosting of health data with Microsoft Azure, as part of the Health Data Hub platform, which brings together all the health data of people being treated in France.

This decision of the CJEU, although it relates to a specific adequacy decision, nevertheless weakens the adequacy decisions adopted by the Commission with respect to other countries, as it is not certain at first sight that their legislation really provides a level of protection of personal data that is equivalent to the GDPR. At any time, a preliminary question could be submitted to the CJEU regarding another adequacy decision.

To ensure the validity and stability of a personal data transfer outside the EU, it is preferable to adopt additional technical safeguards, whether the transfer is justified by an adequacy decision, SCCs or BCRs, since the CJEU emphasises that the transfer of data, regardless of its basis, must be done in a context that guarantees the protection of the rights and freedoms of individuals equivalent to what is provided by the GDPR. These additional safeguards may not be sufficient to justify personal data transfers to certain third countries which do not provide sufficient protection of fundamental rights and which do not have independent courts to ensure the protection of personal data. In this regard, the European Parliament expressed concern in 2016 about the increased number of personal data transfers to China.[42]

*

In conclusion, for the time being, there is still uncertainty about the sustainability of personal data transfers to a country outside the EU. The framework of the GDPR for such transfers and the strict interpretation

---

42 <https://www.europarl.europa.eu/RegData/etudes/ATAG/2016/583836/EPRS_ATA(2016)583836_EN.pdf>.

of the CJEU are, in effect, encouraging data controllers and processors to settle in the EU and invite third countries to adopt a legislative framework that is equivalent to that adopted by the European legislator to facilitate the flow of personal data at a global level. This strengthens the attractiveness of the GDPR, as well as the protection of personal data.

# Human and commercial challenges of the single European market and the Asian market

Michel Bruno

At a time when China displays a growth rate 18 % higher than it experienced before the health crisis, and the same progress is being observed in most Asian countries, European growth is weak.[1] The lagging European market is neither legally nor politically armed to face this competition from Asia. In addition, Europe is still in the grip of the health crisis which is exacerbating her trade problem with Asian countries. This highlights the dependence of all EU Member states on Asian countries for the vast majority of medicines and even some components necessary to manufacture vaccines. The sovereignty of EU Member states is therefore in danger. They depend on Asian countries, beyond drugs (a crucial sector if there is one), in many other products that threaten their sovereignty, in particular electronic components necessary for certain armaments and construction in aeronautics and the space industry. The "investment pump" that Asia in general and China in particular have become for several decades now questions the sovereign rights of all Member states and that of the European Union.

The current commercial challenges to the Single European market (SEM) vis-à-vis Asian countries are therefore sizeable. Behind the bitter observation of Asia's trade power in the face of the EU's commercial powerlessness to deal with it, lie issues that attack the very foundations of European democracies. These are contributing to their own destruction and to that of the EU. Asian industrial products, much cheaper on the European market than European products, lead to the destruction of jobs in Europe and the impoverishment of populations and European companies have been relocating to Asian countries for about thirty years. At the same time, this leads to the

1 This chapter is translated from the French by Pierre Chabal.

impoverishment of EU Member states, which receive less and less tax revenue from businesses and individuals.

This situation is the result of two correlating factors. First of all, at home, Member states are not on the same footing in the face of the globalisation of trade and therefore of the numerous trade agreements concluded by the EU with third states, and in particular with the states of Asia (I). European trade is hampered by trade agreements with Asian countries which accentuate the deindustrialisation of the EU by benefiting multinationals. In addition, these agreements indirectly damage labour law and fundamental rights in most Asian countries and, consequently, workers in the EU (II).

## I. A European market handicapped internally in the face of global economic competition and Asian economic competition in particular

The EU's internal market is not a uniform market and therefore is not a true Single market. We can simply say that this is a very incomplete market in some major areas. Indeed, the rules of law are very different from one EU country to another, both socially and fiscally (A). Competition is therefore acute among EU Member states and among companies from different Member states established on EU territory and among salaried workers established in different EU countries. We are witnessing normative competition among the Member states of the European Union. This situation has dramatic consequences for democracy (B).

### *A. A disunited internal European market*

The single act of 1986 which was to implement a large European market by 1 January 1993 among the Member states of the European Economic Community did not achieve the objective of establishing a genuine European single market. This treaty is very imperfect. If it certainly deepened the common market, it did not provide for the harmonisation of fiscal and social rules among the Member states of the European Economic Community. At the time, this went quite unnoticed for two reasons.

The first relates to the fact that the Treaty of Rome of 1957 establishing the European Economic Community does not allow this possibility of harmonisation among the Member states because direct taxation and social questions remained the competence almost exclusively of the Member states. The second reason concerns the fact that the 12 Member states had fairly similar tax and social rules even if certain states already stood out in tax matters, notably Ireland and the Netherlands. At the time, these two states already had very attractive corporate taxation compared to other Member states.

However, the disunity within the European market was seriously accentuated with the entry into the European Communities and the EU on 1 May 2004 of 10 new Member states. Indeed, these new Member states have very advantageous tax and social rules for companies. Subsequently, the arrival in the EU of Romania and Bulgaria in 2007 further increased social and fiscal differences. The division among the Western European market and the Eastern European market of the EU is an indisputable economic fact. Production costs are much lower in countries which have recently joined the EU. To this must also be added Croatia, which entered the European market in 2013.

Unhealthy competition within the EU immediately manifested itself in 2004, then even more so in 2007. A wave of relocation of companies established in the west of the EU towards the new Member states occurred as early as 2004 One has the bad impression that almost everything had been carefully prepared by the large western companies to relocate as quickly as possible to the eastern European market. A corresponding impoverishment of most western European Member states and of their citizens followed and is still at work. This harsh competition within the European market itself is a legal and political aberration. The losers in this unfair yet legal competition, which is totally paradoxical in a so-called single market, are the working citizens both in west Europe and east Europe. This disruption of the European market among European citizens has dramatic consequences for the very foundations of European democracy under construction and for the very principle of non-discrimination among European citizens.

## B. A European market at the service of large companies

It is indeed surprising to note that the principle of non-discrimination based on nationality is used against European citizens. This is because it can only be invoked by a citizen from another Member state in the host Member state. This principle is also called the principle of equal treatment in the host country. It was therefore initially beneficial to the freedom of movement of workers within the European internal market. But today, it mainly benefits large companies and the relocation system which allows them to benefit from less restrictive social, wage and fiscal standards.

This principle is completely outdated because it has become a legal weapon no longer for the benefit of European citizens but for the benefit of multinational companies. And one can legitimately wonder about the very concepts of European democracy and European citizenship.

European citizenship is not a reality in a European market where workers' rights are segmented and where they are placed in competition with each other. National rules prevail in matters of workers' rights and taxation, and national working citizens are the victims of this. Multinational companies are taking advantage of this and profiting from this lack of harmonisation and complacency towards them. European citizenship seems currently an empty terminology when it comes to workers' rights. One cannot decently speak of European citizenship when workers' rights differ across the EU territory.

The political rights of European citizens covered by the current principle of European citizenship were introduced by the Maastricht Treaty of 1992. However, they hide the sad social reality of the competition among all European workers for the benefit of capitalism in its most antisocial form and of interests of shareholders of multinational companies.

The same applies to the fundamental rights of European citizens enshrined in the European Charter of Fundamental Rights which, since the Treaty of Lisbon of 2007, have legal value for most of the Member states. Indeed, this charter conscientiously obscures the issue of equal rights for workers and social rights in the EU, yet heralded in most of the constitutions of EU Member states.

We can therefore only note that each Member state has an obligation to respect and ensure respect for the rights of national workers and workers from other Member states on its own territory. At the European level, it is a 'war of all against all' (Hobbes). There is therefore no European social pact, the state of nature reigns in terms of workers' rights and the absence of uniform rules to be observed benefits the strongest.

Without a full social pact, European democracy is still a utopia. Indeed, because from the moment when the democracies of the Member states and their various social pacts are put in competition on the social and fiscal levels and thus on the economic level, it is the disunity which reigns. What is even most serious is that this European disunity undermines, to the delight of multinationals and their shareholders, the most elaborate national social pacts brought about, originally, for the benefit of national workers.

Paradoxically, the EU has therefore become a danger for the democracies of the most socially and fiscally advanced Member states. The repercussions of this 'intestine struggle' waged by Member states to attract investors are enormous. Workers' rights in the western EU countries have only declined since 2004. Whether in France, Italy or Spain, successive governments, both right- and left-wing, have been obliged to gradually reduce the rights of their workers. The democratic game in these states has come to be at the expense of workers and the general impoverishment of their respective populations. In France, the milestone of 10 million people living below the poverty-line will soon be crossed and the few remaining public services are increasingly battered. Meanwhile, the richer are getting richer than they already were.

The EU is for the moment only a mosaic of democracies fighting among themselves to obtain investors and to create or maintain jobs in their respective territories, regardless of the rights acquired by their workers. This European social and fiscal disunity thus also undermines the EU's trade policy with regard to Asian countries. The lack of consistency among EU Member states is a weakness in global trade competition.

## II. A European market handicapped externally by the trade agreements signed by the EU with Asian countries

It is therefore clear that the EU, in the absence of common taxation and harmonised workers' rights, is entering the global trade fight in a disorderly manner. Faced with very low production costs in many Asian countries, the EU can hardly fight (A). In addition, the EU's trade agreements signed in particular with Asian countries accentuate the industrial, social and fiscal disorder within the EU. These agreements amplify the economic differences among the Member states of the EU and worsen the violation of workers' rights, whether in Europe or in Asia, and undermine more generally fundamental human rights and democracy. (B).

## A. A European market almost disarmed vis-à-vis third countries

Even if the European Commission can impose anti-dumping duties on products from third countries, this weapon is minimal because it is subject to very strict commercial conditions of use. The absence of sufficient social or environmental standards in trading partner countries cannot be invoked to enforce these anti-dumping duties. Neither can one invoke the failure to respect human rights or democratic principles in such or such a trading partner country.

On the other hand, in bilateral agreements, one can require from trading partners a conditionality in economic exchanges. When looking at the content of EU trade agreements with third countries, one is struck by the inconsistency of the EU's common commercial policy. Indeed, the EU is generally very tough on the issue of respect for democracy and human rights in the trade agreements signed with small, economically weak countries. These include the agreement between the EU and the Kyrgyz Republic or the trade agreement between the EU and Togo. If we are interested in the agreements concluded between the EU and the Republic of Kazakhstan or quite recently between the EU and China on investments made in China, the discourse is no longer the same when it comes to powerful economic partners. Questions of respect for human rights and democracy are carefully set aside in the content of these latest agreements. It is true that in agreements signed with small economically weak countries, given the development aid provided by the EU, the latter is then able to impose the implementation of standards respectful of democracy and human rights. in exchange for the EU providing financial assistance.

Likewise, in order to join the World Trade Organisation (WTO), there is no political conditionality to be observed. China was thus able to join the WTO in 2001 without much difficulty. It was from this date on that this economic and commercial giant was able to develop further and attract even more European and American investors. China has thus been able to benefit from WTO trade rules. The EU, through the European Commission, has tried to enforce respect for social minima within the WTO and environmental rules, but without much success. It must be recognised that recently China converted to the respect for environmental rules by signing the Paris agreements following the COP-21 in 2015.

Multinational companies, for their part, found their interest there since they massively relocated their investments to Asian countries and especially to China, especially from 2001. The 'investment pump' that many Asian countries are, with production costs even lower than in the eastern EU Member states, functioned well. The Chinese 'pump' has been by far the most successful with colossal investments made in China by American and European multinational companies. These paid little attention to the working conditions of workers and their rights. And even less to the respect for democratic rules and respect for human rights.

What are the responsibilities? It is obvious that it is the multinational companies that are really responsible for this situation, having turned a blind eye to the plight of workers in these countries and that of the population in general. They even encouraged not only the perpetuation of this situation by investing massively but they also politically and economically supported the governments in place in all these more or less authoritarian regimes. They validated and consolidated these regimes and the virtual absence of social standards in favour of workers. In some of these countries, children themselves are employed at a very young age in companies and are exploited by American and European multinationals. They have in this manner escaped the social rules in force in Europe and workers' rights but also most often the environmental standards to be respected in Europe.

It is the power of multinational companies that is destroying workers' rights and also slowly destroying the EU. These have been able to profit drastically from the trade agreements concluded by the EU with Asian countries. Is the EU an accomplice? Or has it allowed itself to be fooled by trade agreements which dangled new markets for companies still established in Europe and by the prospect of lucrative contracts? There is probably a bit of both. The truth is often located in a grey area, it is never neither all black nor all white.

But the consequences are palpable because it is the Asian populations and the European and American populations who are the victims of the globalised capitalistic ploy. Multinational companies have thus succeeded in disarming the EU and the Member states, evading almost all rules by investing in Asia. They destroy the Member states and the EU by circumventing or avoiding the enforcement of European standards, particularly in terms of respect for the environment and by no longer paying (or paying little) taxes in Europe… the nerve of the existence of the institutions states and international institutions and of course all national 'public services' or 'European services of general interest'. EU trade deals signed with most Asian countries tend to be beneficial to multinational companies and threaten Western democracies.

The solution adopted by D. Trump was to unilaterally implement tariffs, particularly on many products made in China. His task was to end the haemorrhage from which the USA was suffering with the evasion of capital and investment to Asia. Steadily rising unemployment and the consequent cuts in tax revenues endangered American democracy. So, in order to revive American industry, recreate jobs and at least partially end company outsourcing, D. Trump declared a trade war with China in particular, which retaliated. This showdown was not in vain, but the EU is not the USA and remains a political dwarf. The new US President Biden has decided to maintain this discourse of commercial firmness with China in particular. The EU cannot act in this way for the moment because the Member states have retained their sovereignty in diplomatic matters and therefore in foreign policy. Of course, the European Commission can negotiate trade agreements with third countries within the framework of the common commercial policy, but these must be validated by the Member states and by the European Parliament. And we know very well that the border between politics and commerce is thin.

## B. EU trade agreements with Asian states in the service of multinationals

The EU's trade agreements with third countries and in particular with Asian states are mainly unfavourable to companies still only established in Europe; as well as to European citizens.

Looking in particular at the agreement signed by the EU with South Korea, one sees that the European market, with its 450 million inhabitants, is a boon for Korean companies. and for European and American companies established in South Korea. The Korean market, on the other hand, represents only around 50 million consumers. Indeed, this agreement, which entered into force in 2011, is a vast free trade agreement: from 2011 to 2020, it eliminated 99 % of customs duties on both sides. It also eliminated in principle all measures having an effect equivalent to quantitative restrictions on trade between the two trading partners.

Thus, all companies established in South Korea can profit from the European market as if Korea were a Member state of the EU or almost and at most partially. This is the first such agreement signed by the EU with a third state outside the (non-EU Member) states of the European Economic Area(EEA) and Switzerland. These non-EU states but members of the EEA along with EU Member states are Norway, Iceland and Liechtenstein. With Switzerland, the EU has concluded bilateral agreements, including trade agreements of this type as well. We can say that from 2011, the EEA has become a bit Asian since South Korea since 2020 has roughly the same legal status as all the member countries of the EEA in terms of goods as the EEA also concerns the freedom of movement of persons within the EEA. Turkey since 1995 has had an agreement with the EU similar to that signed with Korea.

Considering the enormous imbalance between the European and Korean markets, one can legitimately wonder if this agreement was not carried out especially to satisfy the interests of the companies established in Korea whatever their origin and to facilitate for them the access to the European market. Since the signing of this agreement, many European companies have invested in South Korea. Social standards and therefore production costs are more favourable there than in many European countries.

However, it must be recognised that South Korea has made significant progress in the right direction over the past thirty years in Korean workers' rights. Production costs in Korea have therefore increased. But the proximity to China enables inputs to come to Korea, that is, products that are used in the design of other products. Korean cars are therefore made in Korea with a lot of Chinese inputs. The agreement with the EU also stipulates that Korean products exported to Europe must not contain more than 50 % of input products of Chinese origin.

But the trick is done and it is now clear that the penetration rate in the EU of cars produced in Korea has increased considerably, notably thanks to the 'input process'. A similar phenomenon has been observed for products made in Turkey, some based on Chinese inputs or from other Asian countries. Products manufactured within EU Member states are not immune to the development of the 'system of inputs' of Chinese origin or inputs from other Asian countries including Vietnam, India or Indonesia. As a result, almost all of the European industry depends on suppliers located in Asia. The only products that are not yet affected by this phenomenon are European food products. EU trade agreements with Asian countries facilitate the entry of Asian products into the European market and the reciprocal is not always true. Certain sectors of European trade stand out under these European agreements, in particular the areas relating to water, its treatment and sanitation, as well as that of public works and road infrastructure. The world leaders in these fields are notably multinational companies of European origin.

The extreme dependence of European states on more and more products manufactured in Asian countries has been revealed in particular with the Covid-19 crisis. Indeed, the finding is alarming since many drugs or components of drugs or vaccines are produced in Asia. Almost all of the electronic components that European countries need are also made in Asia. In addition, there are all the input products that EU Member states use for the manufacturing of other products, which mainly come from Asia. The sovereignty of EU Member states is threatened by this enormous dependence on high-tech products which are sometimes or even often manufactured by European companies relocated to Asia.

Multinationals, whether established in Europe or Asia or on both continents, benefit from trade agreements signed between Asian countries and the EU and are therefore the main beneficiaries. Multinationals in perpetual search for ever more profit are on the lookout for ever more welcoming territories in order to obtain ever lower production costs. Workers in all countries suffer. Trade agreements between Asian countries and the EU are detrimental both to Asian workers who are often exploited and European workers who lose their jobs or who see their rights and wages reduced in order to be able to ensure better 'competitiveness' in the face of competition from Asia.

*

In conclusion, the concerns of the EU are now far removed from the objectives of the founding fathers of the European Communities. The humanism which presided over the foundations of the European Communities has been largely overlooked. The economic and financial interests of 'big business' took precedence over early humanism. Multinational companies have succeeded in taking advantage of

European integration and its shortcomings both internally and externally. The Euro-Asian market today is an example of the power of multinationals by contrast with humanist ideals. Asian and European workers have become instruments to generate ever more profit without regard to workers' rights and even respect for the fundamental rights of individuals.

However, hope was recently reborn. The European Parliament in a burst of humanism adopted a resolution in April 2021 to make accountable European companies that work directly or indirectly with Asia. Thus a 'duty of vigilance' is proposed by this resolution of the European Parliament so that European companies learn about the origin and the manufacturing conditions of the products that they want to import to the EU or/and that they export to the EU. If these products are manufactured under conditions that do not or no longer respect human rights and fundamental human rights then they should no longer import or export them to EU Member states. This is part of what we call 'corporate social responsibility'. It should be remembered that the European Parliament does not take the initiative for European texts. It is the European Commission that has been entrusted with this role since the start of the European construction. The system of Resolutions enables the European Parliament to encourage the European Commission to make a proposal for a European Regulation or Directive. Following the vote on this Resolution by the European Parliament, the European Commission indicated that it would make a proposal for a text on the basis of this Resolution in order to make companies responsible for respecting fundamental rights. The Commission will shortly put to the vote of the Council of the EU and the European Parliament a proposal based on the European Parliament's resolution. Finally, a text which, if adopted, will make it possible to control at least the role played by companies, especially European companies in the non-respect of human rights and to monitor the way in which the conditions under which products imported into Europe have been made by workers.

However, if this Resolution of the European Parliament offers us a glimpse of hope, it is far from giving satisfaction. We would have to go much further. It would in particular be appropriate to create, like Frontex, a European agency endowed with significant funds and responsible for verifying whether the products sold in Europe and coming from third countries are indeed in conformity with all European standards not only with regard to product design but also in relation to the conditions undergone by workers and whether human rights and fundamental workers' rights are respected. Here, it should be noted that, currently, far too many imported products, especially from Asia, do not meet European standards for the manufacture of products. There are not enough national customs officials working to verify products from third countries and in particular whether they comply with European manufacturing standards. This control should therefore be supplemented by the creation of a body of European officials specialising in the control of goods or else the powers of the Frontex agency should be extended.

The economies of Asian and European countries have become extremely interdependent and the states of the two continents need to develop a solid relational base that respects at a minimum the rights of workers and human rights. This could be done through an international agreement negotiated by the European Commission with all Asian trading partners and even with other trading partners. This would force all multinational companies, many of which overlook the abusive practices against workers in many countries, to meet minimum standards. Thus, the whole of this legal arsenal constituted by the text on the 'obligation of vigilance' of companies, plus a new European agency and finally an international trade agreement which really takes into account workers' rights would be likely to counter the abusive practices of certain states, particularly in Asia, but also to counter the behaviour of multinationals, which generally do not care much about the conditions in which workers find themselves and are exploited.

# Covid-19 challenges for China and Central Asia cooperation within the Belt and Road Initiative

Kuralay Baizakova, Fatima Kukeyeva

In a context where the outbreak of the Covid-19 pandemic has brought the world to the brink of an all-encompassing economic crisis, this chapter analyses the main factors influencing cooperation between China and Central Asia within the framework of the Belt and Road Initiative (BRI). The strategic goal of the BRI relates to the construction of a community based on interests, destiny and responsibility embracing political mutual trust, economic and cultural integration.

Despite having different perspectives of national development, each Central Asian country views the BRI as a rare opportunity to bind countries of Central Asia together. As Kazakhstan's President Tokayev highlighted during the Munich Security Conference in February 2020, Central Asia became one of the key regions for the implementation of the Chinese mega-project, the BRI.[1]

*BRI goals in Central Asia* – Implementing the Chinese economy's development tasks requires the connection of external economic resources. Central Asia is viewed as a contributor to the development of the Western Chinese regions. This is Xi Jinping's regional policy priority. It could be reached on a bilateral level but today this task is being implemented within the framework of the BRI. Another goal of the BRI is to create a friendly environment around China. This goal aims to keep Central Asia within the sphere of influence of China.

*Measuring Real Development Initiative (FDI)* – One of the main vectors of concrete BRI development are real investments. Foreign direct

---

[1] Токаев рассказал о внешнеполитических приоритетах Казахстана в Мюнхене (Tokayev spoke about Kazakhstan's foreign policy priorities in Munich) [Electronic document] <https://www.zakon.kz/5007590-tokaev-rasskazal-o-vneshnepolitiches kih.html> (retrieved 04.05.2021).

investment (FDI) should be considered as the main measurement of the BRI results in CA countries. According to Chinese data, the inflow of FDI from China in 2018 to Kazakhstan ($ 3.8 billion), Turkmenistan ($ 1.98 billion), Uzbekistan ($ 412 million), Tajikistan ($ 316 million), Kyrgyzstan ($ 47 million).[2]

## I. How the CA states use these investments

Among Central Asian countries, four are examined as they are more open to scrutiny and available data on this use of the cashflows injected.

### *A. Uzbekistan*

The country is trying to focus Chinese investments on the development of non-resource sectors of production. Most of the 46 projects worth $ 6.8 billion signed by the leaders of Uzbekistan and China in 2018 are directed at the manufacturing industry.

This will strengthen China's interest in investing in non-resource sectors of Uzbek economy. For a number of subjective reasons, Kyrgyzstan used Chinese investments ineffectively, which is explained by the lack of a centralised approach to their distribution. By contrast, in Tajikistan, most of the investments were directed to the development of the mining sector. In Kazakhstan, investments are mainly directed to strengthening the country's transit potential.[3] Including in "Khorgos - Eastern Gate", a dry port on the eastern border with China. COSCO Shipping, one of the world's largest logistics service providers, ShalkarBeyneu railway, Zhezkazgan-Saksaul railway and Kuryk port.

The interests of other member states are defined by the opportunity with the help of the BRI to meet the critical increase in demand for new transportation and technological infrastructure, which in turn is

---

2 Последствия коронавирусного кризиса для инициативы "Пояс и Путь" для Центральной Азии (Effects of the coronavirus crisis on the Belt and Road Initiative in Central Asia) [Electronic document]- <https://cabar.asia/ru/posledstviya-koronavirusnogo-krizisa-dlya-initsiativy-poyas-i-put-v-tsentralnoj-azii> (retrieved 07.05.2021).

3 Последствия коронавирусного кризиса для инициативы "Пояс и Путь" для Центральной Азии (Effects of the coronavirus crisis on the Belt and Road Initiative in Central Asia)…

driven by the rapid modernisation and urbanisation. Apart from a wide range of investments into their national infrastructure and development projects countries involved into the BRI process would also open up new commercial perspectives due to the construction of the new transport and transit corridors. They would also get an access to the new regional and world markets allowing them to integrate on a much more profound scale into the global economy.

Three advantages for Uzbekistan can be synthetised from this project. First, an increase of its own transportation potential as well as its diversification. For example, the construction of an Uzbekistan-Kyrgyzstan-China railway would certainly benefit all participating countries and more.[4] Second, Tashkent plans to develop its "smart" agriculture and create joint venture with China on the latest agricultural technologies. Uzbekistan currently lags behind some latest technological advancements which requires steady and solid funding. The Chinese BRI can provide such funding and assistance.

A third advantage would be assistance in developing Uzbekistan's tourism sector. The country has over 7,400 cultural heritage sites with 209 of them included into the UNESCO World Heritage List.[5] Active cooperation between BRI-involved countries in the field of tourism and protection of the World Heritage sites might bring upon new positive opportunities. This is clearly the case with over 60 countries participating in OBOR from where the tourists might flow into Uzbekistan.

Nevertheless, we should also consider the risks of participating in OBOR for Uzbekistan. Thus, the national economy of the country is still in the process of transitioning towards the market economy with legislation under work and to be completed. The domestic situation is also maintaining its fragile balance. These changes cannot help affecting the country's economic investments politics.

Some security risks also exist. Uzbekistan borders turbulent Afghanistan in the south and mountainous Tajikistan in the east. With

---

4 China-Kyrgyzstan-Uzbekistan railway remains uncertain. [Electronic document] – <https://www.thethirdpole.net/en/regional-cooperation/china-kyrgyzstan-uzbekistan-railway-remains-uncertain/> (retrieved 30.04.2021).

5 I. Turdimambetov, "Development of Tourism in Uzbekistan and Cultural-Historical Tourist Resource Potential of Kashkadarya Region", *Journal of Environmental Management and Tourism*, 2020, 11, pp. 794–801. 10.14505//jemt.v11.4(44).02.

the former engulfed into a lasting civil war and the latter witnessing acts of violence, Tashkent has to carefully manoeuvre the relations with its neighbours. Particularly in view of combatting "three evils": terrorism, separatism and extremism. In this regard, Uzbekistan, as well as other Central Asian states, would have to cooperate with China both bilaterally and within the framework of regional organisations, particularly the Shanghai Cooperation Organisation (SCO).[6]

At the same time, we need to bear in mind the complex geopolitical situation in the region. There are other great powers vying against each other for their own specific interests, such as the Russian Federation and the United States. Neither of them can offer any equivalent to the Chinese Silk Road initiative today.

## B. Kyrgyzstan

This second country is getting deeply involved into regional cooperation with China. Both are working closely to advance some large projects, including the overhaul of Bishkek's road system, the development and transformation of the agricultural irrigation systems and the supply of fresh drinking water.

China successfully funded the transmission lines Datka-Kemin connecting the North and South of Kyrgyzstan over 410 km and 500 kv power lines.[7] In February 2018, an international China-Kyrgyzstan-Uzbekistan highway was opened allowing to curb the overland transportation time of the goods from 10 days to 2 days between the countries. Another highway project is to connect Kyrgyzstan's South and North, funded by China's Road and Bridge Company. The aim is to turn into the most modern and fastest highway facilitating economic, trade and commercial development along the route including the major Balykchy

---

6 Yang Sheng, "China, Central Asian countries to strengthen cooperation on Afghan issue, counterterrorism and diversify energy sources" [Electronic document] <https://www.globaltimes.cn/page/202105/1223313.shtml> (retrieved 30.04.2021).

7 F. Aminjonov, "Central Asian Countries' Power Systems Are Now Isolated, But Not Everyone Is Happy!"[Electronic document] <https://eurasian-research.org/publication/central-asian-countries-power-systems-are-now-isolated-but-not-every one-is-happy/> (retrieved 03.05.2021).

port on the western shore of Lake Ysyk Kul.[8] Thus, by participating in the BRI, Bishkek plans to decrease its international trade and transportation costs as well as boosting its export.

There are however some negative aspects. So far Bishkek's external debt had reached 5 billion USD, 40 % of which is owed to The Export-Import Bank of China for the implemented infrastructure projects for the last decade as part of the BRI.[9] Already Kyrgyz government officials are discussing the issue of extinguishing the debt by transferring part of state assets. This would most surely result in the future destabilisation and even loss of economic sovereignty.

Similar issue of being indebted to China are being faced by other Central Asian countries including Kazakhstan, Tajikistan and Pakistan. Covid-19 also drastically affected the national economies of CA states and resulted in increasing debts and loans from Beijing to fund critical infrastructure projects.

## C. *Tajikistan*

Here, the country developed with China a smooth mechanism for cooperation and dialogue in political, economic, trade and other areas. China even replaced Russia as the main trade partner of Tajikistan. Imported Chinese goods take up over 90 % of the bilateral trade turnover. Beijing also stands as the number one investor into the national economy with 1.2 billion USD which makes roughly around 47 % of the total investment volumes in the country.[10] Over 300 Chinese companies are currently operating in Tajikistan, including different private enterprises, state-owned enterprises, joint-stock companies, and others. Along with loans and FDI, Beijing also provides Dushanbe with gratuitous financial assistance.

---

8 Balykchy Investment profile. <https://invest.gov.kg/wp-content/uploads/2019/11/2019081-Balykchy-Investment-Profile-final-ENG.pdf> (retrieved 28.04.2021).

9 Куда ведет "Один пояс - один путь", или Как Бишкек намерен выплачивать Пекину долги? (Where does "One Belt - One Road" lead, or How does Bishkek intend to pay Beijing debts?) [Electronic document] <https://centrasia.org/newsA.php?st=1614291900> (retrieved 02.03.2021).

10 Чоршанбиев Пайрав, "5 крупнейших иностранных компаний, которые делают деньги в Таджикистане" (P. Chorshanbiev, "5 largest foreign companies that make money in Tajikistan"). [Electronic document] <https://centrasia.org/newsA.php?st=1572372540> (retrieved 02.03.2021).

Chinese companies mostly work in the areas of transport, energy infrastructure, mining, gas pipeline construction, growing and processing of agricultural products, production of building materials, etc. Currently, China heavily invests into Tajikistan's infrastructure projects. One of them is the Dushanbe-Kulyab-Kumbh-Khorog-Murghab-Kulma-Kashgar highway which is to link major Tajik cities with network hubs of the North Western China. The Dushanbe-Jirgatal-Sary-Tash roads connects Tajikistan with Kyrgyzstan. LEP-500 power transmission line united the south and north of the country. The construction of The Dushanbe-2 CHP power plant helped resolving the issue of energy supply to the capital and its environs.[11]

Tajikistan presents an interest for Beijing not only as investment project but as a transit territory with an access to Turkmenistan, Iran and Afghanistan. Dushanbe is also regarded as a useful ally for advancing China-Iran relations.

Being a member to key regional organisations like SCO, CSTO, Eurasian Economic Union (EEU) and others, Tajikistan supports the idea of integrating projects offered by the latter with the Chinese BRI. It also perceives itself as an interaction platform between the EEU and China. By manoeuvring between Russia and China and sometimes knowingly clashing their interests against each other, Dushanbe is mobilising regional geopolitics.

Yet, with the increasing role and particularly the debt Tajikistan owes Beijing comes cautious politics. Indeed, Chinese loans continue developing and advancing Tajik economy as well as infrastructure but that comes with a certain price: over 1.3 billion USD debt or 40 % of the total amount of the combined external debt. Considering that poverty levels remain high in the country, this raises the question about the cost-efficiency. Experts believe that Tajikistan is yet to clearly identify the long-term perspectives of participating in the BRI.

---

11 Dushanbe-2 CHP plant directs generated electricity to the country's power grid. [Electronic document] <https://asiaplustj.info/en/news/tajikistan/economic/20210119/dushanbe-2-chp-plant-directs-generated-electricity-to-the-countrys-power-grid> (retrieved 05.03.2021).

## D. Kazakhstan

Nursultan plays its own key role in advancing in the BRI, bearing in mind it was in Nur-Sultan that Chinese President Xi Jinping first announced the Silk Road Economic Belt initiative (2014).[12] Chinese officials list advantages of dealing with Kazakhstan: the country's transit capabilities; its stable political situation; the favourable investment climate.

Chinese experts perceive Kazakhstan as a regional leader that would assist in implementing various infrastructure projects that Beijing has in mind, both within the region and beyond. On the one hand, Kazakhstan can become an intermediary in the construction of cost-effective and profitable routes through the territory of Kazakhstan, Turkmenistan, Azerbaijan and Turkey to Europe. On the other hand, the country can facilitate Moscow's positive policy towards implementing BRI projects in Central Asia. Moreover, according to the Chinese authorities, Kazakhstan has another important advantage: its experienced leadership pursuing long-term foreign policy with the focus on regional integration. Considering all these factors Beijing chose Kazakhstan as a key partner to implement OBOR's Central Asian segment.

As for risks, China and its BRI are considered in the official discourse of Kazakhstan as a condition and factor that can have a negative impact on the military security of Kazakhstan: both i/ through a possible violation of the balance of forces and interests that have developed around Kazakhstan, and ii/ through the expansion of China's sphere of influence in Kazakhstan and Central Asia.

That is why the foreign policy strategy of Kazakhstan is based on the multi-vector principle. Kazakhstan, actively participating in the Chinese BRI, simultaneously participates in the processes of Eurasian integration, supports the C5+1 mechanism, and also closely interacts with European partners. Generally, it is difficult not only for Kazakhstan, but also for all Central Asian countries, to cooperate on an equal footing with such a large partner as China. And the point is not only in the volume and scale

---

12 Silk Road forum showcases China's power – and the power of its propaganda. [Electronic document] <https://www.washingtonpost.com/news/worldviews/wp/2017/05/15/silk-road-forum-showcases-chinas-power-and-the-power-of-its-propaganda/> (retrieved 10.03.2021).

of the Chinese economy, but also in the training of personnel working in the area.

Nevertheless, as emphasised by the President of Kazakhstan, experts do not share fears about the excessive influence of the Chinese economy on the development of the country. And ultimately it would even certainly increase the geopolitical significance of Central Asia.

## II. Challenges in cooperation between the PRC and CA countries

Such a large-scale initiative as the BRI carries a number of potential prospects and risks for the countries of Central Asia. The analysis shows that BRI transport corridors can significantly improve the situation in the field of trade and foreign investment, as well as the living standards of the population of the participating countries, but only if China and the countries through which these corridors pass adopt more fundamental political reforms to enhance transparency, expand trade, increase debt sustainability and reduce environmental, social and corruption risks.

First, political instability in individual countries of the region does not contribute to sustainable, stable and healthy development of the region. Second, the construction of the Silk Road is viewed as a threat due to the US strategic interests in Central Asia. The US is not only capitalising on the rich natural resources of Central Asia, but also constricting Russia's traditional spheres of influence. Third, contradictions between Russia and China may become an obstacle to the implementation of the BRI projects, thereby negatively affecting their Central Asian neighbours. Russian scepticism will to a certain extent affect the dynamics of participation of the Central Asian countries. But with the stable and friendly development of Chinese-Russian relations, the development of BRI in the countries of Central Asia can develop for the better.

The implementation of the Chinese Initiative in Central Asia may also be hampered by the risks associated with the threat of international terrorism.

Despite the growing opportunities, the China project is also facing many challenges at the local level due to the Covid-19 pandemic.

## III. Impact of the pandemic on cooperation within the Belt and Road Initiative

In analysing this problem, we tried to understand the degree of negative impact of the pandemic on the cooperation between China and Central Asia. Due to the pandemic, Beijing faces the following challenges in the CA region.

The first is economic. According to statistics from the Chinese customs, the volume of trade between China and the four Central Asian countries (not Turkmenistan) in the first half of 2020 amounted to only $ 13.78 billion, which is 27.3 % less than in 2019.[13]

Second is the issue of social problems. Instability increases protest moods in Central Asia, which may negatively affect the implementation of the BRI. Moreover, this is due to instability in political circles, which may negatively affect the position of Chinese investors. On the other hand, against the background of the growth of the Chinese presence and the global information war, which is likely to only intensify, anti-Chinese sentiments are growing in Central Asian society.

The economies of the Central Asian countries were shocked and shaken Covid-19. Quarantine measures and border closures led to a decline in trade under the BRI. Oil exporting countries have been hit twice by self-isolation measures and by strong fluctuations in oil prices

Third, organisational problem. Uneven application of quarantine measures in different countries, depending on the epidemiological situation. For example, when China began to resume production and remove restrictive measures, the CA countries began to quarantine and closed their borders, including those with China. And some projects of the Initiative were suspended or shifted in terms of implementation.

---

[13] Чжан Нин Как пандемия дала толчок расширению китайской инициативы в Центральной Азии (Tzhan Nine, "How the pandemic gave impetus to the expansion of the Chinese initiative in Central Asia") [Electronic document] <https://asiaplustj.info/ru/news/tajikistan/politics/20210224/kak-pandemiya-dala-tolchok-rasshireniyu-kitaiskoi-initsiativi-v-tsentralnoi-azii> (retrieved 05.03.2021).

## IV. A window of opportunity for China?

Despite the challenges, the pandemic and the economic crisis have opened a "window of opportunity" for China to increase its political and economic presence in Central Asia at the expense of other external players. Indeed, China may become the only source of aid for the region and Chinese businesses have a chance to increase their importance in the manufacturing sector of Central Asia.

Since the collapse in oil and other natural resource prices has led to a sharp decline in the incomes of the Central Asian countries, these will strive to develop their transport potential and look for possible ways out of the crisis. For example, Kazakhstan can increase exports in the metallurgical and mining sectors. Since the Chinese industry does not plan to reduce metal consumption. Most of China's programmes are likely to be held under the BRI umbrella.

However, given the current development of events, Chinese and Central Asian experts believe that the development trajectory of the Chinese project does not undergo significant changes and twists due to the coronavirus crisis. The crisis is significantly reinforcing the trends that have emerged in recent years. This, in particular, is the orientation of investments towards practical results, the priority of the resource sector.

## V. Response of the BRI participants to the pandemic challenges

Some concise remarks can be ventured here, six of them. First, there is a consensus on cooperation. Second, the epidemic only changed the way China and Central Asia communicate, but it did not weaken ties. Third, China-Europe trains continue to play as the strategic channels. About half of the express trains pass through two ports in Kazakhstan: Alashankou and Khorgos. In the first half of 2020, the cargo turnover of these two ports reached 10 million tons, up 30.2 % compared to the same period in 2019.[14] While maritime powers are closing ports, this land-based

---

14 Как коронавирус повлиял на проекты "Пояса и пути" в Центральной Азии. Взгляд из Китая ("How coronavirus influenced Belt and Path projects in Central Asia. Looking from China") [Electronic document] <http://inozpress.kg/caa-network> (retrieved 27.02.2021).

intermodal container route has become a "lifeline" for the international transportation on the route China-Central Asia-Europe.

Fourth, China has taken an initiative to reduce or write off the debts of Central Asian countries. In order to implement the G20 initiative to suspend payments. Fifth, the rapid development of the digital Silk Road has helped countries transform their economies. Before the epidemic, the countries of Central Asia formulated strategies for the development of the digital economy, and the epidemic enabled countries to accelerate their implementation. Last, the "Silk Road of Health" has been developed.

*

In conclusion, the emergence and implementation of the BRI undoubtedly gave a noticeable impetus to cooperation between countries of Central Asia and China. A large number of new projects emerged in different fields. Despite the pandemic in Central Asia, economic growth is expected to recover by 3 % in 2021 fuelled by modest increases in commodity prices and foreign direct investment as the region, intensifying its involvement in China's BRI.

Naturally, the BRI might also face several challenges in Central Asia, like the influence of Turkey and its pan-Turkism, the Chinese "theory of threats" and the Russian "imperial" policy. Faced with challenges, the BRI can still be well implemented in Central Asia, provided that countries respond appropriately.

Kazakhstan and its neighbours in the region should proceed from the fact that the BRI reflects an open, inclusive platform for multilateral cooperation, in the process of which it is quite possible to observe the vital national interests of each participant, regardless of the size of its economy ot its political weight.

# GATT principles during Covid-19: Focusing on export-restrictions of face-masks

Chan-Mo Chung

Covid-19 is altering human behaviour, community culture, how society works and trades It reveals the limits of outdated socio-economic paradigms, of which trade rules play a role.[1] Free-trade principles embedded in the World Trade Organisation (WTO) agreements, and the General Agreement on Tariffs and Trade (GATT) in particular, face unprecedented challenges from economic *and* normative perspectives.[2] Self-isolation of the public combined with lockdown of production facilities caused a massive slowdown and reduction in trade. Governments exacerbated the situation by imposing export prohibitions/restrictions, government monopsony and planned distribution.[3] Such measures raise legal concerns for the WTO.

This chapter analyses the challenges facing GATT principles by examining their application to restrictions imposed on the export of face-masks. From early 2021, the world seems to relieve the shortage problem of face-masks but confronts that of effective Covid vaccines.[4] New problems have additional issues but benefit from the analysis of the old. As from 18 February 2021, 98 countries have enacted at least

---

1 See OECD, *Tackling coronavirus (Covid-19)* <https://www.oecd.org/coronavirus/en/> (acc. 20 May 2021). All websites acc. on this date.

2 WTO, *Covid-19 and world trade*, <https://www.wto.org/english/tratop_e/covid19_e/covid19_e.htm>; I. Carreño, T. Dolle, L. Medina and M. Brandenburger, *The Implications of the Covid-19 Pandemic on Trade*, 11(2) *European Journal of Risk Regulation* 402 (2020).

3 WTO Secretariat, *Export Prohibitions and Restrictions*, Information Note (23 April 2020).

4 "Coronavirus: WHO criticises EU over vaccine export controls", *BBC* (30 January, 2021).

one export restriction.[5] Many measures were temporarily, have expired or loosened after some time.

This chapter discusses GATT provisions applicable to export prohibitions/restrictions of face-masks during the Covid-19 pandemic. First, From existing studies on export restrictions,[6] it discusses applicable provisions, especially GATT XI, XIII, XX and XXI, echoing statements by previous commentators[7] that export prohibitions/restrictions of face-masks are justifiable under WTO/GATT regulations when imposed temporarily at the time of a critical shortage. Second, it goes further, pointing that quantitative restrictions should be limited only to the degree necessary and not be prolonged beyond a reasonable period based on scientific risk assessment. Third, it recommends that restrictions be loosened in a phased manner with the goal of full removal. Fourth, it argues that the market is the favoured mechanism vs. the government for the production/distribution of face-masks, except for humanitarian or official development assistance (ODA) purposes.

# I. Application of GATT principles to export restrictions

## *A. Elimination of quantitative restrictions: GATT XI:1*

GATT drafters regarded quantitative restrictions, whether import or export restriction, as most harmful barriers to trade and banned them as follows:

---

5 International Trade Centre, *Market Access Map*; WTO and World Customs Organization also maintain webpages on the list of countries having adopted export control measures for medical supplies, <https://www.wto.org/english/tratop_e/covid19_e/trade_related_goods_measure_e.htm>; <http://www.wcoomd.org/en/topics/facilitation/activities-and-programmes/natural-disaster/list-of-countries-coronavirus.aspx>.

6 B. Karapinar, *Export Restrictions and the WTO Law: How to Reform the 'Regulatory Deficiency'*, 45(6) J. World Trade 1139 (2011); G. Marceau, *WTO and Export Restrictions*, 50(4) J. World Trade 563 (2016).

7 N. M. Hart, *Covid-19: An Overview of Trade-Related Measures to Address Access to Medical Goods*, CRS Legal Sidebar: LSB 10424 (March 20, 2020); Sutter, Schwarzenberg and Sutherland; J. J. Zhou, *Facilitating WTO-compliant Responses to International Public Health Emergencies, International Economic Law and Policy Blog* (2020); J. Pauwelyn, *Export Restrictions in Times of Pandemic: Options and Limits under International Trade Agreements* (April 30, 2020), <https://ssrn.com/abstract=3579965> or <http://dx.doi.org/10.2139/ssrn.3579965>.

> Article XI: General Elimination of Quantitative Restrictions: 1. No prohibitions or restrictions other than duties, taxes or other charges, whether made effective through quotas, import or export licences or other measures, shall be instituted or maintained by any contracting party on the importation of any product of the territory of any other contracting party or on the exportation or sale for export of any product destined for the territory of any other contracting party.

State practices show that restrictions on the export of face-masks come in various forms: *de jure* as well as *de facto*, total ban, partial restriction based on a certain percentage of production, requisition by government for domestic supply, time-consuming approval procedures, minimum export prices, etc. The wording of Article XI is flexible enough to cover various forms of quantitative restrictions.

Export restrictions may take the form of 'duties, taxes or other charges', which is explicitly excluded from the scope of Article XI:1 prohibition. If an export tariff does not contravene Articles I, II, and III of the GATT or any other WTO commitments,[8] then it could be a WTO-consistent policy choice for a WTO Member facing a pandemic. However, export tariffs would not be as effective as quantitative restrictions, as evidenced in the Covid-19 situation. A slight increase in the price of masks does not quell high demand on behalf of fearful and needy buyers. Likewise, 'duties, taxes or other charges' seems to be a less effective policy in curbing the export of face-masks during a pandemic.

How Members of the WTO can impose quantitative restrictions on the export of face-masks despite this general elimination by GATT Article XI:1 is explained in the next sections.

## B. Exemption from the elimination: GATT XI:2(a)

The provision that proclaims general elimination of quantitative restriction is immediately followed by a series of exemption provisions among which most related to our discussion is paragraph 2(a).

> 2. The provisions in paragraph 1 of this Article shall not extend to the following: (a) Export prohibitions or restrictions temporarily applied to

---

8 Some new Members of the WTO have made additional commitments in their accession protocols to refrain from export tariff. See Marceau, *supra* note 6, at 576–581.

prevent or relieve critical shortages of foodstuffs or other products essential to the exporting contracting party;

The Panel in *China – Raw Materials* found that refractory-grade bauxite is "essential" to China because of its importance in steel production. However, the Panel also found that the export restriction of this product was not "temporarily applied", as it had been in place for at least a decade, and that China currently does not face a "critical shortage" of refractory bauxite.[9] The Appellate Body in this case recognised that Article XI:2(a) describes measures applied for a limited duration in the interim, adopted in order to bridge a passing need.[10] Concerning the meaning of "critical shortage", the Appellate Body defined it as referring to "those deficiencies in quantity that are crucial, that amount to a situation of decisive importance, or that reach a vitally important or decisive stage, or a turning point".[11]

In the drafting stage of the GATT, the relevant Sub-Committee altered the wording to the present "essential to the exporting contracting party" in order to clearly communicate the view, for the purposes of this provision, that the importance of any product should be judged in relation to the particular country concerned.[12] Although the drafting history is not obliged to be considered in the interpretation of the GATT, it confirms an ordinary meaning of the words,[13] which has been consistently used through the GATT.[14]

It is evident that masks and other personal protective equipment are to be considered as essential products during the pandemic, and thus export restrictions of those medical products during critical times such as a pandemic can satisfy the conditions of subparagraph (a). Masks during the time of a pandemic are at least equally important as foodstuffs, as there is a strong possibility of a critical shortage. No specific time span was defined

---

9 Panel Report, *China – Measures Related to the Exportation of Various Raw Materials*, WTO Doc. WT/DS394/R (adopted 22 February 2012), 7.354–7.355.

10 Appellate Body Report, *China – Measures Related to the Exportation of Various Raw Materials*, WTO Doc. WT/DS394/AB/R (adopted 22 February 2012) [hereinafter *China – Raw Materials*], 323.

11 *Id.* 324.

12 EPCT/141, at 2 quoted from WTO, ANALYTICAL INDEX OF THE GATT (2012), at 326.

13 Article 32 of the Vienna Convention on the Law of Treaties.

14 The word "essential" appears 10 times through the GATT.

for "temporarily", which means it could be extended to some extent while the critical shortage remains. However, it cannot be extended for a long period or forever, nor can it remain after concerns about the critical shortage have disappeared. For example, export restrictions may be exempt under Article XI:2(a) from the time of the coronavirus outbreak up to the plateau stage, i.e. justified when the daily infection rate is high but not at the time of stabilisation when the queues to buy masks have disappeared. Preventive stockpiling may be excused to some extent, but stockpiling after the infection rate stabilises or drops is not.

## C. Obligations in implementing quantitative restrictions: GATT XIII

If a Member restrains export of a product on the basis of Article XI:2, Article XIII requires that exportation of the like product to all third countries is similarly prohibited or restricted.

> Article XIII: Non-discriminatory Administration of Quantitative Restrictions
>
> 1. No prohibition or restriction shall be applied by any contracting party on the importation of any product of the territory of any other contracting party or on the exportation of any product destined for the territory of any other contracting party, unless the importation of the like product of all third countries or the exportation of the like product to all third countries is similarly prohibited or restricted.
>
> 2. In applying import restrictions to any product, contracting parties shall aim at a distribution of trade in such product approaching as closely as possible the shares which the various contracting parties might be expected to obtain in the absence of such restrictions …
>
> 5....... in so far as applicable, the principles of this Article shall also extend to export restrictions.

It is noteworthy that the wording of Article XIII of the GATT does not require that a Member limit domestic demand in a similar manner as it does for foreign demand. GATT drafters seemingly recognised the global reality of individual nation states in which governments put the necessity of their nationals before that of foreigners, especially in a time of crisis. As a counterargument, one may point out the WTO case law[15]

[15] Appellate Body Report, *United States – Import Prohibition of Certain Shrimp and Shrimp Products, WTO* Doc. WT/DS58/AB/R (adopted 6 November 1998) [hereinafter *US – Shrimp*], 150.

concerning the non-discrimination condition of the *chapeau* clause of Article XX, which we will examine later.

In response, it may be tentatively submitted that Article XIII differs from Article XX in that it presupposes quantitative restrictions in favour of domestic production or consumption, and the scope of the Article XI:2 exemption is more specific than the list of Article XX exceptions.

While a prime objective that the global community should pursue in the time of public health crisis such as Covid-19 is 'provision of heath products to the most needed people as quickly as possible', the global public objective is not properly reflected in the mechanism of Article XIII. A simple extension to export restrictions would rather obstruct achieving the objective in terms of quantity and timeliness. First, one must distinguish between foodstuffs and other essential products with low price elasticity of supply and those with high elasticity. For grains or nuts, which can be harvested only once or twice a year and whose cultivation amount cannot be increased in a short time, it would be appropriate to apply quantitative restrictions, as envisioned in Article XIII, with minor modifications. Raw materials with limited reserves would be the same. However, for products such as face-masks, the production amount of which can be adjusted in a relatively short time, applying Article XIII strictly may result in undesirable consequences. If the exporting country determines only the total amount or percentage of domestic requirements of the produce and allows producers to decide how much to produce, to whom to sell, and at what price, then producers would have the incentive to quickly adjust their export supply to meet overseas market demand. On the other hand, if they are required to comply with quotas specifically allocated among overseas markets, they would lose any interest or benefit in predicting changes in market demand and would not be able to expand their supply to certain markets showing rapidly growing demand for their product.

In the case of face-masks, acquiescing to commercial considerations would achieve the dual goals of distributing the product to the most-needy while providing incentives to increase supply of the product. A market solution is most workable when the supply of a relevant product is elastic to price changes, as in the case of face-masks. One concern is that, with this limited approach, the price of masks might rise to a level that developing/least developed countries could not afford. This is a legitimate concern from a global fairness perspective. A complex system of quota allocation is, however, not the solution. The problem should be solved by the international community, especially collaborative efforts involving international finance, development and health organisations, and national ODA programs.[16]

Lastly, export restrictions may trigger a domino effect of additional restrictions in other countries and input markets. The WTO and IMF have expressed caution that export restrictions can be counterproductive.[17] They have called for international efforts building on existing cross-border production and distribution networks. At this stage, however, it is uncertain whether countries of the world will share the same lesson from this pandemic. Some would insist that a prudent country should not rely wholly upon foreign sources for supply of personal protective equipment and must at least have a contingency plan for self-sufficiency in preparation of a worst scenario.[18] Limitation of state discretion in legitimate export restriction will help build confidence among states in the market-based supply chain, which is essential to prevent an inefficient contingency plan from putting in practice.

## D. General exceptions: GATT XX

Even though a quantitative restriction is allowable under Article XI:2(a), it should further satisfy the requirement of non-discrimination under Article XIII. If a restriction fails to satisfy the latter, irrespective of its satisfaction of the former, the restriction must rely on other broader exceptions such as Articles XX or XXI for its consistency with the GATT. Thus, we will examine the applicability of Article XX to export restriction of face-masks during the Covid-19 pandemic.

> Article XX: General Exceptions: Subject to the requirement that such measures are not applied in a manner which would constitute a means of arbitrary or unjustifiable discrimination between countries where the same conditions prevail, or a disguised restriction on international trade, nothing in this Agreement shall be construed to prevent the adoption or enforcement by any contracting party of measures:

---

16 For a similar opinion, S. Evenett, *Sickening thy neighbor: Export restraints on medical supplies during a pandemic*, VOX: CEPR Policy Portal (March 19, 2020).

17 WTO and IMF, *WTO and IMF Joint statement on Trade and the Covid-19 Response* (April 24, 2020). <https://www.wto.org/english/news_e/news20_e/igo_15apr20_e.pdf>.

18 *Europe Needs 'Self-sufficiency' In Mask Production: Merkel*, Barron's (April 6, 2020).

> (b) necessary to protect human, animal or plant life or health;
>
> (j) essential to the acquisition or distribution of products in general or local short supply; Provided that any such measures shall be consistent with the principle that all contracting parties are entitled to an equitable share of the international supply of such products, and that any such measures, which are inconsistent with the other provisions of this Agreement, shall be discontinued as soon as the conditions giving rise to them have ceased to exist.

Pursuant to the established case law perceiving Article XX as a two-tier test consisting of justifications under one of the paragraphs and then the chapeau,[19] we first examine whether or not export restriction of face-masks may be allowable under paragraphs (b) or (j) of Article XX.

Although some health officials made statements in the initial period of the COVID-19 pandemic that wearing a face-mask does not help protect against coronavirus, it has been since accepted as common sense as well as a majority opinion among health specialists that wearing masks does help.[20] Opposing opinions are only understood as reflecting the unique dire situation of some countries in which the supply of face-masks is not sufficient even for the use of health workers. Wearing a mask is now regarded as a prerequisite for loosening so-called social distancing measures. Based on these circumstances, we may confirm that states' efforts to secure a sufficient supply of face-masks for their own citizens, including export prohibitions or restrictions, are necessary measures to protect human life or health under paragraph (b) of Article XX.

Considering the situation from a global perspective, one may question whether the prohibition or restriction of face-mask exports actually contributes to human life or health. If protecting human life or health is compared with that of observing trade rules, it is obviously easier to place more value in the former. If the situation of an export-restricting Member is graver than those of other Members whose imports are restricted, it would also be easy to argue that those restrictions fall under paragraph (b) of Article XX. However, what will happen if the situation of an exporting Member is less grave than those of importing Members?

---

19 Appellate Body Report, *United States – Standards for Reformulated and Conventional Gasoline*, WTO Doc. WT/DS2/AB/R (adopted 20 May 1996), at 22.

20 *Coronavirus: Should you be wearing a face-mask? – Government has changed its policy on face coverings*, THE INDEPENDENT (June 6, 2020).

When health risks are limited geographically within a country, the principle of necessity allows for the breach of minor duty if it is the only way to perform the greater duty. In the context of the Covid-19 pandemic, the risk is worldwide. Policymakers of exporting countries cannot pretend that they do not see comparable or worse situations in importing countries.

In contrast to Article XX(b) and most other exceptions and exemptions of the GATT, Article XX(j) explicitly prescribes that authorities consider the situation beyond national boundaries. The drafting history shows that Article XX(j) was enacted in consideration of product shortages or breakdown of distribution systems after World War.[21] The phrase "general or local short supply" was "understood to include cases where a product, although in international short supply, was not necessarily in short supply in all markets throughout the world."[22]

The Covid-19 pandemic put the world in a situation similar to the aftermath of the Second World War. Countries are in disarray in organising efforts to protect their own people. Some failed to supply enough face-masks even to healthcare workers. Thus, it is submitted that Article XX(j) is one of the most applicable provisions of the GATT to quantitative restrictions in the midst of the pandemic.

While Article XX(j) requires that authorities consider equitable shares of other countries and limit the duration of restriction measures as soon as the situation improves, paragraph (b) does not require that such conditions be met. As far as export restrictions are necessary to protect human health in the country imposing the restrictions, Members would be able to satisfy the conditions of paragraph (b) with relative ease.[23] Therefore, Members tend to rely on paragraph (b) than (j), which requires meeting double conditions in the administration of quantitative restrictions.

Concerning the necessity test under paragraph (b), panels and the Appellate Body have placed high priority on the protection of human life or health as an objective of state measures in the situation like the current pandemic, which in turn raises the possibility of satisfying the

---

21 London Report, at 11, III.C.1(b); EPCT/A/PV/30; EPCT/A/PV/33.

22 EPCT/A/SR.40(2), at 15.

23 Note "relative ease" due to its difficulty in absolute terms.

necessity test.[24] The existence of a less trade-restrictive alternative should be proved *prima facie* by the complainant. Considering the effectiveness and low cost of face-masks, it would not be easy for a complainant to find an alternative, which is equally effective and widely available, to a guaranteed supply of face-masks, at least in the short-term before the full scale delivery of a vaccine. Therefore, unless the strictness and period of restriction exceed the necessary degree of export restriction as required by the situation confronting the particular Member, the prohibition or restriction of face-mask exports would satisfy all conditions of paragraph (b).

From a long-term perspective, however, the contribution or effectiveness of the measure to protect human life or health can be questioned. The anticipated domino effect of export restrictions in other countries would result in disruption of the supply chain. Only countries with self-sustainable manufacturers may obtain the pursued objective of export restrictions. The fact that export restrictions would go against the primary objective for most countries if the application of the measure is prolonged may suggest that it is actually not a "necessary" measure as it fails to achieve the primary health objective in the long run. The increase of production and stability of trade may be a better solution in the end.

In the case of export restrictions of inputs for face-masks such as spun bond fabrics and melt-blown filters, they are not directly related to human health. Side effects such as disruption of the supply chain of inputs due to retaliatory cuts by affected countries and reduced production due to domestic low prices would overwhelm any short-term beneficial effects. Thus, export restrictions of inputs are far less likely to be justified under paragraph (b).

Therefore, the current pandemic suggests that export restrictions should normally not expand beyond a relatively short time. Further, any country implementing quantitative restrictions should try to empower, not weaken, the market in terms of production and distribution of masks. The time point upon which long queues to buy masks disappear will be the deciding point to return back to the free market mechanism as well as question the necessity of export restrictions.

---

24 Panel Report, *US-Gambling*, WTO Doc. WT/DS285/R (adopted 20 April 2005), 6.489–6.492; Appellate Body Report, *Brazil – Measures Affecting Imports of Retreaded Tyres*, WTO Doc. WT/DS332/AB/R (adopted 17 December 2007) [hereinafter *Brazil – Retreaded Tyres*], 179.

In order to achieve the benefits of the exception under Article XX, all measures implemented by a Member should meet the conditions in the chapeau of the Article in addition to belonging to one of the paragraphs. First, one must examine the condition of not being "a means of arbitrary or unjustifiable discrimination between countries where the same conditions prevail". If the objects of examination are confined to the measures taken towards various importing countries, arbitrary or unjustifiable discrimination would normally be found in the allocation of export quotas. In order to satisfy the non-discrimination condition of the chapeau, the principles mentioned in relation to Article XIII should be followed. However, if Article XIII is the only viable method, Article XX would have little meaning regarding quantitative restrictions. The expression "nothing in the Agreement" in Article XX would include Article XIII but is not limited to that. Other types of quantitative measures that may not comply with Article XIII may indeed be allowed pursuant to the Article XX criteria. This implies that exporting Members have room for maneuvering and imagination in the selection of protective measures in the face of the pandemic. For example, relying on the free-market mechanism would be recognised as not arbitrary or discriminatory. Administration of a quota or permits based on political motives would, however, raise problems in passing this test.

Preceding WTO decisions have indicated that countries in comparison in the chapeau condition are not limited to importing countries but include the exporting country as well.[25] Export prohibitions or restrictions often involve discrimination between domestic buyers and foreign buyers. If the importing country does not experience the effects of coronavirus or its situation is better than the exporting country, then it would be difficult to successfully argue that export restrictions are arbitrary or discriminatory. If the situation is equally bad or worse in the importing country than the exporting country, then assessment should be more delicate. As mentioned, an export restriction without accompanying equivalent domestic restriction would be a discrimination on face value. Whether or not it would be an 'arbitrary or unjustifiable' discrimination, however, needs more discussion.

---

25 Appellate Body Report, *US – Shrimp*, *supra* note 15, 150.

The Appellate Body has held that analysis must focus on the cause or rationale of discrimination.[26] Export prohibition or restriction enacted in the time of an emergency to meet surging domestic demand has a rational connection to the objective of protecting human life or health. Distinction between domestic needs and foreign needs is also based on some sort of plan and reason, although the validity of the plan and reason could be questioned. Thus, it cannot be described as "arbitrary", which ordinarily means "based on chance rather than being planned or based on reason".[27] Whether or not such an action would be "unjustifiable" depends on many factors. First, it needs to be mentioned that the concept of "just" or "unjustifiable" cannot be defined with arithmetic precision. "unjustifiable" is defined as "unacceptable and wrong because there is no good or fair reason for it".[28] "Reasonableness", however, also varies depending on the period, culture, and specific situation. Export prohibition or restriction of masks favouring domestic needs during a pandemic may not be "just" but can be argued as "acceptable". The acceptability may depend on the relative abundance of the supply in the domestic market and the dire shortage in the foreign market as well as the traditional patterns of trade before the pandemic. Unless there is an outrageous disregard of a tragic situation among a country's traditional trading partners, putting domestic needs first would be acceptable and not "unjustifiable" in the current development stage of the international community.

Face-masks have relatively minor importance from an industrial policy perspective.[29] Thus, countries seldom employ restrictions on export of face-masks or inputs thereof by citing protection of human life or health as a means to disguise their industrial policy objectives. Quantitative restrictions based on political motives, however, may be viewed as arbitrary discrimination and a disguised restriction on international trade, thus failing to satisfy the chapeau of Article XX.

---

26 Appellate Body Report, *Brazil – Retreaded Tyres*, *supra* note 24, 229–230; Appellate Body Report, *United States – Measures Concerning the Importation, Marketing and Sale of Tuna and Tuna Products – Recourse to article 21.5 of the DSU by Mexico*, WTO Doc. WT/DS381/AB/RW (adopted 3 December 2015), 7.316.

27 Cambridge English Dictionary (Online).

28 *Id.*

29 This does not preclude the possibility that wearing a mask in a crowded area could become etiquette in Western culture after-Covid-19.

## E. Security exceptions: GATT XXI

Some commentators[30] also noted Article XXI, which reads:

> Nothing in this Agreement shall be construed
>
> (a) to require any contracting party to furnish any information the disclosure of which it considers contrary to its essential security interests; or
>
> (b) to prevent any contracting party from taking any action which it considers necessary for the protection of its essential security interests
>
> (i) relating to fissionable materials or the materials from which they are derived;
>
> (ii) relating to the traffic in arms, ammunition and implements of war and to such traffic in other goods and materials as is carried on directly or indirectly for the purpose of supplying a military establishment;
>
> (iii) taken in time of war or other emergency in international relations; or
>
> (c) to prevent any contracting party from taking any action in pursuance of its obligations under the United Nations Charter for the maintenance of international peace and security.

Article XXI has long been regarded as a last resort, which Members should restrain from invoking. On such limited occasions, small Members tend to petition for judicial review of the measures in this Article while large Members tend to reject judicial review, claiming that the text of the Article clearly expresses self-judgment of the invoking Member. Recent years, however, have seen more frequent invocations of Article XXI, among which the *Russia-Transit* panel delivered its report first, which was adopted by the DSB without appeal.[31]

Application of Article XXI to export restrictions during the Covid-19 pandemic should first satisfy the requirement of "other emergency in international relations." Most experts and officials agree that this pandemic is an emergent situation.[32] The question is then whether it is an

---

30 Pauwelyn, *supra* note 7, at 12–13; V. Lapa, *GATT Article XXI as a way to justify food trade restrictions adopted as a response to Covid-19?*, Regulating for Globalization (April 10, 2020).

31 Panel Report, *Russia – Measures Concerning Traffic in Transit*, WTO Doc. WT/DS512/R (adopted 26 April 2019).

32 The WHO declared the coronavirus a public health 'emergency' of international concern (PHEIC) on January 30, 2020.

emergency "in international relations". The GATT precedents quoted as "emergency in international relations" under this Article involve the state of conflicts between or among countries.[33] Coronavirus is an enemy within or outside, not between or among, the community of nations. One may argue that relations between and among nations ameliorated rather than deteriorated due to Covid-19. On the other hand, we may distinguish an emergency coming from inside versus outside of a country and understand subparagraph (iii) as meaning emergency coming outside of a country. From this perspective, whether the state of emergency is between or among nations is irrelevant. An international emergency may include any emergency against an extraterrestrial intelligence or viruses. The history of GATT has witnessed that generic terms such as "exhaustible natural resources" in Article XX(g) have evolved along with development of the human community.[34] "Emergency in international relations" may also have evolved and now includes threats to regional or global communities irrespective of origin.

Once a measure falls into subparagraph (iii), one should examine its satisfaction of the conditions of the head provisions of paragraph (b), i.e. "necessary for the protection of its essential security interests". "Security" is also a generic term having a very flexible meaning. Generally, it means "free from danger" and includes "protection of a person, building, organisation, or country against threats such as crime or attacks by foreign countries".[35]

However, this general meaning needs to be confined by the context of the provision. "Security" in GATT Article XXI obviously does not include protection of person, building, or organisation. Neither does it include protection against an economic, cultural, environmental, or political threat, in general. Actions against such threats are specified in other places of the GATT such as Articles III: 8–10, XIX, and XX. Considering the subject-matter of each paragraph of Article XXI and especially subparagraphs of paragraph (b), i.e. fissionable materials, arms, and ammunitions, etc., we are led to the conclusion that "security" in Article XXI means "protection of a country against foreign military threats". Spread of viruses would be a military threat if employed

---

33 WTO, ANALYTICAL INDEX OF THE GATT (2012), at 602–605.

34 Appellate Body Report, *US – Shrimp*, *supra* note 15, 129–130.

35 Cambridge English Dictionary (Online).

as a means of biological warfare. Covid-19 is certainly not such a case. Therefore, GATT Article XXI does not apply to export restrictions against the Covid-19 pandemic.

*

In conclusion, as to the elaboration of GATT principles, despite the statement in paragraph 5 of Article XIII that "in so far as applicable, the principles of this Article shall also extend to export restrictions", no authority seems to exist today on how the principles shall apply to export restrictions, leaving the vagueness that must have been a compromise for the purpose of negotiating efficiency. Now that export restrictions have become a more frequent issue of WTO disputes, it would be worthwhile elaborate explanation of the principles as extended to export restrictions. Adoption of an understanding in the coming Ministerial Conference could be an option,[36] e.g., an Understanding on the Export Restrictions of Personal Protective Equipment during a Public Health Crisis.

Members of the WTO[37] and scholars[38] began to make valuable proposals to find a better way to tackle the Covid-19. Most related to our discussion, on April 15, 2020, New Zealand and Singapore made a joint declaration not to apply any export restriction on certain essential goods.[39] It has been well received by other Members[40] and elaborated by scholars for wider acceptance.[41] 47 Member ministers responsible for the WTO called for that any trade restrictive emergency measures shall

36 Art. IX:2 of the Agreement Establishing the World Trade Organization.

37 For a collection of proposals, see <https://www.wto.org/english/tratop_e/covid19_e/proposals_e.htm>.

38 M. Pinchis-Paulsen, *Covid-19 Symposium: Thinking Creatively and Learning from Covid-19 – How the WTO can Maintain Open Trade on Critical Supplies*, OpinioJuris (02.04.20). For more resources, see *Bibliography of Covid-19 Legal Literature*, compiled by Melbourne Law School Covid-19 Research Network, Issue 1 (11 May 2020) and Issue 2 (20 May 2020).

39 *Declaration on Trade in Essential Goods for Combating the Covid-19 Pandemic*, WTO Doc. G/C/W/777 (16 April 2020).

40 Among others, *June 2020 statement of the Ottawa Group: Focusing action on Covid-19*, WTO Doc. WT/GC/217 (16 June 2020).

41 S. Evenett and L.A. Winters, *Preparing for a second wave of Covid-19: A trade bargain to secure supplies of medical goods*, UKTPO Briefing Paper No. 40, (2020).

be targeted, proportionate, transparent and temporary.[42] Many WTO Members indeed have taken measures to remove even WTO-consistent barriers to trade to improve access to Covid-19 essential supplies.[43] These practices can provide bases for a Non-binding Best Practices, which may be annexed to the Understanding on the PPE suggested above.

Without prejudice to Members' wisdom to find different solutions, it is recommended that limiting legitimate quantitative restrictions to be based on scientific risk assessment while widening the scope of traders' decision-making be the common ground for negotiation.

42 WTO General Council, *statement on Covid-19 and the Multilateral Trading System by Ministers Responsible for the WTO from Afghanistan and Others*, WT/GC/212/Rev.1 (28 May 2020).

43 WTO Secretariat, *How WTO Members Have Used Trade Measures to Expedite Access to Covid-19 Critical Medical Goods and Services* (Information Note, 18 September 2020).

# US military presence in Korea and the operational control over the South Korean army

Tai-Uk CHUNG

The US army (United States Forces Korea: USFK) is stationed in South Korea on the Korean Peninsula as part of its overall world presence, and has the second largest number of troops in Korea after Germany and Japan. It is important to remember that the US military has operational control over the Korean military. Such US military dominance has a dual form. One is the so-called United Nations Command (UNC), and the other is the Korea-US Combined Forces Command (ROK-US CFC).

The UNC can command the Korean military on the management of the Korean Armistice. The ROK-US CFC can exercise operational control over the Korean forces in the event of a war on the Korean Peninsula. These two types of armies differ in character, but they have one command system. A general of the US Army serves as the commander of both units. Based on these facts, North Korea insists that South Korea is subordinate to the United States.

The situation on the Korean Peninsula changed markedly in the late 20th century with the dissolution of the Cold War. Some people in South Korea are advocating for the restoration of SK military sovereignty. They want to take over the power on the management of the armistice from the UNC, and they want to regain wartime operational control from the ROK-US CFC. On the other hand, others have the opposite thoughts. They prefer the US military command of the South Korean army and believe that the US army will protect the security of South Korea.

The problem of the US forces stationed in Korea is related to the confrontation between the US and China in Northeast Asia in the 21st century. Those who advocate for the restoration of military sovereignty in South Korea would say that South Korea should maintain an independent position in the context of conflict between the United States and

China, while those who oppose it would say that South Korea should join the US strategy of the siege of China.

## I. United Nations Command and ROK-US Combined Forces Command

### A. The Korean war and the United Nations Command

First, let's take a look at how the US troops were stationed in South Korea, how the two types of US army came into existence, and the relationship between the two.

The origins of US forces in Korea can be traced back to the Pacific War against Japanese imperialism. Together with the Soviet Union, the US occupied Korea, a former Japanese colony, and carried out its military administration. After that, separate governments were established on the Korean peninsula. Both US and Soviet troops withdrew, and the crisis rose. South Korea and North Korea argued that they were the only legitimate governments on the entire Korean peninsula, defined the other as a "rebel group," and finally (June 1950) North Korea launched a full-scale invasion of the South.

In response to the all-out attack by North Korea, South Korea has requested assistance from the United States and the United Nations. The US government and the UN Security Council took action. In accordance with the UN Charter, the Security Council defined the armed attack by North Korea as a "breach of peace," and recommended military assistance to its Member states to repel it. It was recommended that the United States establish a unified command and that the US President appoint a commander. It also authorises the contingents to use the United Nations flag along with their national flags.[1] The United States appointed General MacArthur in Japan as the commander of the united forces, and named the command "United Nations Command".[2]

The South Korean government handed over the command of the South Korean military to the United Nations Command under MacArthur. On 14 July 1950, President Syngman Rhee sent a memorandum to General

1 UN SC Resolution. 82(25. June, 1950), 83(27. June, 1950), 84(7. July, 1950).

2 R. Higgins, *United Nations Peacekeeping: 1946–1967 (Documents and Commentary II, Asia)*, Oxford University Press, 1970, p. 196.

MacArthur stating that "I [Syngman Rhee] am happy to assign to you command authority over all land, sea, and air forces of the Republic of Korea during the period of the continuation of the present state of hostilities, such command to be exercised either by you personally or by such military commander or commanders to whom you may delegate the exercise of this authority within Korea or in adjacent seas".

There is controversy over the legal nature of this "UN Command". Because its name is "United Nations Command," it tends to be misunderstood as a subsidiary organ of the United Nations, that is, a formal UN force. However, as mentioned earlier, the United Nations Command was arbitrarily attached by General MacArthur, and the armed forces are not a UN agency. One should distinguish between the armed forces supported by the United Nations and those belonging to the United Nations.

In order to become an official UN forces, a special treaty must be made with the United Nations in accordance with Article 43 of the Charter of the United Nations, and the United Nations, not the United States, must exercise command of the armed forces. However, the countries that sent troops to South Korea during Korean War only signed an agreement with the United States, and the United Nations has not exercised any control. Both the appointment and replacement of commanders were decided independently by the US government. The UNC in Korea has not registered as a UN agency in its yearbook. The United States also paid the finances of the so-called UN forces in Korea. Thus, the forces in Korea should be viewed as multinational forces commanded by the United States. It is essentially not different from the US-led multinational forces seen in the wars in Iraq and Afghanistan in the late 20th century.

The United Nations Charter envisions the United Nations' armed forces for international law enforcement, but the charter-scheduled armies have not yet been organised. Until now, the UN forces as an auxiliary organ to the UN exist only as UN peacekeepers (often referred to as "Blue Helmets"). These UN peacekeepers are only able to monitor the cease-fire or take measures to prevent war at the request of the country, and they cannot exercise military force unless it is for self-defence. UN Peacekeepers cannot wage war against invading countries. The so-called UN forces sent to Korea during the Korean War are different from these peacekeepers.

The Korean War began with North Korea's invasion of the South, but eventually became a global war. The Korean War began in June 1950 and reached an armistice in July 1953. From October 1950 when China entered the war more than two and a half years were actually a war between China and the United States. And the armistice line on the Korean peninsula was fixed as the borderline of the East-West Cold War.

## B. *The Korean armistice and the United Nations Command*

The Korean War ended with an armistice. The Korean Armistice Agreement was not merely meant to cease fighting, but to prohibit all hostilities and restore peace. The Korean Armistice Agreement made the withdrawal of all foreign troops an important agenda.[3]

However, South Korea, which was afraid of the second invasion by North Korea at the time, continued to need protection by the US military. South Korea demanded a military alliance from the United States, and the Mutual Defence Treaty was signed in October 1953. The treaty gave US troops new grounds for continued presence in South Korea. In "Minutes of Agreement on Military and Economic Assistance to Korea" signed on 17 November 1954. ROK troops were placed under the operational control of UNC command while UNC command is responsible for the defence of Korea.

On the other hand, though North Korea was substantially commanded by the Chinese army during the Korean War, but formally maintained joint command. After the armistice, the Chinese troops promised to withdraw, and in 1958 all Chinese troops returned home. However, in 1961, North Korea also maintained a military alliance by signing Sino-North Korean Mutual Aid and Cooperation Friendship Treaty.

---

3 Korean Armistice Agreement Article IV, 60: In order to insure the peaceful settlement of the Korean question, the military Commanders of both sides hereby recommend to the governments of the countries concerned on both sides that, within three (3) months after the Armistice Agreement is signed and becomes effective, a political conference of a higher level of both sides be held by representatives appointed respectively to settle through negotiation the questions of the withdrawal of all foreign forces from Korea, the peaceful settlement of the Korean question, etc.

After the withdrawal of Chinese troops, North Korea insisted on the withdrawal of US troops in Korea, as well as the dissolution of the UNC. In 1971, China took over as a permanent membership of the UN Security Council in the stead of Taiwan. And a large number of third world countries have joined the United Nations. North Korea's assertion was further strengthened.

In addition, the relation between the United States and China then began to improve. As China and the Soviet Union entered into conflict and competition, the interests of the United States and China to contain the Soviet Union coincided. President Nixon announced the "Nixon Doctrine" in 1969, proclaiming that the United States will minimise military intervention in Asia, including the Vietnam War. In 1972, he visited China and held a summit meeting with Mao Zedong, and recognised Taiwan as a part of China. Later, in 1973, the United States and China set up liaison offices in Washington and Beijing, which would lead to the establishment of diplomatic relations in 1979. This improvement in US-China relations led to discussions between the US and China on a peaceful solution to the Korean issue.

Finally, the 30th United Nations General Assembly in 1975 dealt with the UNC issue. UN General Assembly Resolution 3390[4] was adopted as two distinct decisions, A and B. Resolution 3390 A declared that if an armistice agreement on the Korean peninsula was replaced by a peace agreement, the UN Command could be disbanded. This reflected South Korea's position. On the other hand, Resolution 3390 B recommended the dismantling of the United Nations Command and the withdrawal of all foreign troops stationed in South Korea. And it recommended a peace agreement and disarmament between the two Koreas and independent peaceful unification. This reflected North Korea's position.

## C. Establishment of ROK-US Combined Forces Command

As peace on the Korean Peninsula and the dissolution of the UNC were becoming of international interests, the issue of withdrawal of US troops also emerged. Nixon withdrew some of the US troops in Korea. However, the withdrawal of US troops was halted as Nixon failed to be re-elected due to the Watergate incident. Later, Carter also planned to

---

4 UN GA Resolution 3390(17. Dec. 1974), "Question of Korea".

withdraw US forces from Korea. However, the opposition of the South Korean government and the US military prevented it.

In this situation, South Korean President Park Chung-hee and the US military pushed forward to strengthen the ROK-US alliance based on the ROK-US Mutual Defence Treaty. Even if the UNC were disbanded and a peace treaty on the Korean Peninsula could be signed, the presence of US troops in Korea could be possible. This is because Article 4 of the Treaty stipulates that "the Republic of Korea grants the right to deploy the US Army, Navy and Air Force within and near the territory of the Republic of Korea by mutual agreement, and the United States accepts it."

Thus, in 1978, the ROK-US Combined Forces Command was founded. The commander of US Forces in Korea was appointed as the commander of the ROK-US allied forces, and a general of the Korean army was appointed as the deputy commander. The US-Korea CFC took over the operational control over the South Korean military from the UNC.

The ROK-US Combined Forces Command is guided by the Military Committee (MC) composed of the Joint Chiefs of Staff of both countries and the Security Consultative Meeting (SCM), which is a meeting of the defence ministers of both countries. Such a consultative body gives the impression that the ROK-US CFC is an equal consultative organisation between the US and Korea. However, the commander of the ROK-US CFC is the commander of USFK who belongs to the US Pacific Command. Also, the gap in military and intelligence power between US and ROK is real. Therefore, in actual military operations, the ROK-US CFC should be seen as ultimately under the command of the US military authorities.

As the ROK-US CFC took over the mission of defence of South Korea, which was previously in charge of the UNC, the UNC is only responsible for the maintenance of the Korean Armistice. All combat forces have now been transferred to the ROK-US CFC. However, the command of the CFC and UNC belongs to the same commander, the USFK General. And the officers of the ROK-US CFC also serve as the staff of the UNC.

As such, the USFK currently controls South Korean troops in the dual form of the US-ROK CFC and the UNC.

## II. The issue of returning the operational control of the Korean army

The ROK-US CFC has a fixed unit structure. This is different from other allied forces such as NATO. While NATO operates in the form of assigning certain troops to each Member state in carrying out specific operations, the ROK-US CFC basically includes most of the South Korean military.

With the dissolution of the Cold War between the US and the Soviet Union at the end of the 1980s, the independence of national defence began to become a public debate in South Korea. Thus, President Kim Young-sam's administration started negotiations with the US government on the return of the ROK-US CFC's operational control, and in 1994 it took over the operational control in "peace time".

This return of peacetime operational control can be said to be an event that represents a new change in US-ROK relation. However, the real significance of the return of operational control was not great. The reason is that it was nothing but *peacetime* operational control, and *wartime* operational control was still reserved by the ROK-US CFC. Assuming that the military's peacetime training was prepared for the war, as long as the wartime operation control was reserved, the return of peacetime operation control could even be meaningless.

Since 1994, South Korea has continued to insist that even wartime operational control must be redeemed. The United States also pursued a strategy of relocating of troops stationed abroad while engrossed in the war on terror. Accordingly, the 2006 annual ROK-US Security Consultation Meeting reached an agreement to dismantle the ROK-US CFC in 2012 and return wartime operational control to the South Korean military. This was a landmark agreement in modern Korean history.

However, the situation changed again as the North Korean nuclear crisis escalated and confrontation between the United States and China became visible. The assertion of the US-centred ROK-US coalition response system to the North Korean threat gained sympathy again in South Korea, and the US also hesitated to give up control of the South Korean military. As a result, the timing of the return of wartime operational control was postponed to 2015.

The Park Geun-hye' administration came up with prerequisites for the return of wartime operational control. The preconditions proposed by the United States were threefold: i/ the South Korean military would have the military capability to lead the combined defence of the ROK-US, ii/ the South Korean military would have the initial response capability to the North Korean nuclear and missile threat and iii/ the return of operational control should be consistent with the regional security environment of Korean Peninsula.

As a result, the return of wartime operational control was delayed *sine die*. And, as can be seen from the expression "regional security environment," the issue of the ROK-U.S. CFC has been linked not only to North Korea, but also to military strategies against China.

## III. The issue of the revitalisation of the United Nations Command

As we have already seen, the return of operational control from the ROK-US CFC means the dissolution of the ROK-US CFC. However, in line with that discussion, the UNC's revitalisation is being promoted. Since the US-ROK CFC and the UNC are virtually integrated, if the CFC is disbanded, it may be anticipated that the UNC should also be disbanded. Rather, the UNC is being strengthened newly.

The US President George W. Bush's administration, involved in the war on terrorism, was active in returning the ROK-US CFC's operational control. At the same time, Defence Secretary Rumsfeld ordered the UNC policy to involve more countries in addition to the original Member states (participating in the Korean War). Similarly, in 2005, then UNC Commander Burwell Bell emphasised the reinforcement of the UNC's organisation. And in 2013, Commander Curtis Scarparotti also made the revitalisation of the UNC as a key task.

In 2018 a lieutenant general of the Canadian Army was appointed as deputy commander of the UNC.[5] It was the first time in the history of UNC history that the general of a third country, not the US, was appointed vice-commander of the UNC. In addition, in Vancouver, Canada, the 'Diplomatic Ministers' Meeting on Security and Stability

5 Korean Yonhap News Agency, 19:01 July 30, 2018. <https://en.yna.co.kr/view/AEN20180730008500315>.

of the Korean Peninsula' was held, including 17 countries participating in the Korean War *and Japan*. Finally, the 2018 ROK-US Defence Ministers' Annual Meeting (SCM) confirmed that even if the ROK-US CFC is disbanded, the UNC will continue to exist.[6]

This reactivation of the UNC was originally understood to be for the maintenance of the Korean Armistice after the dissolution of the ROK-US CFC. However, the UNC is already carrying out the maintenance and management functions of the Armistice through the ROK military. Even though the ROK-US CFC were disbanded, there could be no problem with maintaining the armistice on the Korean Peninsula. Therefore, it is understood that the purpose of revitalisation of the UNC is to maintain control of the ROK military through the UNC even after the dissolution of the ROK-US CFC. Furthermore, it is suspected that the revitalisation of the UNC will go beyond that and promote a so-called "Asia's NATO". It is speculated that the reorganisation of the UNC is being promoted as part of the United States' global strategy targeting China.

From the standpoint of the United States, there are several advantages of the UNC over the ROK-US CFC. The CFC is just a bilateral organisation between South Korea and the United States, but the UNC is an international organisation of multinational forces. It could be far more useful for the United States to use its coalition strategy on a global scale. In addition, the UNC has a rear base in Japan. The facilities and bases provided by Japan to the US military could be used by the UNC in Korea as well. In other words, in case of emergency in East Asia, Japan can serve as a military base for the UNC.

As such, the UNC is not just playing a role in maintaining and managing the Korean Armistice, but it is reborn as a multinational combat unit in times of emergency on the Korean Peninsula and East Asia. This change in the role of the UNC in Korea suggests the danger of Korea being involved in the struggle for supremacy in East Asia due to the US military.

Furthermore, this is contrary to the original purpose of transferring operational control from the UNC to the ROK-US CFC. Even if the South Korean military took over operational control from the ROK-US

---

6 Joint communique of 50th U.S.-ROK Security Consultative Meeting (Oct. 31, 2018), <https://www.usfk.mil/Media/News/Article/1679753/joint-communique-of-50th-us-rok-security-consultative-meeting/>.

CFC, if South Korean forces were assigned to multinational forces under the US command through the UNC, the US command over the South Korean forces could remain unchanged.

*

In conclusion, as to the confrontation between US-China and the future of the Korean peninsula, as mentioned at the outset, the situation in which the United States is reluctant for the dissolution of the US-ROK CFC and is seeking the possibility of a new multinational forces through the revitalisation of the UNC is understood in the backdrop of confrontation between the United States and China.

The Korean War in 1950 was between South Korea and North Korea, and between the United States and China. However, it can be said that the Korean War almost ended with the establishment of diplomatic relations between the United States and China in the 1970s and the normalisation of relations between South Korea and China in the 1990s. However, hostile relations between the US and North Korea have not yet been resolved. Progress in inter-Korean relations is unstable.

Now, relations between the United States and China are falling into a dangerous situation again. As can be seen from the disputes in the South China Sea, the Taiwan issue, and economic disputes, the US and China are facing all-round confrontation. The United States is currently envisioning a strategy to contain China in the Pacific Indian Ocean. The so-called "Quad" initiative is just an example. The Korean Peninsula lies on the front of such a confrontation between the United States and China. Will South Korea join the US siege strategy of China?

The United States has command over the South Korean army. Militarily, the US can control South Korea. However, South Korea has formed close economic ties with China. The South Korean economy is dependent on trade. The country to which South Korea exports the most is China, and the country from which South Korea imports the most is China, too. If South Korea is cut off from China, the South Korean economy will not be sustainable.

In this way, South Korea is militarily subordinated to the US and economically dependent on China. Here is the South Korean dilemma. Do South Koreans really need more military or more economics? The future of the Korean Peninsula depends on this.

# Part III

# Sectoral and socio-economic issues

# Introduction

Amandine CAYOL

The third part of this book deals with sectoral and socio-economic issues. Its seven chapters ascribe to three broad categories of such issues. Some deal mainly with the health crisis, others with intellectual property rights, finally some address the consequences of the crisis in the performing arts and in tourism.

Several articles focus on the health crisis related to the COVID-19 pandemic. The first emphasises the need to ensure equal access to care for all. Gulmira MASHIMBAYEVA and Aidana OTYNSHIYEVA, intent on ensuring the right to health in the terms and times of global epidemics, regret the "vaccine nationalism" which has created inequality among countries on the issue of access to vaccines. The fight against COVID-19 requires a global response and cooperation among states. It also requires solidarity among individuals. The COVID-19 has unfortunately increased xenophobia, nationalism, discrimination against migrants and refugees, denying them access to treatment. The authors conclude that "Governments have a responsibility to protect people not only by guaranteeing universal access to health services, but also by ensuring their economic and social rights"

The second article shows that health systems have had to adapt in order to cope with the COVID-19 pandemic. Amandine CAYOL, looking at the development of e-health in the context of the COVID-19 pandemic, highlights the use of telemedicine that developed very strongly in France in this context, in order to overcome the problems of access to doctors in person. Its practical interest was brought to light by the health crisis, which facilitated its social acceptance by health professionals and patients, and led to the relaxation of the regulatory and conventional framework. However, the development of telemedicine has raised concerns about the protection of health data and the respect of patients' rights.

The third article emphasises the importance of legal consciousness of citizens in overcoming the current pandemic. Yesbol Omirzhanov and Almagul Tusupova, looking at the level of legal consciousness of citizens as a determining factor in the fight against Covid-19, explain that whatever the political decisions and technical means implemented to fight the pandemic, the psychological acceptance of the measures by the citizens is essential. In consequence, governments should take into account the psychological attitude of the population to their decision to ensure compliance with them.

Other chapters deal with the question of the protection of intellectual property rights. The first one addresses the implementation of WTO standards in this field in the legislation of the Republic of Kazakhstan. Zhuldyz Sairambaeva and Madina Nurtay, looking at the implementation of WTO standards in the field of intellectual property in the legislation of the Republic of Kazakhstan: protecting of intellectual property rights during Covid-19, insist that globalisation and technological advances have made it necessary to create an effective and universal international mechanism for protection of intellectual property rights between states.

The second one, focusing on the evolution of intellectual property rights: international and regional evolution, by Philippe Gast, traces recent developments in this area at the European and international levels: the literary and artistic property, questioned by internet and GAFAM from one side, and industrial property questioned by trademark and patent infringement on another side

Finally, the last two articles deal with the consequences of the health crisis on two particularly affected sectors: the performing arts industry in a text by Sung-Kee Hong, looking at the the prospect of the performing-arts industry in the pandemic era: Korean perspective on copyright issues, and on tourism in a text by Odgerel Purevdorj and Erbakhit Badelgaji, addressing the Covid-induced challenging losses to a national economy of East Asia: the 2020 economic case of the tourism sector in the Ulaanbaatar area of Mongolia.

# Ensuring the right to health in the terms and times of a global epidemics

Gulmira Mashimbayeva,
Aidana Otynshiyeva

Since the end of 2019, the world has faced an unprecedented crisis, based on the global public health emergency created by the Covid-19 pandemic. The scale of this situation cannot be compared to any other emergency that has occurred over the past century and that now requires a global response.

The coronavirus has thus proved to be a serious test for the pros and cons of international cooperation. From the onset of the pandemic, the slogan "every man for himself" has genuinely threatened international relations. Fear of the virus has forced developed countries to fence themselves off from each other, with borders and other barriers. Today, we would like to forget how, in the spring of 2020, EU countries reluctantly responded to Italy's desperate requests for medical care or Germany's tough position on banning the export of medical masks to other EU Member states or that Brussels announced a ban on the export of medicines and medical equipment for the treatment of coronavirus outside the EU.

A so-called "vaccine nationalism" created inequality among countries on the issue of access to vaccines. Today, after the world has lived in a state of pandemic for over 18 months, humanity must realise that only together can we defeat the coronavirus crisis.

## I. Measures taken by the United Nations

Awareness that the coronavirus epidemic could threaten human rights around the world let the UN to call on countries to adopt a more coherent, global and human rights-oriented approach to the pandemic, which Secretary-General A. Guterres called a "universal crisis". Since the beginning of the Covid-19 coronavirus outbreak, human rights officials and UN-appointed independent experts have emphasised the importance of protecting people's rights. This was enshrined in Resolution 74/270 "Global Solidarity in the fight against coronavirus disease 2019 (Covid-19)", adopted by the UN General Assembly on 2 April 2020.[1]

Covid-19 is not only a health problem but also a virus that increases xenophobia, nationalism, discrimination against migrants and refugees, denying them access to treatment and other social benefits. The rights of the elderly, those of women and children suffering from domestic violence in lockdowns and home isolation; access to health care for persons in prison, the rights of persons with disabilities, etc. The incomplete list of human rights concerns that have emerged since the arrival of Covid-19[2] can be supplemented:

- The Office of the UN High Commissioner for Human Rights (OHCHR) provided recommendations for a human rights-focused response to the spread of the Covid-19 coronavirus infection:
- Health policies should take into account not only the health aspects of the pandemic, but also the human rights and gender implications of the health response.
- Emergency powers should be used legally, in the interests of public health, and not as a basis for suppressing dissent or silencing the activities of human rights defenders or journalists.
- Restrictive measures, such as social distancing and self-isolation, should take into account the needs of people who rely on other people's support for food, clothing, and bathing. Many people, including people with disabilities, rely on family and social services for these aspects.
- It is also essential that any tightening of border controls, travel restrictions or restrictions on freedom of movement do not hinder people who are forced to flee war or persecution.
- Tax incentives and social protection packages aimed directly at those least able to cope with the crisis are essential to mitigate the devastating effects of the pandemic. Immediate economic assistance measures, such as guaranteed paid sick leave, expanded unemployment benefits, food distribution, and universal basic earnings, can help avoid the acute effects of the crisis.

---

1 Resolution adopted by the General Assembly on 2 April 2020 <https://undocs.org/ru/A/RES/74/270> (accessed on 16 May 2021).

2 <https://www.un.org/ru/coronavirus/protecting-human-rights-amid-covid-19-crisis> (accessed on 16 May 2021).

- Members of the LGBTI community also face increased risks during this pandemic. Specific actions should be included in the response plans to address the challenges in this area.
- states should take into account the specific health concepts of indigenous peoples, including their traditional medicine, consult and take into account the free prior and informed consent of indigenous peoples when developing preventive measures for Covid-19 coronavirus infection.
- People deprived of their liberty, including in prisons, pre-trial detention centers, immigration centers, institutions and other places of detention, are at increased risk of infection in the event of an outbreak. Their situation should be considered separately when planning and responding to crisis situations.
- Health professionals and relevant experts, including scientists, should be able to speak freely and share information with each other and the public.[3]

It is thus clear that the present sanitary crisis serves as a test challenging global governance, including in its institutional aspects, way beyond the still urgent medical and sanitary measures indispensable to (try and) curb the spread of the disease and its variants.

## II. The right to health in the human rights system

The priority of the international community – to save lives –, in view of the exceptional situation, will manage to do so – to save lives – if countries accept that they have no choice but to take emergency measures.

Three fundamental rights stand out at the forefront of the fight against the current pandemic: i/ the right to life and the duty to protect life, ii/ the right to health and access to health care, and iii/ freedom of movement. These rights were proclaimed in the 1948 Universal Declaration of Human Rights and in the 1966 International Covenant on Economic, Social and Cultural Rights.

As the modern fight against Covid-19 is aimed at protecting the lives of all people, reference to the right to life reminds us that all states have an obligation to protect human life, including by addressing the

3 Covid-19 Control Guide <https://www.ohchr.org/ru/NewsEvents/Pages/COVID19Guidance.aspx> (accessed on 17 May 2021).

basic conditions in society that pose direct threats to life. states are making great efforts to do this, and this right must remain at the centre of attention.

The right to health is an integral part of the right to life. The Covid-19 crisis is also testing the ability of states to protect the right to health. Everyone has the right to the highest attainable standard of health providing them with decent living conditions. Everyone, regardless of their social or economic status, should have access to the health care they need. The age-old underfunding of health systems has weakened their ability to respond to the pandemic and simultaneously provide other critical health services. The experience of the fight against Covid-19 shows that universal access to health services is imperative. Those states that have effective and sustainable health systems are better equipped to respond to crises. Health systems around the world are overloaded, and some of them are on the verge of collapse.

Universal access to health services promotes effective and sustainable health systems, reaches vulnerable populations, and promotes pandemic preparedness and prevention. Achieving universal health coverage is one of the challenges of sustainable development. Universal, affordable health systems help fight the pandemic by ensuring that everyone has access, without discrimination, to basic measures to contain the spread of the virus. These measures include testing, specialised care for the most vulnerable patients, intensive care, and vaccination whenever possible, regardless of the ability to pay. In response to the pandemic, some countries provided universal access to health services for all residents; others entered into agreements with private-sector health facilities to use their facilities and equipment to fight the pandemic.

In order to control the spread of the virus and protect the right to life, it is necessary to break the chain of infection: people must stop moving and interacting with each other. The most common public health measure taken by states in the fight against Covid-19 is the restriction of freedom of movement, which can take the form of a lockdown or an instruction to stay at home. This is a practical method that is necessary to stop the spread of the virus, prevent the overload of health systems and thus save lives. However, exclusion can have very serious consequences for employment, economic conditions, access to services, including access to health, food, water, education and social services, as well as for the safety of the home, an adequate standard of living and family life.

It is thus clear that freedom of movement is one of the most important rights, which contributes to the realisation of many other rights. While international law allows for some restrictions on freedom of movement, including for security reasons and in connection with national emergencies, such as in the field of health, restrictions on freedom of movement must be strictly necessary, proportionate and non-discriminatory. The ability to conduct effective and generalised testing and contact tracing, and to implement targeted quarantine measures, may reduce the need for more indiscriminate restrictions.

The Universal Declaration of Human Rights (article 25), the International Covenant on Economic, Social and Cultural Rights (article 12) enshrine the right of everyone to the enjoyment of the highest attainable standard of physical and mental health.

The right to health refers to social rights. The French WHO legal expert N. Delpere argued that "social rights are established in order to ensure a safe existence for everyone".[4] With the advent of a number of international documents of the last fifty years, health has become the object of legal analysis. The nature of the definition of health, as set out in the preamble to the WHO Constitution, suggests that such a definition of health goes beyond the competence of medicine. This is evidenced by the presence of a non-medical factor that makes up health – "social well-being". That is, despite the fact that health is a personal good of an individual, it has a social character.

> Human health is the most important condition for the harmonious development of each individual, the collective in which he lives and works, and society as a whole. The health of a person depends both on himself and on how the society in which he lives protects and multiplies this priceless gift of a person, and ultimately, how it organised the health system.[5]

A new definition of health was proposed at the WHO 101st session: "Health is a dynamic state of complete physical, mental and social well-being, not only the absence of diseases or physical defects".[6] This

4 G.L. Burci, "Shifting Norms in International Health Law", *Am Socy Intl L Proc.* 2004, 98, p. 34; N. Delpere, (1993) *Protection of the rights and freedoms of citizens of old age*, p. 35.

5 The World Health Organization, *Report 1998: Life in the 21st Century, A Vision for All*, 1998, p. 39.

6 Criteria for the Development of Health Promotion Policies. Adopted on 21 September 2000 (722nd Meeting of the Ministers' Deputies).

definition of health remains the most widely used. This interpretation of the concept of health makes it possible to adapt it more widely to the changing priorities and principles of international cooperation in the field of public health, especially in the context of new medical and social problems associated, for example, with global epidemics.

Health protection is usually understood as a set of measures of a political, economic, legal, social, cultural, scientific, medical, sanitary-hygienic, anti-epidemic nature, aimed at preserving and strengthening the physical and mental health of a person, maintaining his long-term active life, providing him with medical care in case of loss of health.[7]

We must always remember that the health of every person depends on the health of the whole society. Therefore, the responsibility for health should be mutual. In order to demand that the state ensure the right to health, each individual must understand the extent of their responsibility to the health of the entire society.

## III. The role and importance of the WHO in health protection and in the fight against global problems and epidemics

The WHO, as a professional medical, scientific and legal platform, provides international cooperation and global control in the fight against the coronavirus pandemic. For a year and a half, the WHO has been criticised for not responding in time to the crisis surrounding the coronavirus pandemic. There is a certain amount of truth in these reproaches. However, we must be realistic and understand that today the WHO is the only administrative platform in the world that can manage joint projects to combat the pandemic. It was within the framework of the WHO that important international legal acts were adopted in the fight against Covid-19 and other serious epidemics.

The World Health Organisation as important global focal point for the exchange of information between Governments, scientists at universities, government institutions, and pharmaceutical companies, is not omnipotent. Only national health systems, research institutes, and

---

7 World Health Assembly Res No WHA56.28, *Revision of the International Health Regulations*, P 3(1) (2003), available online at <http://www.who.int/gb/ebwha/pdffiles/WHA56/ea56r28.pdf> (accessed on 17 May 2021).

industry can and should do the real work to combat emerging diseases. Despite its name, the WHO cannot compensate for the shortcomings in health care or fluctuations in the markets for medicines, personal protective equipment, etc.[8]

## IV. The WHO's international legal instruments and bodies

In 2005, the International Health Regulations (IHR) were adopted, as international legal instruments binding 196 states parties, including 194 Member states of the WHO, as well as the WHO Secretariat. Their purpose and scope are (article 2) "to prevent, prevent, control and respond to the international spread of diseases at the public health level, which are commensurate with and limited to the risks to public health and which do not unnecessarily hinder international transport and trade".

The Committee to Review the Functioning of the International Health Regulations (2005) during the Response to the Covid-19 pandemic was formed by the Director-General of the WHO on 8 September 2020.

In accordance with resolution WHA73.1, the Committee was requested to review the functioning of the IHR during the Covid-19 response period with respect to the application of the relevant IHR provisions, which relate to, but are not limited to, the following issues:

- Outbreak alert, event check and risk assessment, information exchange;
- International coordination and cooperation, including the role of national IHR Focal Points (NCS);
- Working arrangements for the IHR Emergency Committee and the declaration of a public health emergency of international concern, including consideration of an interim level of preparedness;
- Additional health measures taken by states Parties with regard to international travel;
- Implementing and reporting on core IHR capabilities, including the possibility of implementing peer review processes, etc.

In addition, a WHO Emergency Committee was specially convened to combat the coronavirus epidemic in January 2020.

---

8 <https://www.dw.com/ru/комментарий-упреки-в-адрес-воз-несправедливы/a-53152652> (accessed on 17 May 2021).

In 2010, the WHO Committee to Review the Functioning of the International Health Regulations (2005) during the response to the influenza pandemic (H1N1) – 2009 – concluded that: "The world is ill-prepared to respond to severe influenza pandemics or to any similar global, prolonged and public health-threatening emergencies".[9] The post-H1N1 review highlighted numerous vulnerabilities limiting the capacity of national public health systems such as lack of scientific knowledge, difficulties in making decisions in an uncertain environment, difficulties in implementing international cooperation, and communication challenges. It also stressed the need for the WHO Secretariat to further strengthen its "internal capacity to respond" to long-term public health emergencies of international concern, in particular pandemics.

Subsequent public health efforts have focused on strengthening health systems and building capacity to prevent, detect and respond to health emergencies at the national, regional and global levels.

Today, however, there is reason to believe that these efforts were insufficient. Indeed, a number of countries that appeared to be best equipped to detect the deadly virus and respond were among the least able to prevent or contain the spread of severe acute respiratory syndrome 2 (SARS-CoV-2) coronavirus domestically or internationally. The unprecedented intensification of international cooperation in response to the pandemic has been accompanied by alarming isolationism. Countries with a robust public health system in place have been able to successfully contain the spread of SARS-CoV-2.

It is clear that the localisation of a pandemic caused by a new pathogen for which there is no vaccine or effective treatment is possible only if a strong and strategically calibrated response is taken to protect public health.

In its analysis of global responses to the pandemic, the WHO has concluded that too many countries still lack sufficient public health capacity to protect their own populations and provide timely warnings to other countries and the WHO. The lack of capacity, especially in terms of resources, is also experienced by the WHO itself. The WHO proposes to establish a peer review system, where countries can work

---

9 Document A64/10, section IV, Conclusions and recommendations, paragraph 31 // <https://apps.who.int/gb/ebwha/pdf_files/WHA64/A64_10-ru.pdf> (accessed on 17 May 2021).

together to assess their capacity, publicise the results and, crucially, support each other. It is hoped that such a system, with the support of the WHO Secretariat, will serve as a single mechanism for ensuring country accountability. Since this unprecedented health crisis affects more than just people's health, ensuring accountability must be the focus of serious attention by all public authorities.

It is clear that in the context of the 2020 pandemic, the countries that approved the IHR in 2005 applied the Rules only partially, and were not sufficiently aware of them. In this context, the Latin saying *ignorantia juris non excusat* (ignorance of the law is not an excuse) may be valid. However, there is less need to look for blame than to consider options for making the IHR more feasible, especially in order to prevent as well as effectively address pandemics and other global health crises. For example, the current Rules do not mention such important issues as the exchange of samples and genetic sequences of pathogens, the introduction of digital technologies, the impact of social networks on the operation of the alert system and the degree of implementation of recommendations.

Thus, despite the thoughtful nature of the IHR provisions, they will never be able to fully ensure the safety of people if all countries – their governments, local communities, civil society, businesses and public health leaders – do not work with each other and with WHO, as well as other regional and international institutions, to apply the Rules in a spirit of solidarity. Such fruitful cooperation can be fully realised only on the basis of the principles of trust and transparency: without these two conditions, it is difficult to imagine a more secure future.

*

In conclusion, one short chapter as this one cannot consider all the components of the measures taken to ensure the right to health in the period of global epidemics. In this regard, the practice of responding to the challenges of the pandemic of national health systems is of interest. In particular, it is relevant to compare the experience of China, Russia and South Korea. Why some countries managed to prevent the collapse of health care, while others did not. Serious analysis and revision of approaches to the organisation of the health care system are needed.

Legal and other aspects of creating vaccines against coronavirus infection deserve a separate study. It is interesting to study the significance of the WHO's work on vaccine development and WHO's collaboration with national research centres. It is with regret that the creation and acceptance of vaccines is becoming an instrument of international politics. All this is improper for ensuring the right to health of people.

Based on the above, governments have a responsibility to protect people not only by guaranteeing universal access to health services, but also by ensuring their economic and social rights: effective food distribution systems; social security and protection systems; gender equality; protection of people and jobs through respect for labour rights, minimum wages, etc.

Another important conclusion is that ensuring the right to health during a global epidemic is not only a task for governments, but also for each individual, and it is necessary to ensure collective responsibility. To do this, governments need to be more open and transparent, responsive and accountable to the people they seek to protect than ever before. To participate effectively in the response, people must be informed and involved in the decisions that affect them, and any measures taken must be necessary, reasonable and proportionate to fight the virus and save lives.

Those who want to abandon the protection of human rights in order to take advantage of the crisis should think carefully; such actions can only undermine the effectiveness of the global and national response to the pandemic.

Governments have a responsibility to do everything they can to mitigate the enormous pressure placed on health workers in the fight against the pandemic. Their safety at work is critical, and they should have access to effective protective equipment, regular coronavirus screening, antibody testing, and psychosocial support.

Thus, as the UN Secretary-General noted in his Call to Action, "the only response to the many crises facing humanity is collective action".[10]

---

10 <https://www.un.org/sites/un2.un.org/files/human_rights_and_covid19> (accessed on 16 May 2021).

# The development of *e*-health in the context of the Covid-19 pandemic

Amandine Cayol

Digital health, or "e-health",[1] refers to all areas where information and communication technologies are used to improve health.[2] Telemedicine, defined as "a form of remote medical practice using information and communication technologies",[3] is only one of its components.[4]

Although it began in the 1990s, the use of telemedicine in France has really developed with the health crisis linked to the Covid-19 pandemic since the beginning of 2020.

The law of 13 August 2004 timidly established telemedicine, specifying that it allows "among other things, to perform medical acts (...) at a distance, under the control and responsibility of a doctor in contact with the patient by means of communication appropriate to the performance of the medical act".[5] Following the recommendations of the European Commission,[6] the law of 21 July

---

1 The term e-Health was born at the end of 1999 during the 7th International Telemedicine Congress. John Mitchell defined it as "the combined use of the Internet and information technology for clinical, educational and administrative purposes, both locally and remotely".

2 This was broadly defined by the World Health Organization (WHO) in 1945 as "a state of complete physical, mental and social well-being".

3 Public health code, art. L6316-1, al. 1.

4 More specifically, it is a component of telehealth, since the consecration by Law No. 2019-774 of July 24, 2019 on the organization and transformation of the health system, of telecare (art. 53 et seq.), defined as "a form of remote care practice using information and communication technologies (in order to put) a patient in touch with one or more pharmacists or medical auxiliaries" (Public health code, art. L6316-2).

5 Law No. 2004-810, August 13, 2004 on health insurance, art. 32.

6 Already favourable to the development of digital health care since the early 2000s (European Commission, *eHealth – improving healthcare for European citizens*, (2004) 356, Apr. 2004), in November 2008, the European Commission expressly

2009[7] defined telemedicine more precisely,[8] while the decree of 19 October 2010 detailed the conditions of implementation.

The latter provides for five types of telemedicine acts:[9] teleconsultation, tele-expertise, remote medical monitoring, remote medical assistance and the medical response provided as part of the regulation produced by the emergency medical services (SAMU). Teleconsultation allows a patient to consult a medical professional at a distance. Tele-expertise refers to the situation in which a medical professional gives his expert opinion at a distance. Remote medical monitoring is the way to follow a patient suffering from a chronic disease (heart failure, diabetes, etc.) at a distance thanks to indicators (which can be collected by medical devices). Finally, we speak of medical tele-assistance when a health professional assists another health professional remotely during the performance of a procedure.

Telemedicine is often presented as a relevant solution to meet the challenges facing the French healthcare system: changes in medical demographics, territorial inequalities in access to care,[10] an increase in chronic diseases, an ageing population, and dependency care. The decree of 29 December 2017 defining the National Health Strategy (NHS) for the period 2018–2022 considers it necessary to "generalise the use of telemedicine in daily practice, primarily teleconsultations and tele-expertise and build an ethical framework for the use of telemedicine so that it benefits the entire population",[11] and to "develop the use of technologies in the prevention and monitoring of chronic pathologies".[12]

The decree of 13 September 2018, and the ministerial order of 1 August 2018, approving amendment No. 6 to the national agreement organising relations between independent physicians and health

---

encouraged Member states to "allow better access to telemedicine services by adapting their national legislation" (European Commission, *Telemedicine at the service of patients*, (2008) 699, Nov. 2008).

7 It repealed the articles on telemedicine from the law of August 13, 2004.

8 Law No. 2009-879 of July 21, 2009 on hospital reform and on patients, health and territories, art. 78.

9 Decree No. 2010-1229 of October 19, 2010.

10 M.-L. Moquet-Anger, "Télémédecine et égal accès aux soins", *RDSS*, 2020, p. 13.

11 Decree No. 2017-1866 of December 29, 2017, p. 23.

12 *Ibid.*, p. 39.

insurance (itself signed on 25 August 2016)[13] enabled the practice of telemedicine by private practitioners:[14] as of 15 September 2018, teleconsultations have been integrated into the care pathway and have opened the right to billing from health insurance.[15] The financial set-back on the development of telemedicine has thus been removed. However, this has been accompanied by "a fairly strict framework for this practice [so as not to] run the risk of a significant drift in medical expenditure".[16]

The law of 24 July 2019 also aimed to increase the use of digital technology in the field of health,[17] in particular by "fully deploying telemedicine and telecare".[18] However, until the Covid-19 pandemic, the use of telemedicine remained low, especially in liberal medicine.

Its practical interest was brought to light by the 2019–2020 health crisis, which facilitated its social acceptance by health professionals and patients, and led to the relaxation of the regulatory and conventional framework. The number of teleconsultations has thus increased from 60,000 in 2019 to nearly 20 million in 2020! Telemedicine has indeed been the means, both to curb the health crisis and to ensure continuity of care. However, this acceleration in the use of telemedicine during the health crisis is not without raising numerous ethical and legal questions. Indeed, according to Dr. Pierre Simon, "more than half of the teleconsultations [in 2020] were characterised by a practice that did not comply with fundamental rules such as the General Data Protection Regulation (GDPR) or the respect of patients' rights".[19]

---

13 Ministerial order of Aug. 1, 2018, approving amendment No. 6 to the national agreement organizing relations between independent physicians and health insurance signed on Aug. 25, 2016, and Decree No. 2018-788 of Sept. 13, 2018, on the terms and conditions for implementing telemedicine activities.

14 Amendment No. 2 first created in 2017 two follow-up procedures for patients in residential facilities for the dependent elderly (EHPAD): tele-expertise (coded TDT) and tele-consultation (coded TTE).

15 See on this issue, B. Apollis, "Télémédecine et remboursement des actes", *RDSS*, 2020, p. 23.

16 M. Borgetto, "La télémédecine", *RDSS*, 2020, p. 3.

17 It thus implements the measures announced by Emmanuel Macron, in his speech of September 18, 2018, regarding the "My Health 2022" plan.

18 Law No. 2019-774 of July 24, 2019, art. 53 et seq.

19 P. Simon, "La téléconsultation est une pratique légale et réglementaire, mais est-elle toujours une pratique éthique?", *Managersante.com*, 41, mai 2021.

If the interest of developing telemedicine in times of health crisis is undeniable (I), it is important to verify which risks are really generated, in order to allow for the implementation of regulations that reconcile easy access to telemedicine and protection of patients' rights (II).

## I. The interest of developing telemedicine in times of health crisis

As underlined in the ministerial order of 23 March 2020, telemedicine "makes it possible to provide medical and health care management at home for patients with symptoms of infection or recognised as having (the) Covid-19 and to protect health professionals from infection as well as the patients they care for".

Thus, during the health crisis linked to the Covid-19 pandemic, the value of using telemedicine was revealed both for people who had contracted this virus (A) and for people requiring particularly strong protection against any risk of infection (B).

### *A. For those who have contracted Covid-19*

Patients presenting symptoms of infection caused by Covid-19 were initially invited to call the SAMU (centre 15). This was the only entry point in the management of stages 1 and 2, i.e. before 14 March 2020. However, the medical response provided within the framework of medical regulation is one of the five acts covered by telemedicine according to the decree of 19 October 2010.

Starting with the upgrade to stage 3, the use of teleconsultations and remote monitoring has increased significantly to ensure follow-up, at home, of patients with Covid-19. The use of telemedicine has been facilitated by abandoning some of the conditions set by amendment No. 6 to the national agreement organising relations between independent physicians and health insurance. The latter in fact made the reimbursement of teleconsultation procedures conditional on compliance with the coordinated care pathway. Patients had to be referred by the attending physician, to have consulted the teleconsulting physician during at least one face-to-face consultation in the last 12 months, and then alternate face-to-face and remote consultations.[20] This limited the use of teleconsultation, which was "not intended to supplant 'face-to-face' medical procedures [...], clearly promised to remain an alternative in the minds of the partners to the agreement".[21] Amendment No. 6 also required the use of video transmission to obtain reimbursement.[22] The purpose of this clarification was to exclude telephone platforms offering medical consultations.

A decree of 9 March 2020,[23] established derogatory conditions for the reimbursement of telemedicine procedures for people infected or potentially infected by the coronavirus. It thus provided that teleconsultation by video transmission with a physician be reimbursed, even for patients who are outside the care pathway coordinated by the attending physician, including for a primary consultation. A decree of 23 March 2020 even allowed, as a derogation, to deal with the Covid-19 pandemic, that healthcare professionals use digital tools and "general public" communication applications when they take care of patients with symptoms of the infection or recognised as suffering from Covid-19.[24]

### B. For persons requiring special protection from Covid-19 contamination

The fear of contamination has been particularly strong persons requiring special protection, such as the elderly, patients with chronic diseases, and pregnant women.

In its 14 March 2020 opinion on the prevention and management of Covid-19 in patients at risk of severe forms, the high council of public health (HCSP) recommended "reducing to a strict minimum the risk of contact with the virus for these fragile individuals". To do this, the HCSP recommended "restricting face-to-face consultations" and "giving preference to telemedicine or telephone consultations".

---

20 Art. 28.6.1.1.

21 B. Apollis, "Télémédecine et remboursement des actes", *RDSS*, 2020, p. 23.

22 Art. 28.6.1.3.

23 Decree No. 2020-227 of March 9, 2020 adapting the conditions for receiving health insurance cash benefits and coverage of telemedicine procedures for persons exposed to covid-19.

24 Ministerial order of March 23, 2020, art. 8, I.

In order to facilitate the use of telemedicine for the medical follow-up of these persons requiring special protection from Covid-19 contamination, a decree of 21 April 2020[25] has, once again, established derogatory conditions for the reimbursement of teleconsultation procedures, which can now be performed by telephone for persons who do not have the necessary equipment to perform a video transmission and who fall into one of the following situations: a person aged 70 years or older, a person suffering from a long-term illness (ALD) or a pregnant woman.

## II. The risks generated by the development of telemedicine

The development of telemedicine has raised concerns about the protection of health data (A) and the respect of patients' rights (B).

### A. *On the protection of health data*

The health care relationship between a doctor and his patient has always been based on the sharing of information about the patient's health.[26] Whether it is transmitted directly by the patient[27] or brought to the physician's attention during the examination of the patient's body or after biological tests, this information is covered by medical secrecy in France.[28] Doctors are forbidden to pass it on to others, although this principle was relaxed in 2016[29] to allow for the exchange of information within the same medical team to ensure better continuity of care.

However, the development of telemedicine has profoundly changed the issue of the protection of health-related information,[30]

---

[25] Decree No. 2020-459 of April 21, 2020 amending Decree No. 2020-73 of January 31, 2020.

[26] C. Zorn-Macrez, *Données de santé et secret partagé*, PU Nancy, 2010.

[27] Particularly concerning his personal or family history.

[28] Public health code, art. L. 1110-4.

[29] By Law No. 2016-41, known as the "modernization of our health system" law, of January 26, 2016.

[30] See on medical confidentiality in the use of telemedicine, C. Daver, "La télémédecine, entre progrès techniques et responsabilités", *D.* 2000, p. 527.

due to "the dispersion of data in spaces that are not always perfectly secure".[31]

The use of telemedicine requires the processing of numerous personal data,[32] including (but not limited to) health data, broadly defined as those "relating to the physical or mental health of a natural person, including the provision of health care services, which reveal information about the health status of that person".[33] The physician practicing telemedicine is, as a result, subject to the obligations arising from the General Data Protection Regulation (GDPR),[34] which came into force in May 2018. The latter has strengthened the individual's right of control over the data that concerns him or her: right of access to data, right of rectification and opposition to processing, "right to be forgotten".

A practical guide for physicians on the protection of personal data was published by the National Council of the Order of Physicians (CNOM) and the National Commission on Information Technology and Liberties (CNIL) on 20 July 2018.[35] Under the terms of Article R. 6316-10 of the Public Health Code, healthcare professionals must ensure that the use of technologies used for their teleconsultation complies with the terms and conditions for hosting personal health data. Amendment No. 6 to the national agreement organising relations between independent physicians and health insurance also specifies that teleconsultation "must be carried out under conditions that guarantee the security of the data transmitted".[36]

However, the health crisis has led to a relaxation of the technical conditions initially set.[37] "More than half of the teleconsultations carried

---

31 L. Cluzel-Metayer and A. François, "La protection des données personnelles à l'épreuve de la télémédecine", *RDSS*, 2020, p. 51.

32 This is defined as any "information relating to an identified or identifiable natural person (...) by reference to an identifier, such as a name, a registration number, location data, an online identifier, or to one or more factors specific to his or her physical, physiological, genetic, mental, economic, cultural or social identity" (GDPR, art. 4). Consequently, any information that allows the direct or indirect identification of the person is qualified as such.

33 GDPR, art. 4, 15.

34 European regulation 2016/679 of 27 April 2016. See on this issue, O. de Maison Rouge, "Les conséquences du RGPD pour les acteurs de la santé", *D. IP/IT* 2020, p. 298.

35 <https://www.cnil.fr/sites/default/files/atoms/files/guide-cnom-cnil.pdf>.

36 Art. 28.6.2.2.

37 Cf. the first part of this paper.

out in 2020 were done by telephone."[38] The use of the telephone or non-secure platforms (such as *Facetime*, *Whatsapp* or *Skype*) has created a significant risk of infringement of health data protection.[39]

It is therefore important not to maintain the possibility of using such means of communication once the health crisis is over.

## B. Respecting patients' rights

Teleconsultation must not become a degraded practice of medicine: it is important to ensure that the quality of care is assured and patients' rights are respected.[40]

First of all, it is often feared that telemedicine will not provide the same quality of care as a face-to-face consultation. The distancing induced by digital tools would disrupt the "one-on-one discussion" between the doctor and his patient and would not allow for a sufficiently reliable diagnosis due to the absence of physical examination of the patient's body. However, as Dr. Pierre Simon points out, "a medical diagnosis for a first-line treatment can be obtained in 70 % of cases by questioning the patient properly, [...] the physical examination contributes to the diagnosis in only 7 % of cases, and [...] complementary examinations contribute in 23 %".[41] Teleconsultation would thus offer a relevant solution in the majority of cases.

Patients' rights are also guaranteed. The decree of 19 October 2010 recalls the requirement for informed consent from the patient. The specifications for telemedicine experiments are particularly demanding: "the duty to inform is duplicated, if not de-tripled". Firstly, and classically, it concerns the "methods of carrying out the procedure,[42] secondly, the transmission of useful data to the health professional who will carry out the telemedicine procedures, and thirdly, the processing of personal data".

---

38 P. Simon, "La téléconsultation est une pratique légale et réglementaire, mais est-elle toujours une pratique éthique?", *Managersante.com*, 41, mai 2021.

39 D. Jaafar and M. Gautier, "Covid-19 et données de santé: Raison et sentiments", *Gaz. Pal.* 16 juin 2020, p. 15.

40 See on medical ethics in the face of telemedicine, D. Truchet, "Télémédecine et déontologie", *RDSS*, 2020, p. 44.

41 P. Simon, "La téléconsultation est une pratique légale et réglementaire, mais est-elle toujours une pratique éthique?", *Managersante.com*, 41, mai 2021.

42 Public health code, art. L. 1111-2.

The doctor must therefore inform the patient, both on purely medical aspects (proposed treatments: usefulness, risks, etc.) and on his or her rights regarding the processing of personal data.

The "basic rights" even seem to be strengthened by telemedicine.[43] Thus, the right to equal access to and continuity of care,[44] and the right to receive appropriate care "throughout the territory"[45] – which condition the right to health protection[46] – are consolidated by the development of telemedicine. The main advantage of telemedicine is that it counteracts territorial inequalities in access to health professionals.[47]

Finally, telemedicine could be an effective "bulwark against the commodification of the medical relationship".[48] The outsourcing of health care through online medical services has long been a source of concern for the National Council of the Order of Physicians (CNOM).[49] It is reasonable to think that "it is precisely because of the inertia of the law in deploying telemedicine [...] and then because of its excessive rigor that the risk has been created".

Telemedicine does not create a new risk for the health care relationship; on the contrary, it must be the counter-offensive.[50]

*

In conclusion, the health crisis has enabled the development of telemedicine, whose usefulness has become clear, both in treating patients with Covid-19 and in limiting the spread of the virus while ensuring continuity of care for other patients, particularly those at high risk of severe forms.

However, this unprecedented development of telemedicine uses has raised many fears. It is true that the technical flexibilities authorised

---

43 C. Lantero, "Télémédecine et droits des patients", *RDSS*, 2020, p. 61.

44 Public health code, art. L. 1110-1.

45 Public health code, art. L. 1110-5.

46 Preamble of the Constitution of 1946, al. 11.

47 See on this issue, M.-L. Moquet-Auger, "Télémédecine et égal accès aux soins", *RDSS*, 2020, p. 13.

48 C. Lantero, "Télémédecine et droits des patients", *RDSS*, 2020, p. 61.

49 CNOM, *Télémédecine et autres prestations médicales électroniques*, févr. 2016.

50 C. Lantero, "Télémédecine et droits des patients", *RDSS*, 2020, p. 61.

during health crises to facilitate the use of teleconsultation have increased the risk of losing control over patients' health data. It is therefore important not to maintain them in the future.

On the other hand, patients' rights have not been infringed upon, "observation clearly showing not only that a large part of these rights are entirely compatible – subject to adaptation, if necessary (information, consent, medical secrecy) – with [telemedicine] (choice of doctor, access to medical records, etc.), but also that those rights that constitute 'basic rights' (equal access to care, coverage by social security, right to receive appropriate care, etc.) could, on the contrary, be strengthened by the deployment of telemedicine…".[51]

---

[51] M. Borghetto, "La télémédecine", *RDSS*, 2020, p. 3.

# The level of legal consciousness of citizens as determining factor in fighting Covid-19

Yesbol Omirzhanov, Almagul Tusupova

Implementation of all the tasks of the state depends on many factors. Among these, the level of *legal* consciousness of the citizens of this state stands out. Legal consciousness is one of the forms of *social* consciousness and has its own specificity. Above all, legal consciousness reflects almost the entire set of legal phenomena of public life (legal order, legal system, legal regulation, etc.) and makes it possible to assess the state's ability to implement certain tasks. Legal consciousness can reveal a system of legal emotions, ideas, feelings, assessments, views, attitudes that express the attitude of each person both to the current legal system, to the rights, freedoms, duties of citizens, and to the positive aspects of the desired law, legal phenomena.

When making decisions, the government should take into account the level of legal consciousness of its citizens, their psychological attitude to this decision. Legal consciousness has an active influence on the regulation of many life processes occurring in the state and society, namely, it stimulates the process of consolidation of citizens and social groups, forms a general idea, and as a result pushes citizens to support or reject decisions made by the state. With a developed sense of justice and a high level of legal culture of citizens, the basis of the rule of law is formed, citizens evaluate the decisions made by the state and give their own assessment.

For 30 years Kazakhstan has been building a law-abiding state, where special attention is paid to the formation of legal consciousness and legal culture of citizens. The development of legal consciousness and legal culture in Kazakhstan makes it possible to develop interaction between the individual, society and the state and unites Kazakhstanis, develops civil society. Legal consciousness and legal culture in Kazakhstan are becoming a real instrument of social, political and economic transformations, modernisations that have a significant impact on the functioning of the political and legal system of the state and civil society as a whole.

This chapter analyzes how the level of citizens legal consciousness influenced the fight against Covid-19 in Kazakhstan.

## I. Stating the facts

The Covid-19 pandemic caused by the SARS-CoV-2 coronavirus has exposed the problems that previously existed in Kazakhstan. Cities were quarantined, medium and small businesses stopped, unemployment rose. The work of small and medium entrepreneurs in Kazakhstan is paralyzed by restrictive measures in connection with the state of emergency. Thousands of businessmen have suspended their activities and are forced to send workers on vacation without pay or to lay them off. According to political scientist A. Sarym: "The most important thing the virus did is that it nullified the previous ideologemes. Kazakhstan will no longer be able to claim that it is the leader of the region and a prosperous country but focus instead on overcoming unemployment and poverty."[1]

During the pandemic, many types of public relations have undergone changes in the country, some industries have developed, many types of services and works have switched to online mode. Schools, universities, public service centers and other institutions have switched to online mode. Like many countries, Kazakhstan began to revise its internal policy and make new decisions in the field of social support for the population. The state has adopted a number of regulations aimed at regulating public relations related to the Covid-19 Pandemic. On 16 March 2020, the President of Kazakhstan K.-J. Tokayev, following a televised address, issued a Decree introducing a state of emergency throughout the country due to the spread of coronavirus.[2]

Although a state of emergency was introduced throughout the Republic of Kazakhstan for the period from 08:00 on 16 March to 07:00

---

1 V. Volkov, "How the second wave of coronavirus changed Kazakhstan" // Deutsche Welle website. 08/13/2020 <https://www.dw.com/ru/kak-izmenila-kazahstan-vtoraja-volna-koronavirusa/a-54559893>.

2 Decree of the President of the Republic of Kazakhstan On the introduction of a state of emergency in the Republic of Kazakhstan // Website Lawyer, March 15, 2020 <https://online.zakon.kz/document/?doc_id=32648341>.

on 15 April, the state of emergency in the country lasted until mid-May 2020. During this period, the authorities twice paid income-loss benefits to Kazakhstanis left without income in the amount of the minimum wage – 42,500 tenge. According to the authorities, in the first month, over 4.5 million people received benefits, in the second – more than 2 million.[3]

On 29 June 2020, the President of Kazakhstan, during a meeting on measures to counter the spread of coronavirus infection, instructed the state commission to make proposals on the introduction of strict quarantine. Taking into account the complication of the epidemiological situation and the increase in the incidence of coronavirus infection in Kazakhstan, the state commission decided to introduce restrictive measures for 14 days from 5 July 2020.

According to the decree of the Chief state Sanitary Doctor of the Republic of Kazakhstan, the volume of passenger rail transportation has been reduced; suspended the movement of suburban passenger trains (electric trains, except for working trains), intercity bus transportation. Public transport is restricted. At the same time, Kazakhstanis were allowed to travel by private vehicles between regions. It was forbidden to hold entertainment, sports events, exhibitions, forums, conferences, as well as family, commemorative events, including at home, and other events with a large crowd of people. The activities of shopping and entertainment centers, trading houses, trading networks have been suspended, with the exception of grocery supermarkets and pharmacies located in them; entertainment establishments, cinemas; all cultural objects (theatres, concert halls, museums, exhibitions, etc.); religious objects (mosques, churches, cathedrals, synagogues, etc.) etc.[4]

On 13 July 2020, the Kazakh President said on *Twitter* that due to the epidemiological situation in the country, the quarantine regime was

3 K.J. Tokayev, the quarantine regime will be extended until the end of July, benefits will be paid // Website of Radio Azattyқ, July 13, 2020 <https: //rus.azattyq.org/a/30723846.html>.

4 The lockdown regime came into force in Kazakhstan // Website Inform.kz, July 5, 2020 <https://www.inform.kz/ru/rezhim-lokdauna-vstupil-v-silu-v-kazahstane_a3669293>.

to be extended for another two weeks.[5] As a result, Kazakhstanis lived in quarantine for another month. After the quarantine, the state retained many restrictions. In total, Kazakhstanis lived under strict restrictions from 16 March to 11 May 2020, in total for almost three months.

## II. Accounting for adaptive measures

Making sure that the Covid-19 Pandemic is not short-term, the Government of Kazakhstan developed a National Plan to protect the life and health of Kazakhstanis in a pandemic, which was approved by the Government of the Republic of Kazakhstan dated 30 July 2020 №489. According to this plan, the following main activities are highlighted: (1) Organisation of medical care, including for people from risk groups (elderly people and people with chronic diseases); (2) Strengthening the infrastructure and material and technical equipment of medical organisations; (3) Provision of medicines and personal protective equipment; (4) Provision and training of personnel; (5) Digitalisation; (6) Outreach work; (7) Anti-epidemic measures; (8) Ensuring the efficient operation of Covid-19 testing laboratories; (9) Financing and tariff policy; (10) Measures to stabilise public order during the introduction of quarantine restrictive measures.

In addition to measures for social support of the population, the state has decided to toughen the punishment for violating the quarantine regime, and new penalties have been introduced for violating quarantine. New types of administrative violations have been identified. A joint order of the Minister of Health of the Republic of Kazakhstan dated 5 July 2020 № RK MH-77/2020 and the Minister of National Economy of the Republic of Kazakhstan dated 6 July 2020 № 52 On amendments and additions to the joint order of the Minister of Health of the Republic of Kazakhstan dated 27 June 2017 № 463 and the Minister of National Economy of the Republic of Kazakhstan dated 20 July 2017 № 285 "On approval of the criteria for assessing the degree of risk and checklists in the field of sanitary and epidemiological welfare of the population." According to this order, the basic requirements (24 points in

5 Tokayev: the quarantine regime will be extended until the end of July, benefits will be paid // Website of Radio Азаттық, July 13, 2020 <https: //rus.azattyq.org/a/30723846.html>.

total) are determined for violation of which a fine is imposed for individuals 30 monthly calculation index (83,340 tenge); fine for small businesses – 230 monthly calculation index (638,940 tenge); medium business – 310 monthly calculation index (861,180 tenge); large business – 1,600 monthly calculation index (4,444,800 tenge).[6]

In early 2020, the authorities took up informing the public about the dangers of the virus. Many actions, flash mobs, television programs have been organised to explain the need to comply with the quarantine regime, personal hygiene, communication norms, etc. A huge amount of money was spent on billboards, posters, brochures on compliance with the quarantine regime. This, in turn, helped to bring to the consciousness of every citizen of Kazakhstan to observe security measures.

During the 2020 year in Kazakhstan, the situation with the spread of the virus was not clear cut. In each area, the situation was different, if some areas were in the green zone, others were in the yellow zone, and some were in the red zone. A year after the start of the Pandemic, cases of coronavirus infection have not stopped in Kazakhstan. Despite the measures taken, the state was unable to defeat the virus; in early March 2021, three people died from coronavirus infection. According to official data, as of the morning of 13 March 2021, the number of people infected with coronavirus infection was 222,671 people, 2,840 people died.[7]

## III. Presenting public reaction

Although the state turned on all its resources to inform the population, Kazakhstani society reacted in its own way to quarantine measures organised by the state. During the quarantine, there were many cases of violation of quarantine measures by citizens. Many cases were revealed when citizens organized various festive events, sacrificial treats despite the ban.

---

6 For what violations of sanitary norms can entrepreneurs be fined during quarantine? // Website kapital.kz, 07.07.2020 <https://kapital.kz/business/88368/za-kakiye-narusheniya-sannorm-mogut-oshtrafovat-predprinimateley-vo-vremya-karantina.html>.

7 Cases of coronavirus infection have been registered in all regions of Kazakhstan. What's happening? // Website of Radio Azattyq, March 12, 2021 <https://rus.azattyq.org/a/kazakhstan-coronavirus-first-cases/30485416.html>.

Many violations were reported in the media. There were also funny situations, for example, on 21 April, a resident of Nur-Sultan tried to break into the quarantine zone through a checkpoint. The 30-year-old man responded rudely, without choosing expressions, while threatening police officers when asked by police officers to show their documents and introduce themselves. "Do you know who you are touching?! I will find out where you live. I answer. I'm Pablo Escobar here! I contacted you with the wrong one, I will devour you," said the man in the video.

A man who attacked a policeman was detained in Almaty on 19 April. According to the Police Department of Almaty, the guards who went on patrol noticed 10 people having a picnic in the courtyard of the house. At the request of the police to comply with the quarantine regime, one of the instigators of the event attacked the policeman, the rest began throwing stones and shouting obscene language.

The Almaty resident publicly insulted the police officers. He published a monologue with obscene language addressed to the police on his page on social networks.

Residents of Kapshagai had a picnic in the yard. Young people wanted to celebrate their birthday in nature during quarantine.

On 21 April, residents of Karaganda staged a disco in the midst of quarantine. Dozens of people with children went out into the yard and began dancing to loud music.[8]

Interestingly, during the quarantine, some Kazakhstani celebrities ignored the recommendations of experts. Some artists held rallies, visited underground bars, visited beauty salons, that is, they grossly violated quarantine requirements.[9]

At first, some citizens did not trust the authorities, and there were those who opposed quarantine measures. With the deterioration of the

---

8 Y. Fatikhova, It is forbidden to do this: the most malicious violations of Kazakhstanis in quarantine // Website of the newspaper Liter, April 22, 2020 <https://liter.kz/43920-2>.

9 How media personalities and law enforcement officers violated the state of emergency in Kazakhstan // Baigenews.kz website, June 11, 2020 <https://baigenews.kz/news>.

social situation, Kazakhstanis began to openly express their dissatisfaction with government policy and the crisis of mistrust in the authorities worsened. Many accused the government of distorting statistics for the fact that Kazakhstan recorded deaths from coronavirus separately from pneumonia.[10]

Representatives of the Kazakh authorities in the spread of the disease mainly blamed the citizens themselves. "Quarantine measures in cities are not observed, which leads to an increase in the number of infected. The government, regional akims, cities must rectify the situation" – K. Tokayev wrote on Twitter.[11]

International experts also urged citizens to comply with quarantine measures. Head of the World Health Organisation Country Office in Kazakhstan Dr. Caroline Clarinval urged Kazakh residents to strictly observe the restrictive quarantine measures introduced in the country. Most of all, the World Health Organisation is worried about the behavior of the country's population. Experts believe that after the nationwide state of emergency ended, not all Kazakh residents continued to observe the social distancing and necessary precautions, especially in families.[12]

## IV. Highlighting the limits of public action

The current economic situation in the country did not allow the authorities to maintain strict quarantine measures. With the onset of spring, circuses, billiard clubs, and children's entertainment centers were allowed to work in the regions located in the "green" zone for seven days. It was allowed to hold sports events, Friday prayer and commemoration. In the regions that are in the "yellow" zone for seven days, covered markets (grocery, non-food), shopping and entertainment centers, trading houses, retail chains can work on Sundays. "The general relaxation of restrictive measures has led to an increase in the incidence. The largest

---

10 N. Ryskulova. "Discontent is growing." How Kazakhstan is democratizing and arresting oppositionists // BBC website, September 29, 2020 <https://www.bbc.com/russian/features-54333280>.

11 Kazakhstanis do not comply with quarantine, decisive measures are needed // Sputnik website, 05/25/2020 <https://ru.sputnik.kz/society/20200525/14065923/Tokaev-anonsiroval-novye-mery-dlya-zaschity-zdorovya-kazakhstantsev.html>.

12 Together against Covid-19: WHO to send group of experts to Kazakhstan // Website of Qazaq tv, 15.07.2020 <https://old.qazaqtv.com/en>.

number of cases falls on Almaty and Nur-Sultan, where, due to the epidemiological situation, restrictive measures have been introduced in the high-risk zone," said Chief state Sanitary Doctor Y. Kiyasov.[13]

On social networks, citizens discussed all the quarantine measures taken by the state, urging each other to comply with them. There were bloggers who were skeptical about everything and called not to trust the authorities. Especially in social networks, vaccination of the population against the virus was vigorously discussed. Kazakhstanis on social networks expressed dissatisfaction with the likelihood of making vaccination against Covid-19 mandatory. Many then motivated their fears by the fact that vaccines were experimental.[14]

The above showed that some of the Kazakhstanis are not ready to fight against the virus without the direction and control of the state. Ordinary citizens did not understand that the fight against the virus should be waged by society too, that they should help the state in the fight against the virus. Some part of the citizens complied with the requirements of quarantine only in order not to be punished.

## V. The enduring public adhesion

However, we cannot deny that during the quarantine, most of the Kazakhstanis were sympathetic to the measures taken by the authorities. Many were at home, worked online, and did not violate quarantine requirements. The peak of the coronavirus was in July 2020. At this time, a shortage of drugs, speculation, a shortage of beds in hospitals, the untimely arrival of an ambulance heated up the situation. But the difficulties brought the people of Kazakhstan together. On social networks, people began to share the coordinates of pharmacies where one could find the necessary medicines. Caring citizens massively raised funds for

---

[13] I. Ogurtsov, Reliefs led to an increase in the incidence of coronavirus in Kazakhstan // Website of the newspaper Liter, March 17, 2021 <https://liter.kz/kiyasov-pro-rost-zabolevaemosti/>.

[14] M. Mamyrkhanova, Will vaccination against coronavirus be mandatory, the Ministry of Health told // Website of the newspaper Liter, January 6, 2021 <https://liter.kz/108455-2/>.

the purchase of ventilators for hospitals. Everyone tried to show care and help.[15]

Socially active citizens tried to help those in need, raised money to help families who had lost their breadwinners. Various NGOs, religious organisations, foundations helped needy citizens. There were also those who brought cumus to hospitals. This showed that one part of Kazakhstanis have a very high level of legal consciousness.

## VI. A case for social discontent?

It cannot be noted here that not only ordinary citizens, but also civil servants violated quarantine measures. state bodies reacted quickly to such violations, and appropriate measures were taken. Each incident had a great public response, citizens discussed on social networks, criticised government agencies. For example, a video was uploaded on social networks of a wedding cortege of elite cars quietly crossing one of the city's checkpoints, thereby violating the state of emergency and traffic rules. Later it turned out that they were going to a celebration organised by the head of the criminal police of Almaty. Five people were detained on the fact of illegal passage through the checkpoint and for violating the state of emergency. All four cars, on which the violators of the law were driving, were placed in an impound lot. On 17 April, the "hero of the occasion", the head of the criminal police of Almaty Zh. Ziadin, was suspended from work. On 22 April, it was decided to fire him. The deputy commander of the patrol police regiment was also relieved of his post.[16]

Also, a video appeared on social networks, which captured how several officials were resting in a bath complex. An official investigation was carried out according to the results of which the head of the investigation department of the Department of the Agency of the Republic of Kazakhstan for Combating Corruption of the Akmola region and four

---

15 M. Holdorbekov, One year with coronavirus: what quarantine restrictions Kazakhstanis faced // Kazinform website, March 13, 2021 <https: //www.coronavirus2020.kz/ru/god-s-koronavirusom>.

16 The head of the criminal police of Almaty was suspended from work for the passage of a wedding cortege through the checkpoint // Website of the newspaper Liter, April 17, 2020 <https://liter.kz/nachalnika-kriminalnoj-policzii-alm>.

of his subordinates who violated the state of emergency were dismissed for negative reasons.[17]

In early May 2020, a video from a sauna in Zharkent, Almaty region, appeared on the social networks. Its author led a tour of the sauna and showed how he and his colleagues were resting during an emergency. The judge of the district court and the district prosecutor of the Almaty region were next to him. The prosecutor of the Panfilov district of the Almaty region, who was resting in a sauna with colleagues and a judge during the state of emergency, was dismissed from the supervisory authority. The Chief Justice of the Supreme Court also reacted to the video and suspended the powers of the Chairman of the Kerbulak District Court of the Almaty Region.[18]

On 24 May, 2020, an event in honor of the 20th anniversary of graduation was held at the Zhetigen restaurant in Zhetysay district Shymkent region. It was attended by 15 people, including an employee of the Enbekshi District Police Department.[19]

## VII. A lowering of social and legal consciousness?

These facts showed that some civil servants have a very low level of legal consciousness and, being a defender of laws, they themselves violated the same norms that they were supposed to protect. This, in turn, reduced the authority of law enforcement agencies among the population.

There were cases when scammers also wanted to take advantage of the opportunity and make money at this difficult time. For example, in the city of Taldykorgan, a 27-year-old resident of the city, pretending to

---

17 Employees of the Anti-Corruption Service who were resting in the bathhouse during quarantine were fired for negative reasons // Inform Bureau website, April 20, 2020 <https://informburo.kz/novosti/v-akmolinskoy-oblasti-pyateryh-sotrudnikov-antikorrupcionnoy-sluzhby- uvolili-za-narushenie-rezhima-chp-105413.html>.

18 The prosecutor who became the hero of the scandalous video in the sauna of the Almaty region was fired // Sputnik website, 05/20/2020 <https://ru.sputnik.kz/regions/20200520/14024312/uvolili-prokurora-skandalnoe-video-v-saune-almatinskaya- oblast.html>.

19 A. Akhmetbekov, Celebrated in a restaurant during quarantine: a Shymkent policeman was suspended from work // Azattyk ruhy website, 05/30/2020 <https://rus.azattyq-ruhy.kz/incidents/10059>.

be a civil servant, checked restaurants for violations of the quarantine regime. Then he extorted money, allegedly for providing protection from the monitoring group.[20]

*

In conclusion, after analysing the available materials, it is suggested that majority of Kazakhstanis have a level of legal consciousness above average. Since during quarantine and after the weakening of quarantine measures, most of the population adhered to the recommendations of the authorities. The above examples were published in the media, discussed and condemned by the majority on social networks. Interestingly, every video about wrongdoings by civil servants was published on social networks and after that the relevant government authorities responded to them. This shows the increased level of social activity of the average citizen of Kazakhstan, his attitude to the violations taking place around him.

In final analysis, when making decisions, the state should take into account the current socio-economic situation in the country, pay attention to how the standard of living of ordinary Kazakhstanis has changed. It is also necessary to continue work to improve the legal consciousness of citizens, pay more attention to explanatory work. An increase in the level of fines and tougher penalties for violating the quarantine regime will not give positive results, since during quarantine measures, citizens do not have the opportunity to pay fines, and many entrepreneurs are on the verge of bankruptcy without it. The imposition of fines increases the protest mood of the population and leads to various clashes between the population and law enforcement agencies.

As indicated above, there were many cases of violation of quarantine measures by the officials themselves, this is to say about the need to reform the law enforcement system and tighten the requirements for entering the civil service.

---

20 Fraudster "fined" Taldykorgan residents for violation of quarantine // Website of TV channel "Khabar 24", March 16, 2021 <https://24.kz/ru/news/social/item/461539-moshennik-shtrafoval-taldykorgantsev-za-narushenie-karantina>.

# Implementing WTO standards protecting intellectual property rights in Kazakhstan during Covid-19

Zhuldyz Sairambaeva, Madina Nurtay

The development of science and technology, global computerisation and international trade have led to the widespread use of the results of intellectual and creative activities. In this regard, the issue of protection of intellectual property rights is becoming more relevant for states. The latter need an effective mechanism for legal regulation of the Institute of intellectual property.

In order to create an effective and universal international legal mechanism for the protection of intellectual property rights among states, international legal acts were adopted. However, these international legal acts did not sufficiently regulate issues related to trade.

Under these circumstances, a mechanism for the protection of intellectual property rights was created within the framework of the World Trade Organisation (WTO). It will act on the basis of the systematisation and improvement of all achievements enshrined in the adopted international agreements in the field of intellectual property. It becomes an effective international legal mechanism for countering violations in the field of intellectual property rights. This regulatory mechanism operates on the basis of the agreement on Trade Related Intellectual Property Rights (TRIPS Agreement).[1]

Kazakhstan, as a member of the WTO, undertakes to implement the requirements of the TRIPS Agreement in the domestic national legislation in the field of intellectual property.

---

1 Agreement on Trade-Related Aspects of Intellectual Property Rights (TRIPS Agreement). Available on the website <https://www.wto.org/english/tratop_e/trips_e/ta_modules_e.htm> (date of access: 15.04.2020).

## I. Formation of the system of legal protection of intellectual property in Kazakhstan

Kazakhstan's legal system is the result of the introduction of various institutions into the current national legal system. Since 1991, some institutions and other legal systems have been adapted to the Kazakh legal system, which passed numerous laws, amendments and additions to the existing legal acts, noted Y.T. Omirzhanov.[2] Today Institute of intellectual property is one of the most important institutions.

The first stage of the formation of legislation on the legal protection of intellectual property in Kazakhstan took place during 1992–1996. The National Patent Office of the Republic of Kazakhstan and the Committee on copyright and related rights were the first specialised organisations in the field of legal protection of intellectual property. During these years, the country adopted laws regulating the field of intellectual property. Resolutions were adopted that characterise the status of bodies and organisations that make up the infrastructure of intellectual property relations, and regulations on service inventions.

The second stage of the development of intellectual property legislation was associated with the decision of the country's leadership to join the WTO. The first of the measures was to bring the legislation of Kazakhstan on intellectual property in line with the requirements of the WTO, in particular, with the TRIPS Agreement. Among the institutional changes, the committee on intellectual property rights was established as part of the Ministry of Justice of the Republic of Kazakhstan. The National Institute of intellectual property of the Committee on intellectual property rights of the Ministry of Justice of Kazakhstan was presented as an expert body for all types of intellectual property objects.[3]

Kazakhstan has gradually expanded its participation in World agreements on certain issues of intellectual property protection.

---

2 Y. T. Omirzhanov, "The influence of European and Asian Values on the features of Kazakhstan's legal system" (in English), Book chapter, 2018, pp. 67–73.

3 Analytical report: "Improvement of the legislation of the Republic of Kazakhstan: trends and prospects" (Prepared by the Institute of Legislation of the Republic of Kazakhstan based on the results of scientific research in 2011), pp. 92–93.

## II. Implementation of TRIPS Agreement in the legislation of the Republic of Kazakhstan

From 2004 to 2012, measures to bring the legislation in line with the agreement on trade-related aspects of intellectual property rights were carried out. By making appropriate changes to the current legislation, a number of amendments to the current legislation were adopted.

As a result of the work carried out, copyright was extended to works of any form. The period of protection of objects of copyright and related rights was increased (70 years were introduced instead of 50 years after the death of the author). The protection of computer programmes was equated with the protection of literary works.[4]

Taking into account the recommendations of WTO member countries, Kazakhstan will introduce protection of the rights of authors and performers on the *Internet*. Therefore, Kazakhstan adopted the laws of the Republic of Kazakhstan on 16 April 2004 on the accession of the Republic of Kazakhstan to the treaty of the World Intellectual Property Organisation on copyright[5] and on 16 April 2004 on the accession of the Republic of Kazakhstan to the treaty of the World Intellectual Property Organisation on Performers and phonograms.[6]

One of the conditions of the TRIPS agreement is to provide citizens of other WTO member countries with treatment no less than that which it offers to its own citizens.

In order to suppress the facts of import (export) of goods violating intellectual property rights, the Kazakh customs authorities were given the right to act on their own initiative in cases where goods passing

---

4 Scientific and production enterprise Brochure for the round table 3.06.2015. Available on the website <https://atameken.kz> (date of access: 19.04.2020).

5 Law of the Republic of Kazakhstan dated April 16, 2004 N 547 "On accession of the Republic of Kazakhstan to the copyright agreement of the World Intellectual Property Organization" Available on the website <http://adilet.zan.kz/kaz/docs/Z040000547_> (date of access: 19.03.2020).

6 Law of the Republic of Kazakhstan dated April 16, 2004 N 546 "On accession of the Republic of Kazakhstan to the Treaty of the World Intellectual Property Organization on performances and Phonograms" Available on the website <http://adilet.zan.kz/kaz/docs/Z040000546_> (date of access: 22.03.2020).

through the customs border are suspected of violating intellectual property rights (principle "ex officio").[7]

## III. Improving legislation in the field of intellectual property

Kazakhstan's legislation in the field of legal protection of intellectual property, despite the fact that it has been formed to a large extent and meets the main international requirements, requires amendments and additions to a number of issues.

On 3 July 2018, the Law "On Amendments and Additions to Certain Legislative Acts of the Republic of Kazakhstan on Improving Legislation in the field of Intellectual Property"[8] came into force. The law is largely aimed at regulating the following areas: improvement of legislation in the field of intellectual property; simplification of the procedure for registration of intellectual property objects; elimination of administrative barriers in the field of intellectual property protection. In accordance with this law, amendments were also made to the Civil Code of the Republic of Kazakhstan, the Patent Law of the Republic of Kazakhstan, the tax code and some other normative acts.

*The procedure for reviewing applications for patents for inventions, utility models and industrial designs has changed.*

The "two-level" procedure for the examination of applications in the expert organisation and the authorised body has passed only to the "one-level" procedure in the expert organisation. The expert organisation "Republican state Enterprise on the right of economic Management" National Institute of Intellectual Property (NIIP) after the examination still does not give an opinion, makes a decision to grant a patent.

*The procedure for issuing a patent for industrial property objects has changed.*

---

7 Scientific and production enterprise Brochure for the round table 3.06.2015. Available on the website <https://atameken.kz> (date of access: 19.04.2020).

8 Law of the Republic of Kazakhstan "On Amendments and Additions to Certain Legislative Acts of the Republic of Kazakhstan on improving Legislation in the field of Intellectual Property" dated June 20, 2018 No. 161-VI Available on the website <http://adilet.zan.kz/rus/docs/Z1800000161> (date of access: 22.04.2020).

NIIP not only register inventions, utility models and industrial designs in the relevant state registers, but also issue patents for these objects of industrial property, that is, the grant of a patent is removed from the competence of the Ministry of Justice of the Republic of Kazakhstan and transferred to the competence of NIIP. It is also stipulated by law that the relevant state registers will be posted on the internet resource of the NIIP, and information on the registration of NIIP will be published in the bulletin on a weekly basis. These changes will ensure the issuance of a patent and timely access to patent information as quickly as possible.

*The definition of the scope of legal protection provided by a patent for an industrial design has changed.*

The scope of legal protection is now determined only in conjunction with its essential features, which are presented in the images on the appearance of the product. The product is now a protected industrial design, provided that it contains all the important features presented in the images of its appearance. When determining the scope of protection of an industrial design, the set of features listed in the list of essential features of an industrial design described in words was not used.

*The norms related to the terms of granting rights to industrial property objects and license agreements and their registration have changed.*

The law on amendments under the new procedure, in accordance with the "single-level" procedure for registering contracts, the NIIP registers the contract in the relevant state Register of inventions, utility models or industrial designs. In addition, information about the agreement is published in the official bulletin. Now the entire procedure for registration of the contract will take place in the NIIP.[9]

*Most of the changes were related to the license terms.*

The definition of two types of licenses has been clarified. The license agreement states that the licensor grants the licensee the right to use an industrial property object in the following cases: with the preservation of the licensor's ability to use it, but without the right to transfer the license to other persons (the only license); does not retain the licensor's ability to use it, but may provide for the transfer of the license to other persons without the right (exclusive license).

---

[9] Civil Code of the Republic of Kazakhstan (Special part) dated July 1, 1999, as amended on June 20, 2018. Available on the website <https://online.zakon.kz/document/?doc_id=1013880> (date of access: 22.04.2020).

In addition to the registration of license agreements and sublicense agreements, it is planned to register comprehensive license agreements and register another agreement containing the terms of the license agreement. The six-month restriction on issuing a license agreement for registration has been lifted. The term of validity of the license is determined by law and, if it is not specified in the contract, it is established in the usual manner for a period equal to five years.[10]

*Reduced terms of examination of applications for intellectual property objects.*

An important change is the reduction of the terms of the examination of applications for intellectual property objects, according to which: examination of applications for a trademark has been reduced from 9 to 7 months; in the name of the place of origin of the product from 3 months to 30 working days; in the topology of integrated circuits from 35 working days to 10 working days.

The total terms of registration of industrial property objects have been significantly reduced, and the deadline for entering information and their changes in the state Register of rights to copyright-protected objects is one working day.[11] Information about applications for trademark registration will now be published in the Bulletin within five working days from the date of completion of the preliminary examination.[12]

*In connection with non-use, an amendment was made to cancel the sign.*

If it was previously possible to cancel the mark due to its non-use within three years from the date of registration or from the date preceding the date of filing the objection, at present the interested person can

---

10 Law of the Republic of Kazakhstan No. 422-I of 13 July 1999 On the protection of breeding achievement, as amended on June 20, 2018. Available on the website <https://online.zakon.kz/document/?doc_id=1014046&doc_id2=1014046#pos=5;-98&pos2=349;-96> (date of access: 25.04.2020).

11 Law of the Republic of Kazakhstan "On Amendments and Additions to Certain Legislative Acts of the Republic of Kazakhstan on improving Legislation in the field of Intellectual Property" dated June 20, 2018 No. 161-VI Available on the website <http://adilet.zan.kz/rus/docs/Z1800000161> (date of access: 22.04.2020).

12 Law of the Republic of Kazakhstan "On Trademarks, Service Marks and Appellations of Origin of Goods" of July 26, 1999 N 456 as amended on January 01, 2016, June 20, 2018 Available on the website <https://online.zakon.kz/document/?doc_id=1014203> (date of access: 22.04.2020).

challenge the registration due to non-use of the mark only within three years preceding the date of filing the objection.[13]

*The term "counterfeit goods and their packaging" are defined.*

Counterfeit goods and their packaging, in which a trademark or similar mark is placed without the consent of the copyright holder to the degree of confusion, are recognised as counterfeit. Counterfeit goods and their packaging, as well as weapons, equipment or other means and materials used for their manufacture, are subject to withdrawal from circulation and destruction at the expense of the offender on the basis of a court decision that has entered into legal force.[14]

Although the law on amendments has already been introduced, the work on improving the legislation in the field of intellectual property will not stop.

## IV. Protecting of intellectual property rights during Covid-19

Today, the national constitutions of many states and international treaties legally binding on human rights fully recognise the right of every person to the highest accessible level of health. Currently, a generally recognised part of the right to health is access to the most necessary medicines.

Article 25 of the Universal Declaration of human rights states that everyone has the right to a standard of living adequate for the health and well-being of himself and of his family, including food, clothing, housing and medical care and necessary social services, and the right to security in the event of unemployment, sickness, disability, widowhood, old age or other lack of livelihood in circumstances beyond his control.[15]

---

13 Law of the Republic of Kazakhstan "On Trademarks, Service Marks and Appellations of Origin of Goods" of July 26, 1999 N 456 as amended on January 01, 2016, June 20, 2018 Available on the website <https://online.zakon.kz/document/?doc_id=1014203> (date of access: 23.04.2020).

14 Civil Code of the Republic of Kazakhstan (Special part) dated July 1, 1999, as amended on June 20, 2018. Available on the website <https://online.zakon.kz/document/?doc_id=1013880> (date of access: 22.04.2020).

15 Universal Declaration of Human Rights. Available on the website <https://www.un.org/sites/un2.un.org/files/udhr.pdf> (date of access: 22.03.2020).

Article 12 of the International Covenant on economic, social and cultural rights is binding on almost 85 % of WTO member countries. H. Hestermeyer noted, that in the context of access to medicines, subparagraphs 12 (2) (c) and (d) are very important, as they clarify that the content of the right to health includes the prevention, treatment of epidemic and other diseases and the availability of health care and medical care in the event of illness. Access to medicines is an integral part of therapy for most and is therefore essential in the prevention, treatment and control of diseases, as well as for health care in the event of illness.[16]

The TRIPS agreement obliges all WTO members to introduce protection of intellectual property rights, including patent protection for medicines. Fortunately, some provisions of the TRIPS Agreement allow WTO member countries to take into account their health interests in the process of introducing the TRIPS Agreement into national legislation. These rules are called the "flexible TRIPS rules in the field of health care", which help countries balance the interests of public health with the personal rights granted by patents.[17]

Recovery from Covid-19 requires all countries and all people to have access to cheap medicines, vaccines, diagnostics, and other medical products. However, the monopoly powers granted to pharmaceutical companies under the WTO agreement on trade-related Aspects of Intellectual property Rights allow companies to artificially restrict global supply and generate extravagant profits and set prices that may be banned for most countries in the world.

In order to prevent, contain and treat Covid-19, early October 2020, India and South Africa made an official recommendation to the WTO to abandon some provisions of the TRIPS Agreement. The reason for this refusal is that pharmaceutical companies block other manufacturers from producing Covid-19 vaccines and medicines and prevent the expansion of production.

The WTO agreement treats the pandemic as an exception and recognises that intellectual property rights can be revoked. Experts believe

---

[16] H. Hestermeyer, *Human Rights and the WTO: The Case of Patents and Access to Medicines*, OUP 2008, p. 105, available on the website <https://www.corteidh.or.cr/tablas/25644.pdf> (date of access: 29.03.2020).

[17] OSI, Playing by the rules: Using Intellectual Property Law and Policy to Improve Access. Available on the website file: <///C:/Users/user/Downloads/playing_20080818.pdf> (Date of access: 29.03.2020).

that the flexibility in the TRIPS Agreement is not enough to meet global needs, and therefore point out that it should be abandoned.

The proposal to waive the trip rights, submitted on 2 October 2020, assumes that WTO member countries should not fulfil, apply or ensure compliance with certain obligations in the field of intellectual property rights in the TRIPS Agreement as an obstacle to the prevention, treatment and containment of Covid-19.

These provisions apply to the following sections of the TRIPS Agreement: Copyright and related Rights (Section 1); Industrial Designs (Section 4); Patents (Section 5); Protection of Undisclosed Information (Section 7).

The exclusion proposal applies to Covid-19 health products, including medicines, vaccines, diagnostics and other technologies such as masks and fans.

This is not a waiver of all the obligations under the TRIPS agreement, but only applies to the rules necessary for the prevention, containment and treatment of Covid-19.

The exact deadline for refusal is not clearly stated. However, the rejection proposal states that it is necessary to continue until a large-scale vaccination is carried out in the world and most people around the world have developed immunity. The exact duration depends on the negotiations of the members and is limited in time (according to WTO rules). This refusal applies to all WTO members and is not mandatory. Any country that does not want to give up its intellectual property obligations can continue to fulfil them.

On 17 December 2020, based on the proposal of the TRIPS Council, the WTO General Council will agree to extend the discussion of the waiver proposal until 2021.

Informal and official sessions of the TRIPS Council were to be held in mid-January and February 2021, and meetings of the general council on 1–2 March. A number of questions and additional evidence of refusal in connection with the circumstances were considered.

For example, *proponents* of the rejection proposal argue that IP (Internet Protocol) contributes to innovation. Many pharmaceutical corporations are trying to commercialise scientific achievements that are taking place in public laboratories and through government funding around the world. IP rules guarantee a large pharmaceutical company a monopoly on the market and may even require offer and pricing from governments through other measures to improve the economy. These rules prevent pharmaceutical companies from producing vaccines and medicines by other manufacturers, prevent production expansion, restrict supply, and artificially keep prices high.

*Opponents* of the waiver said the intellectual property would hinder Covid-19 medicines and technologies, such as diagnostics, medical equipment, treatments and vaccines. For example, South Africa has faced problems accessing essential chemicals for Covid-19 diagnostic testing due to proprietary testing equipment and reagents. In northern Italy, patent holders threatened manufacturers of vent valves for 3D printing with lawsuits for patent infringement. The South Korean manufacturer has developed an alternative version of the pneumonia vaccine for children (PCV13), but Pfizer's aggressive patent strategy forced the company to stop its development and postpone the release of the available version of the vaccine.[18]

To date, the issue of making a decision in connection with the extension of the term of withdrawal from certain provisions of the TRIPS Agreement remains open. However, WTO members should carefully consider the health issues related to the Covid-19 situation and come to a common solution.

*

In conclusion, the implementation of TRIPS standards requires considerable work from many developing countries to review national legislation and significant financial and human resources necessary to address intellectual property issues.

TRIPS standards are being implemented in the legal system of Kazakhstan through the direct introduction and publication of domestic acts in the field of intellectual property. During the entire period of formation and further development of the system of protection of intellectual property, many changes have been made to the legislation of Kazakhstan. In particular, the authority for registration of rights to

---

18 Available on the website <https://publicservices.international/resources/news/---?id=11516&lang=ru> (date of access: 26.04.2020).

intellectual property objects was transferred to the expert organisation (NIIP).

Currently, this system has reduced the terms of consideration and registration of applications. The possibility of pre-trial consideration of registration disputes has been expanded. In accordance with the Civil Code, disputes related to the registration of industrial property objects are subject to mandatory pre-trial consideration. According to statistics, the appeal Council under the Ministry of Justice of the Republic of Kazakhstan is an effective tool for pre-trial settlement of disputes. According to the law, the right holder had the right to demand compensation from the offender in the amount determined by the court, depending on the nature of the violation, the market value of unique goods, instead of compensation for damage when the fact of the offense was proved. This innovation will ensure transparency in the activities of the expert organisation.

In the case of Covid-19, the TRIPS agreement plays an important role. The TRIPS Agreement requires all WTO members to protect intellectual property rights, including patent protection of medicines. Although some states have temporarily abandoned some TRIPS regulations due to the obstacles caused by Covid-19, their positions on the overall intellectual property protection system have not changed.

# International and regional evolutions of intellectual property rights

Philippe Gast

For a long time during the French *Ancien Régime* of privileges and services, intellectual property was not recognised as a right. Creators, and their heirs, where rarely rewarded by the king, while printers and booksellers were. Before this injustice and under the pressure of many barristers in the parliament of Paris,[1] this privilege became systematic under the reign of Louis XVI. Then the Revolution, while abolishing privileges and services, established such rights as freedom (including property) and duties for all (equality). In particular, the Le Chapelier's Law established a right of property for the creators of works of the mind, 'the most noble property' (Diderot) since these are 'enjoyable by all' and not depriving anyone, contrary to material property which, due to space-time limitation, does not make it possible for several persons to use the same good at the same time. The right of property defined as an exclusive right of exploitation of a good is thus a work of the mind.

During the 19th century, that of the industrial era in full expansion, it seemed necessary to protect equally all creators: not only literary products or ornaments but also inventions: new products, and of course new machines to produce in large numbers these new goods[2] for an increasing number of consumers. This protection appeared through patents,[3] but

---

1 As Marion, who still in the 16th century, invoked freedom of exploitation that the author should have on his creation, idea recovered and developed by d'Hericourt during the 18th, who claimed explicitly the author's right of property (copyright) over his work (See Colombet, *La propriété Litteraire et artistique*, Précis Dalloz, 1999, p. 2).

2 But also a new combination of products yet existing, indeed a new utilization of a product or a combination yet existing (for example, a drug yet existing, but for which one finds a new use) (see A. L611-11 of IPC).

3 Necessary inventive condition, besides novelty and industrial character.

also through distinctive signs (trademarks, PDO), so that the consumers may identify the company producing them, to retain them (commercial dimension, stimulated by liberalism and free concurrence).

At the international level, it seemed necessary also to protect authors through the rule 'equal treatment for the national and the unionist', through several conventions.[4]

The 20th century was marked by an explosion of creativity, at the same time as the development of democracy and the freedom of expression which resulted from it,[5] but also technological invention in the energy field[6] that enabled mass- and accelerated possibilities of transportation (boats, container carrier, fast trains, planes etc.), but also in the medical field, that allow a longer life of retired people (baby-boomers) who have a good purchasing power (which is very new in history), in an exacerbated globalisation that tries to question the legitimate protections of creators despite the rationale of WTO and WIPO[7] but whose rules are often broken, and who, besides, protect the authors only minimally under the pressure of multinational trade, very powerful lobbies that try to limit moral rights of the authors, to assimilate intellectual creations to simple goods.

So we see that because the stakes and problematics are quite different, while originating in the same context and cause: failed globalisation due to the lack of political harmonisation whether material (open to all kinds of dumping) or digital (not yet mastered at the global level), it is

---

4 Convention signed in Berne (1886.9.9) followed by the Convention signed in Genève (1952/ Unesco), less protective but more universal, then the Convention signed in Rome (1961.10.26), protecting the interprets and the one signed in Genève (1971.10.29) protecting the creators of phonograms.

5 For the rights of authors and interprets, due to the development of new arts issued from the technical capacity of recoding images (cinema, photo) and sound: phonograph, vinyl, then CD, DVD…and then, by digitalization of the sounds and images by informatics combined to telematics: internet, last revolution in the matter.

6 The industrial era was born out of coke, its explosion in the 20th century, was made possible by oil and nuclear energy, and the 21st century probably will be able to develop through renewable energies, or at least, non-carbon energies.

7 The protection of industrial property at international level is due to: Convention signed in Paris (1883.3.20); WIPO signed in Stockholm (1967.7.14); WTO signed in Marrakech (1994.4.14) last two attached to UNO; And at the European level: European organization of patent instituted in Munich (1973) to register new patents (OEB); the European Office for intellectual property (EUIPO ex OHMI) instituted in Alicante (1994), to register trademarks, drawings and models.

necessary to differentiate between intellectual property, the literary and artistic property, questioned by internet and GAFAM (I) and industrial property questioned by trademark and patent infringement (II).

# I. Evolution of the situation of literary and artistic property in the globalised system

If, since the antiquity, the authors have been able to get a certain glory (origin of the moral rights of the authors), the patrimonial dimension appeared really only after the invention of paper and mostly of the printing press in the 15th century, that enabled the existence of a sufficient massive production to be able to create a market and then rights for the authors and interpreters. Indeed, the ability to record the performances (sound and visual) have allowed their duplication due to easily accessible and transmissible supports; thereby the market and then the authors and interprets's rights have been able to develop.

Nowadays it is the new telematics, digital support, that is internet, globalised net, that cause the upheaval of the law while this one was well established for the traditional material supports (A), but the dematerialisation, especially delocalised, making difficult the penal prosecution, induced prevention as the essential tool to fight against internet user's counterfeiting through HADOPI (B)

## *A. The literary and artistic property is well protected as concerns classical supports*

Several conventions (Berne, Geneva and various European regulations and directives[8]) protect correctly the creators of mind works in the democracies,[9] all integrated into French Intellectual Property Code (IPC) since 1992, by imposing a right of exclusive exploitation of

---

[8] Treaty of Rome: free circulation of goods (a.3a); free services (a.59); free concurrence and forbidden agreements (a.86); abuse of dominant positions (a. 86), but also and mostly through the derivative rights from it as Directive 91.250 from the council of Europe (1991.5.14); DC: 92.100 (1992.11.19): about location, loan, interpret s rights; DC: 93.83 (1993.9.27):about the radio diffusion (authors and interprets); DC/93.98 (1993.10.29) about rights of authors and interprets, etc.

[9] For a long time, the communists refused the notion of property, he understood intellectual.

representations or reproduction of their works (by cession or concession) to the benefit of the authors during their lives and during 70 years after their death for their heirs -Ib. a.L123-1- (50 years for the interprets after the recording of their interpretations -Ib. a. L211-4-), for the patrimonial dimension, but there is also the protection of their moral, extra patrimonial rights[10] as long as there are heirs, all under penalty of infringement.[11]

However, literary and artistic property is endangered by Internet. Indeed, digitalisation of sound and image by computers made operational by softwares which themselves use binary computer language (developed by Turing during WWII, and by themselves as language work are also protected by copyrights[12]), allow to transmit these works everywhere in the world, instantly. The GAFAM (Google, Apple, Facebook, Amazon, Microsoft) that make possible a huge freedom of expression, because of the decentralisation aspect of *Internet*, pose the problem of the utilisation of personal data: violation of private life, right "to be forgotten", invasive and manipulated advertising, manipulation of information…

European regulations attempted to stop this danger after long debates where the GAFAM lobbies led a fierce opposition especially against article 17 of the directive.[13] But finally the directive has been adopted, especially on the point rejected by the GAFAM to the effect that the platforms are now responsible of the information made public by internet users through their service: so if an internet user shares a protected work, the platform is co-responsible;[14] then to escape from counterfeit the platforms have to sign a contract of license with the authors and interprets or companies of authors and interprets.[15] So now the authors

---

10 The right of paternity (cite the author's name – a. L121-1 of IPC- or of the interpret's – *ibidem* L212-2- upon the support), right of integrity of the work –L121-1- or of the interpretation -L212-2- (not to modify the work without the permission of the author or the interpret); but there is a right of divulgation (L121-2) and of withdrawal (L121-4) specific to the authors, as the right of resale (L122-8)…the right of divulgation also but existing indirectly for the interprets.

11 Punished by three years of jail and 300,000€ of fine for author's (Ib. L335-2); software (L335-2-1) and Phonograms or video grams of interpret's (L335-4) copyright infringement.

12 *Ib.* A. L122-6 and L121-7: so software may itself be counterfeit.

13 EU Directive 2019/790 from European parliament and Council (2019.4.17)about the author's and interpret's rights in the Unique Market modifying the directives 96/9 EC an 2001/29 EC.

14 *Ib.*, Article 17-1.

15 *Ib.*, A.17-2.

and interprets are certain to be retributed for the use of their work. But the Directive grants some temperament[16] when access providers respond to a statement of a beneficiary;[17] also when some content uploads are expressly excluded from the Directive.

Like hyperlinks to new articles accompanied by 'isolated words or very short extracts'[18] that can be shared freely; from the journalist side, they must receive a part of all income from copyrights obtained by editors. Finally, 'start-up' platforms[19] are under less strict obligations.

The same reasoning (but it is not in the Directive) could be extrapolated in case of press offense (defamation, insults, incitement to hatred…) but with more difficulty because from one country to another, there exists more or less freedom of expression.[20]

Mastering these GAFAM require the use of a tax politic, yet existing in France,[21] but some European countries (Ireland) tent to oppose this because certain GAFAM (Google, Facebook) put their European headquarters in them, where corporation tax is law (13 %). So this financial lobbying is very powerfully managed to block European process.[22] Nevertheless, the new US Biden administration seems in favour of a minimum global tax of the multinational corporations as GAFAM.[23]

---

16 *Ib.*, A.17-4.

17 *Ib.*, A.17-9.

18 *Ib.*, A.17-7 (see L122-5 and L211-3 IPC).

19 *Ib.*, A.17-6.

20 Nevertheless, GAFAM spoke up on Twitter in relation to Trump, regarding serious disinformation for public health, but also into politics, in the Capitol invasion affair, where Trump, president defeated but denying his defeat, incited his supporters to go there… platforms from which he was excluded (see the article by S. Mastandreas in *Les Echos* -2021.1.13). But this poses clearly a private censorship problem… but freedom permit to change platform, what Trump deed, creating his own platform (see <https://www.capital.fr/entreprises-marches/donald-trump-va-lancer-son-propre-reseau-social-1397674>).

21 Law No. 2019-759 (2019.7.24) creating a tax on digital services (modifying article 299 of General Tax Code).

22 "GAFAM tax: EU is divided: the Commission wants a tax but don't want to hurt US", Article by LENA (2021.3.19) in *Le Figaro*. This tax has been abandoned in favour of a global tax, negotiation blocked by Trump. See article by Anne Michel and Alexandre Piquard (2020.6.19) in *Le Monde*.

23 See *Le Monde (2021/04/06*).

All this could be easily resolved by a general automatic transaction tax or by adapted algorithms. In order to fight against illegal downloading, in France, a special institution has been created: HADOPI … contested since its creation.

## B. The High Authority for the dissemination of works and the protection of Rights on the Internet (HADOPI)

In the beginning of the 2000s, the penal legislation on counterfeiting was applied with very (too) heavy sanctions against the downloads by internet users (who sometimes were minors) in a first period, then the legislation was sanctioning the platforms that were offering directly access to the mind works through their hard drive (but externalised, almost impossible to sanction) then later sanctioning the sites case by case which were not centralising the works but only the IP addresses, which in itself is not illegal, but it comes down to the same result: counterfeit.

Before these difficulties, in France created the HADOPI[24] which sanctions progressively the downloaders: after sending them emails, then registered letters, with legal information and sites, then threats,[25] HADOPI has the power to impose to the access providers to Internet to cut off Internet access to the recalcitrant … and even as a last resort, to open penal proceedings for counterfeit.

But there are two problems with HADOPI. First, there is an interference into private correspondences (forbidden without permission of a magistrate[26]) in order to prove that the downloading was illegal. Second, there is violation of the principle of presumption of innocence (art. 9 of DDH), because HADOPI presumes that while downloading from a case by case site, it is illegal.

Despite these criticisms, HADOPI survived, because of its efficiency: most of the caveats and other threats have been sufficient to stop the illegal downloading after emailing downloaders.

---

24 Articles L331-12 to 37 of the Code of Intellectual property.

25 *Ibid.*, article L331-25.

26 As the instruction judge (Article 100 and following from the Penal Procedure Code) or the judge of freedoms at the request of the prosecutor (*Ibid.*, art. 706-95) in the event of flagrant or preliminary investigation for offenses committed in an organized group or particularly serious.

A problem remains of whether democracy implies the protection of general, majority interest, and almost all citizens are *Internet* users (likely to download) and, then, downloading mind works from authors or interprets (the majority), which could suggest that we accept even illegal downloads. But if we don't sanction this majority, then the minority (creators) will be disadvantaged and will have to work out of their art … so creation will suffer/

So, we see that it is a difficult choice. Hence the legislations have been hesitating. Yet, the danger of counterfeit is not limited to literary and artistic works, it concerns also industrial property.

## II. The evolution of the industrial property situation at the risk of globalisation

In industrial matter, globalisation also poses a certain number of problems which are grouped together under the term of counterfeit and that oppose democracies to authoritian regimes for the dumping engendered, WTO and WIPO often bypass, for patents (A) as trademarks (B)

### *A. Manufacturing methods right: Patents*

Patents that are well protected in France, in Europe and in International law through various registration procedures imposing verification of priority (a. L661-11 and f. of the IPC), of inventiveness (a. L611-14: non obvious for a person skilled in the art who know the state of the art and all that has been published) and of industrial application (a.L611-15) that constitute the three characteristics necessary for patentability, have since the 19th century, mainly benefit to western democracies that have registered most inventions.

This situation caused, in the second part of the 20th century (after decolonisation), an important debate: in the developing countries, due to the low standard of living of the populations concerned, people could not procure new products or machines before entering into the public domain of inventions (after 20 years – a.L613-1 of the IPC). The question has been glaring in medical matters, especially with the triple therapy against the HIV: poverty and the high drug price were killing thousands of Africans in particular. We find the same situation today with the vaccines against Covid-19.

On the other hand, the laboratories argue that if they cannot get profit from their inventions, they will no longer have the means to do research and therefore find new drugs.

The solution to this situation would be that international institutions finance these therapies for the poor countries… or through allowing patent compulsory license (Ib. a.L613-12,16,18) or even expropriation patent (Ib. L613-20).

But since the 2000s, globalisation through WTO came to upset this imbalance.

And manufacturers outsource their production to developing countries with low production costs due to low wages and by importing back into the West, virtually tax-free, the products thus manufactured, i/ making considerable margins often without tax because these multinational trade companies are often based in tax havens, and ii/ enabling populations to have products (drugs in particular) at prices corresponding to their standards of living and thus access these therapies, that contributed to increasing their standard of living creating an enriched class that has a standard of living comparable to the West (about 300 million people in China and India.) … until finally encouraging Chinese manufacturers to relocate their production and invest in Africa (Ethiopia in particular) where wages are still very low.

But if the opening of markets is indeed useful for the people of developing countries, it should be on the condition that this economic liberalism is coupled with a trade union and political liberalism, which is not at all the case in some developing countries, where these freedoms are violated to benefit the corrupt.

This Asian expansion (particularly towards Europe), especially since China entered the WTO in 2001[27] has led to 16 % of Chinese production being imported into Europe resulting in a double-digit growth rate for about 20 years, making China the second largest economic power in the word (almost 3118 bds $[28] of financial reserve available for

[27] But that doesn't respect the rules of economic liberalism of WTO in the whole area still planned and subsidized like ceramics and aluminium (see the article by R. Hiault in *Le Figaro*, 2018.1.1).

[28] See article in *Le Capital*, 2018.8.7.

investments[29] and research, which explains why it is now the first country to file patents worldwide).

Maurice Allais, first French Nobel prize in economics, in 1989,[30] warned at the time against such globalisation which would in a way make millions of semi-slaves in emerging countries and millions of unemployed in the west. To verify, it, France in particular lost 36 % of its workforce and globally 40 % of its industrial production[31] in 20 years, due to social and political dumping.

While, for an economy to be balanced, a certain agricultural, industrial (mostly energetic, but also manufactured), services (public and private) is necessary, otherwise, interdependence becomes dependence, and dependence drifts towards economic downgrading, impoverishment and even neo-colonialism in reverse.

The dividend industrial loss has also as consequence that the research budgets and therefore the very sensitive patent filing in France which regularly goes down in the world ranking (8th world rank in 2018, behind India, and with 10 times less registered patents than China which became the first[32]). But the question also arises from distinctive signs.

## B. The distinctive signs

In a liberal system, where competition is the rule, if the ornaments of a product make it more attractive[33] compared with the product of

---

29 Without respecting the rules of liberalism in particular for foreign investments limited, when signing joint ventures with Chinese companies, to 49 % of the capital. Cf. point I.8 of the EU commission report (2017.12.20).

30 See his *La mondialisation: la destruction des emplois et de la croissance [Globalisation: destruction of jobs and of growth]*, Paris, Clément Juglar, 1990, where he presents the idea that: "Globalization can only bring instability, unemployment, injustice everywhere" and "globalization is neither inevitable, necessary nor desirable", considering that "unemployment is due to the relocation itself due to the various excessive wages" thus "protectionism reason between countries with very different incomes is not only justify but absolutely necessary" (<http://www.liberation.fr/futurs/2010/10/11/deces-de-maurice-allais-prix-nobel-liberal-et-protectionniste_685598> [archive]).

31 See the article by A.S. Bellaiche in *Usine nouvelle*, 2019.6.13.

32 See <https://atlasocio.com/classements/economie/innovation/classement-etats-par-nombre-de-depots-de-brevets-monde.php> (but the size of the population obviously plays a role in the number of registered patents).

33 Hence the protection of designs under copyright but also industrial as seen above.

other origins having the same function, the identification of its origin is important since it enables customers to find the quality they are looking for as a product or a service, as much for the company through the trademark (a) as by its traditional or geographic origin (b).

(a) The trademark – Trademarks are distinctive signs (forms, colours, sounds, registered by the National Institute of Industrial Property and protected for such product or service – a.L711.1 and following of IPC) that make it possible to identify the company that is at the origin of a product or service. In collectivist countries, the trademark had the function of product traceability. Some consider from this point of view that the liberal marks are useless and futile, that they simply aim to flatter the ego of the 'fashion victims' who will choose such a chic trademark 'because I'm worth it': thus, the trademark Loreal will not have the same social impact – brand image – as Tati.

Nevertheless, liberal globalisation will answer that it is up to everyone to choose this or that trademark and that it is not for the state to judge the private live or motivation of its citizens.

These trademarks impose also a quality and then a price that the citizens of poor countries cannot afford. Yet, the same remark as for the patents maybe applies: since globalisation, the same luxury trademarks have often relocated their production in these countries … making products affordable for locals. In addition, the locals acquiring the know-how of these brands have become able to produce products of almost as good quality …but with at a much lower cost… so that the counterfeit production is growing in these countries, especially in Asia.[34]

In addition, counterfeiting in these countries is difficult to prosecute in local courts because corruption is often widespread, or justice is under the orders of a Party that imposes nationalist judgments.

(b) The designation of origin (PDO's, indications of origin) – This concerns distinctive signs such as brands but which do not indicate the origin of a company but the geographical origin of a product which must meet certain traditional criteria of manufacture and local production. Originally, PDO where born in France to designate cheeses and wines so that the consumer is not

[34] See the article of E. Moreira in les Echos (2019.1.18).

> deceived (for example a Camembert would not be made in Japan or a Champagne in Chili.). Thus, wine and cheese use a PDO to indicate their real origin that must correspond to a production of the indicated zone: the labels "Camembert" or "Champagne" must be produced in the geographically corresponding zone, and by the traditional methods described in a specification text.

Then PDO has become an EU acronym, but in reduced numbers.[35] There exist also other signs as PGI that indicate a local know how … but the product that can be used can come from anywhere (*sic*).[36] Other signs such as the Red Label, biologic acronyms (AB, etc) include exceptions, so that the consumer is better protected by some private labels as Demeter.

*

In conclusion, balanced and fair globalisation needs global rules and, apart from the counterfeit seizure when these products arrive in the West, the fiscal weapon seems to be the only effective one but a kilometric carbon tax would curb these wild imports (for example: 0,001€ by km by kg of product). While awaiting a more radical solution, which would consist in excluding authoritarian regimes from commercial liberal market, the access to liberal market should be conditioned to liberal unions and liberal politics systems.

That requires that the Westerner hiding behind the multinationals via the tax haven cannot make lobbying … not to mention the necessary reciprocity of treaties, meaning that an Asian can buy in France[37] while it is not possible for a French to buy a building in Asia except after marrying a local.

---

35 [36] In France there exist 50 dairy, 50 agrifood (oil, etc.), 363 wines PDO (Rural code: articles R.641-1 to R.641-10)

36 <https://www.economie.gouv.fr/particuliers/aop-aoc-igp-stg-labels-certification-alimentation>.

37 The same applies to buying the major part of a company. See article by H. Prolongeau in *Le Monde*, 2019.1.26.

# Protecting theatre directors and artistic directors of public *troupe* on filming of the performing arts

Sung-Kee Hong

**The copyright industry of Korea** – Korea had experienced Japan's colonial rule from 1910 to 1945 (when Japan surrendered). Unfortunately, after independence, Korea failed to form a unified nation and two separate regimes were established as North and South Korea. Following the North Korean invasion in 1950, the peninsula experienced serious war for three years. Around that time, the national per capita income of South Korea was less than 100 USD, making her one of the poorest countries in the world. In about 50 years, South Korea's per capita income has reached 30,000 USD and the amount of trade has ranked in top 10 countries in the world.

The achievements in intellectual property rights, especially in the copyright sector, are also remarkable. According to the U.S Chamber International IP Index of 2018, Korea ranked 11th for overall intellectual property rights and 6th for copyright. Until about 15 years ago, Korea was listed on the watch list or priority watch list published by the USTR every year. However, Korea is no longer listed, but also became a model country in the field of intellectual property rights. The USTR is evaluating in the sense that "Korea is a country that produces intellectual property rights, so this is a natural result."

As the level of copyright protection increases, the cultural industry is becoming stronger. Around 2012, *Gangnam Style* became very popular all over the world, and now *Dynamite* by BTS is surpassing the previous high. Korean TV dramas have become quite popular in the Middle East, Asia, and South America, and now good news continues in the film industry. The film *Parasite*, released in 2019, won awards at various film festivals, including the American Academy Film Festival, the British Academy Film Festival, and the Golden Globe. This year, the low-budget film *Minari* is delivering another good news. The Webtoon market is also growing and has large sales, but its value as an original work for movies and computer games is also recognised. The production of TV dramas and movies based on webtoons is increasing.

Along with the popularity of Korean contents, its indirect effects on exports are also noticeable. According to the *2020 Intellectual Property Right Trade Balance* released by the Bank of Korea, Korea's copyright exports more than doubled from 4.6 billion USD in 2016 to about 11 billion USD in 2020. Also, the trade balance of the Culture and Art Copyright sector has turned into a surplus for the first time in 2020. Korea's copyright industry revenues are steadily increasing, and the core copyright industry revenues in 2018 recorded 156 billion USD. The overall copyright industry accounted for 8.91 % of Korea's nominal GDP in 2018.

This confirms the importance of the copyright industry in the national economy.

# I. The pandemic era – challenges and response

## A. Challenge and response

The emergence of new media may lead to changes in the copyright system and in the cultural industry. The development of printing following the Reformation made it possible to publish music scores with the publication of the Bible. The printing of Gutenberg, developed around 1450, was applied to the printing of the choir music by about 1470, and in 1501, the first commercial music publication was made by the Venetian printer Petrucci. Music publishing provided an opportunity for the musicians who depended on the nobilities and the churches to become economically independent, and in the late 18th century, musicians who enjoyed the benefits of music publishing along with music publishers appeared.

The technological unemployment brought by the invention of recording and broadcasting technology caused the development of the performer's rights. The phonograph, invented by Thomas A. Edison in late 1877, took its place in the market using the fear of the Spanish flu that occurred in 1918. It was thanks to the advertising phrase, 'You can enjoy opera performances without the risk of being infected'.[1] When TV

1 Chosunilbo, 2020. 9. 16.

and VTR appeared, Hollywood filed a copyright infringement lawsuit against SONY, alleging that the film industry was going to be starving by the new devices.[2] In fact, with the advent of the devices, Hollywood has become much wealthier.

Free online performances appeared as the concert hall closed due to the Corona incident. The live footage of the 25th anniversary of the *Phantom of the Opera*, which was released free of charge through the *YouTube* channel 'The Show Must Go On', was watched by 10 million viewers around the world in only 48 hours.

The widespread pandemic in 2020 is ravaging the venues, however, which can accelerate the filming of the performing arts and could be a blessing for some genres with thin fan base.

## B. Filming of the performing arts

The leading case of the filming of the performing arts is the 'Metropolitan Opera Live in HD' (HD Live) of the Metropolitan Opera House of New York initiated in 2006. The management of the Metropolitan Opera House, who felt a crisis due to the reality of 'ageing of opera audiences', organised a separate budget to promote filming of the performance for 'live cinema' events. Since the mid-2010s, the number of audiences who do not visit the theatre has increased because they enjoy HD in Live in movie theatres comfortably, and the ticket sales has reduced. So, management is said to be grappling with ways to attract corporate sponsorship for free streaming services.[3] 'HD in Live' of the Metropolitan Opera House inspired the British National Theatre, which started the visualisation project in 2009 ('NT Live'). 'NT Live' expanded its genre to 'play' and 'musical'.

The 'Digital Concert Hall' of the Berlin Philharmonic Orchestra, which started in 2008, is a streaming business that is compatible with diverse devices including personal computers, home audio and video devices thanks to SONY's active participation. The Berlin Philharmonic's

---

2 SONY Corp of America v. Universal City Studios Inc., 464 U.S. 417 (1984), a so-called Betamax case, the Supreme Court held that if you record a TV program for later viewing, it is not a copyright infringement.

3 National Theatre of Korea, 『Materials for Performance Visualization』, 2020, p. 37.

venue began in 1949 with the fundraising of Berliners in the ruins of the Second World War, H. von Karajan actively supported the unique design suitable for filming from the beginning. The Berlin Philharmonic is not only relaying live performance through smartphone apps, but also serving archive images and rare documentary videos on demand.

In early 2013, the Seoul Arts Center launched a filming performance project ('SAC on Screen') with ideas from 'HD in Live' of the New York Metropolitan Opera. The Seoul Arts Center's 'SAC on Screen' is a success story that started with the goal of providing the chances to the residents of the isolated regions not easily accessible to the performance venue. Among the commercial producers, EMK Musical Company entered the performance streaming business early. Before the Corona incident, a live video of *Smiley Man* was screened at cinema theatres in 2019, and in June 2020, a live video of *Excalibur* was screened for two weeks through 'Broadway on Demand'. In August 2020, EMK streamed for the Japanese audiences only residing in Japan on the 10th anniversary of *Mozart*.

## II. Some copyright issues in filming of performing arts

Lockdown measures enforced due to the pandemic brought about a surge in on line streaming, which may of much benefit to performing arts. For the stage actors who lost their jobs due to the lockdown, diverse schemes are being devised to support them. For the stage directors and choreographers for the public troupe, we need to look at their status.

### *A. Theatre director: An author or a performer?*

#### *1. Theatre director v. film director*

According to the Korean Copyright Act, the term "performer" is defined as 'a person who gives a stage performance by expressing works through acting, dancing, musical playing, singing, narrating, reciting or other artistic means or by expressing things other than works in a similar way, *including a person who conducts, directs or supervises a stage performance* (Article 2)'. In this paragraph, 'a person who directs' means 'a theatre director', 'a person who supervise' means 'a film director'. Although a film director is defined as a performer in article 2, he/she is interpreted as the author of the audiovisual work and there is no objection to it.

It is because 'Special Rules concerning Cinematographic Works' stipulates that '*a person* who agreed to cooperate in the production of a cinematographic work with a producer obtains a copyright to the said cinematographic work (art. 100 (1))'. "A person" in the said article cannot be other person than 'a film director'.[4]

## 2. *Traditional debate*

Theatre directors have long claimed that they are authors like directors of audiovisual works. They claim that the relationship between a dramatic work and its theatrical production is the same as that between a scenario and the audiovisual work produced on the basis of it.

Such an allegation, however, was hardly considered as appropriate so far. The logic is as follows.

Firstly, an audiovisual work is not a presentation of a scenario but something which is of a completely new quality in relation to it. The creators of an audiovisual work transform the scenario into another artistic language, into the language of images where dialogues and everything else that the scenario contain are only mere contributions to an artistic unity. An audiovisual work still does not exist in the stage of a scenario, it comes into existence by the activity of the director. On the other hand, dramatic works do exist before they are staged. Dramatic works contain not only dialogues but a series of more or less detailed instructions concerning the scenery, the characteristics, costumes and movements of the actors. If follows from the nature of dramatic works that their contents are determined by their creators in an even more detailed manner.[5]

Secondly, the authors of dramatic works create with the intention that those works be staged and be performed in the form which the authors have given them. If their intention is realised, the contribution of a director could hardly be qualified as the creation of a new work. What

---

4 Article 100 (Rights to Cinematographic Works) (1) Where a producer of a cinematographic work and a person who agreed to cooperate in the production of a cinematographic work have obtained a copyright to the said cinematographic work, the rights necessary for the exploitation of such cinematographic work shall be presumed to have been transferred to the producer of the cinematographic work unless otherwise expressly stipulated.

5 "Dramatic, choreographic and Musical Works. Preparatory Document for and Report of the WIPO/Unesco Committee of Governmental Experts (Paris, May 11 to 15, 1987)", Copyright, 23rd year No. 6 June 1987, § 31.

he produces is a performance of the work. Small changes, deletions, certain movements which are not mentioned or are differently described in the written version of the work, the actualisation of the scenery or the costumes may be parts of the contribution of the director, but it can hardly be said that they are creative elements and thus may qualify together as adaptation.[6]

### 3. *Recent debate*

At the 35th meeting of the WIPO's Standing Committee on Copyright and Related Rights (SCCR) in December 2017, the Russian delegation submitted a proposal to strengthen the status of the theatre director.[7] A detailed explanation of the proposal was given at the 36th meeting in May 2018. The Russian delegation alleged,

> In the modern theatre, it is the director's efforts that result in the consolidation of all elements of the stage performance including the following: the play, the acting, the decorations, the sound and musical accompaniment. The activities of a theatrical production director are similar to those of a film director, but the latter, unlike the performer, possesses copyright for the produced film.[8]

In order to strengthen the protection of rights of theatre directors, Russia enacted a new law as of 1 January 2018, by which the director is attributed the right to inviolability of the protected theatrical production[9] both during its public execution and during its reproduction in the recorded form.

As the theatre director was not covered by the Rome Convention[10] of 1961 or the WPPT[11] in 1996, it was a request to the effect that a separate WIPO treaty for the theatre director is needed. As a result, WIPO

---

6 *Ibid.*, § 32.

7 SCCR/35/8, "Proposal on the Part of the Russian Federation with rigid to Strengthening the Protection of Theatre Director's Rights at the International Level".

8 *Ibid.*, p. 2.

9 I.e. the right to protect its production from any distortion, changes leading to corruption of its meaning or to violation of the integrity of perception of the production.

10 Rome Convention for the Protection of Performers, Producers of Phonograms and Broadcasting Organizations.

11 WIPO Performances and Phonograms Treatment.

accepted the proposal of the Russian delegation at the 37th SCCR meeting and asked the secretariat to review it. The secretariat commissioned experts and the research is being conducted currently.[12]

Modern directors create new production using playbook as raw material. The dialogues of the original playbook are largely omitted, some roles are completely removed, the order of the acts is changed, and the events set by the writer are replaced with completely different events. This interpretation of the playbook is something that the writer did not intend at all.[13] If there appears such a change, the theatre director would be regarded as the original author of the new creation. A theatrical production in such a case is different from the original work not because theatrical productions represent a new quality of such works but simply because it is not the original work which has been put on stage but a modified version to it, A modified version of a work is an adaptation. Consequently, a director may enjoy copyright protection not because he is a director, but because he is an adaptor.[14]

As the pandemic era demands filming and streaming service of the stage performance, it became more difficult to distinguish the functions between film directors and theatre directors. The stage actors are acting not in front of the audience but the in front of the cameras, the theatre director directs the acting focusing only on the camera.

### 4. *How to cope with co-production of theatre director and film director?*

Until now, the filming of the performance may have done by the direction of the theatre director. Online streaming market is growing drastically. In order to improve the perfection of the filming, the film director and the theatre director will have to cooperate from the pre-production and think together about the actor's movement, the location and function of the camera, lighting and so on. As the role of film director increases, it is expected that such produced works should be evaluated as a joint work of theatre director and film director. However, if theatre

---

[12] SCCR/37/3. p. 2.

[13] "Dramatic, choreographic and Musical Works. Preparatory Document for and Report of the WIPO/Unesco Committee of Governmental Experts (Paris, May 11 to 15, 1987)", Copyright, 23rd year- No. 6 June 1987, § 33.

[14] *Ibid.*, § 34.

director is literally a performer, he/she cannot share the copyright to the audio-visual work. The theatre director may not bear this consequence.

## B. Choreography v. "Work Made for Hire"

### 1. Filming and choreographer

In Korea, the filming of the performance has been made mainly by public organisations that can easily mobilise the budget. It is common to interpret the works of the artistic director of the public performing organisation as "works made for hire" thus the copyright to the choreography belongs to the organisation. If the performing arts are filmed, the use of the performance will be greatly expanded. This means that the status of the primitive creator of the work be weakened. The term of artistic director of public performance organisations is not long, and this period is when his creativity is most vigorous. However, if the work of that period is treated as work made for hire, audio-visualised and distributed in large quantities, it means that the footing on which he can work after his retirement can almost disappear. This is contrary to the purpose of the copyright law – 'improving and developing the culture'.

'Work made for hire' clause seems to be a regulation for dealing with the industrially produced work. This is a concept that does not match the 'Schöpferprinzip' of copyright law, so it should be interpreted as strictly as possible.

There are several questions regarding the requirements of 'work made for hire' in relation to the creations of artistic directors.

First, whether there is a scheme by the employer, an art director generally plans and executes the entire artistic activities of the organisation. The artistic director characterises the attributes of the artistic activities of the organisation during his/her tenure and the reputation of the organisation itself depends entirely on his/her capacity.

Second, it is doubtful whether there is a supervision of the organisation over the artistic director. The organisation usually gives the artistic director full authority over the artistic elements of the troupe including the evaluation of the members. Third, considering the term of artistic director and not enough remuneration for the responsibilities, copyright attribution to the organisation seems to be unfair. When an artist has the highest artistic prowess, he/she temporarily takes charge of the job of artistic director. If a choreography created during his/her tenure becomes a work made for hire, it would be contrary to the purpose of the copyright system – improving and developing culture.

## 2. Free use of public works?

Recently there was a dispute over copyright ownership of the choreography created by the artistic director of a civic dance troupe. The Court, on the premise that the choreography is 'work made for hire', judged that the choreography is in the public domain according to 'free use of public works' (art. 24-2), and therefore the artistic director who used the choreography personally without the consent of the city government is not to blame.

The Court may have developed this logic to remove the liability from the choreographer, but it seems inappropriate.

The provisions similar to the "free use of public works" stipulated in Article 24-2 of the Korean Copyright Act are found in the 1976 US Copyright Act. The U.S. Copyright Act declares that U.S. government works are not subject to copyright protection (Article 105(a)).[15] In 2019, U.S. revised the Copyright Act by adding (b), (c) and (d) to Article 105. Accordingly, a civilian member of the faculty of a 'covered institution' owns the copyright to the 'covered work'. However, the Secretary of Defense may direct the covered author of a covered work to provide the Federal Government with an irrevocable, royalty-free, world-wide, non-exclusive license.

'Covered work' means literary work produced by a covered author in the course of employment at a covered institution for publication by a scholarly press of journal (§ 105 (d) (3)).

The EU published the Directive on the re-use of the public sector information in 2003 and revised it in 2013.[16] By this revision, the 2003 Directive shall not apply to *documents* held by cultural establishments,

---

15 § 105 Subject matter of copyright: United States Government Works: (a) In General. – Copyright protection under this title is not available for any work of the United States Government, but the United States Government is not precluded from receiving and holding copyrights transferred to it by assignment, bequest, or otherwise. § 101. A "work of the United States Government" is a work prepared by an officer or employee of the United States Government as part of that person's official duties.

16 Directive 2003/98/EC of the European Parliament and of the Council of 17 November 2003 on the re-use of public sector information; Directive 2013/37/EU of the European Parliament and of the Council of 26 June 2012 amending Directive 2003/98/EC on the re-use of public sector information.

such as museums, libraries, archives, orchestras, operas, ballets and theatres (art. 1. 1. (f)).[17] "Documents" in this Directive covers "any representation of acts, facts or information – and any compilation of such acts, facts or information – whatever its medium (written on paper, or stored in electronic form or as a sound, visual or audiovisual recording), held by public sector bodies."[18] 2013s Directive made its exception simpler by subtracting 'libraries, museums and archives.' That means 'documents held by cultural establishments such as *orchestras, operas, ballets and theatres*' only are out of the application of the re-use.

The handling of public works in the copyright law of the United States, Germany and Japan is basically aimed at literary works. The document in the EU Directive also means the fixed medium of the work. The attitude of EU re-use Directives toward "orchestras, operas, ballets and theatres" is significant: it is demanding special protection and handling of the performing arts.

*

In conclusion, the Berne Convention differentiates between 'books, pamphlets and other writings' and 'dramatic and dramatico-musical works' (art. 2(1)), Universal Copyright Convention differentiates between 'writings' and 'dramatic works'(art. 2). In this situation, dramatic works seems to mean 'playbook'. However, in the Korean Copyright Act, 'playbook' is included in the category of 'literary works', and there is other category of 'dramatic work'.

Then 'dramatic work' shall include theatre director's creativity, and the author of the dramatic work shall be theatre director. When the filming of the performing arts under pandemic era demands of the

---

17 Article 1. Subject matter and scope: 1. This Directive establishes a minimum set of rules governing the re-use and the practical means of facilitating re-use of existing documents held by public sector bodies of the Member states. 2. This Directive shall not apply to: … (f) documents held by cultural establishments, such as museums, libraries, archives, orchestras, operas, ballets and theatres.

18 Whereas: … (11) This Directive lays down a generic definition of the term "documents", in line with developments in the information society. It covers any representation of acts, facts or information – and any compilation of such acts, facts or information – whatever its medium (written on paper, or stored in electronic form or as a sound, visual or audiovisual recording), held buy public sector bodies. …

film-director-like function from the theatre director, we can hardly deny authorship to the theatre director.

Regarding artistic director of the public troupe, the Court decision misinterprets the purpose of 'free use of public works'. The case should have been resolved with an active interpretation that the choreography of the artistic director does not fall into the realm of a work made for hire.

# Covid-induced losses in a national economy of East Asia: The case of the tourism sector in the Ulaanbaatar area in 2020

Odgerel Purevdorj, Erbakhit Badelgaji

In just over four months, after the Covid-19 coronavirus spread from December 2019, it had reached throughout the world, causing massive destruction to public health as well as to the world economic situation. Mongolia underwent this contamination for 10 months through an prompt, advanced and effective process after the initial shock all the way to November 2020.

In order to curtail the contagion, the Mongolian government declared a strict public and partial quarantine between February and July 2020, maintained the electoral process, then progressively reopened non-manufacturing organisations. Therefore, on 21 September 2020, the quarantine was totally lifted and every organisation such as schools and other training structures functioned normally.

After that, the government went on with the prevention of Covid-19 by keeping borders closed. Unfortunately, contamination continued by November, despite these publicly well-built schemes until the end of December 2020 and it was necessary to maintain closed all service organisations. Inhibition and quarantine continued almost one whole year, causing massive disaster to the state economic situation.

The tourism sector is the one that faced most factual damage, more than other sectors of the Mongolian economic. It basically stagnated for first time in its history, losing its financial circulation and affecting 88,000 people negatively in their economic activity.

Government services and other field organisations are conducting various kinds of researches and analysing the impact measure and its level. For example, research conducted by the Mongolian National Chamber of Commerce and Industry determined that 90 % of tourism business operators were affected by the coronavirus.[1] The Mongolian Tourism Association announced that 30–70 % of total tourist trips were cancelled, even though this was not confirmed by the research. Tourists number dropped by 21 % in February and 96.8 % in March, compared with the previous year's statistics and the net income of tourism sector decreased by 28 % or 31 billion MNT in February and 216 billion MNT in March based on all the total number of passengers who crossed the border.

As numbers and facts are insufficient to fully address the total loss of Mongolian tourism field in its research methodology, this chapter furthers the study for the Ulaanbaatar city tourism sector. Economic losses of organisations rest on the total of external sources of tourism such as hosting services, tour operators and entertainment services, estimated in total cash.

Aiming thus to estimate economic losses of the tourism field in Ulaanbaatar city during coronavirus-induced restrictions, this chapter conducts analysis report by collecting data and researches from field organisations, collects useful first cases of data, analyses data by choosing research methods on each indication, prepares recommendations by combining all total loss of economy.

Research methods include dynamic analysis method, percentage estimation approaches based on first case of data, regression analysis calculations, input-output measures syntheses. The broad framework of the analysis comprises hotels, motels, resorts and tourist camps in Ulaanbaatar; souvenir shops and entertainment places which directs profit from tourists; car rentals, independents who provide transportation services for tourists; public catering establishments and places.

## I. Estimation result of the research

### *A. Direct loss levels*

In 2019, Mongolia welcomed 570,262 tourists[2] and profited from 1,685,674 MNT or about 600 million USD.[3] One million USD gained

---

1 Mongolian National Chamber of Commerce and Industry. (2020). *Research report of employment impact of Covid-19.*

2 General Authority for Border Protection of Mongolia. (2020). *Number of foreign tourists passed through the Mongolian border.*

3 Ministry of Environment and Tourism (2020). *Annual data of tourists to Mongolia.*

from the tourism sector went into economic circulation, creating 1.42 million USD in trade and affecting economics directly and indirectly by producing 862 million USD or 2.393.657 MNT in sales.

Still in 2019, the Mongolian GDP reached 37,280,841 MNT and 6.48 % of total GDP was brought about by tourism fields income. By advanced estimation for 2020, income from the tourism sector was to reach 668 million USD, making up 5.02 % of total GDP[1].

Finally, for 2019 still, 78.7 % of total tourists (or 452,957 tourists) spent two to three days in Ulaanbaatar after entering at Buyan-Ukhaa airport (49.3 %) or the Altanbulag border (9.3 %), the Zamiin-Uud train station (5.3 %), the Zamiin-Uud transportation road (10.6 %) and Sukhbaatar border point (4.0 %).

In 2020, 36,483 tourists visited to Mongolia throughout the whole year. Precisely, this number is referring to January, February and first half of March of 2020. Tourist numbers decreased by 93.1 % in 2020.

Based on this data, following estimation derived, the direct profit and tourists number passed through Ulaanbaatar city by the percentage estimation method are given.

**Tab. 1. Number of tourists passed through Ulaanbaatar and field income (by USD)**

| Year | By the end of the year | | | Income of year end | | |
|---|---|---|---|---|---|---|
| | Number of passed tourists | Percentage change | Percent of total tourists to Mongolia | Total income | Percentage change | Percent of total income of tourism field |
| 2018 | 406,455 | | | 112,148,121 | | 20.5 % |
| 2019 | 452,957 | 11.4 % | 78.7 % | 155,714,772 | 21.5 % | 25.6 % |
| 2020 | 24,946 | -93.1 % | 68.4 % | 7,071,426 | -95.4 % | ? |

Income from tourists injected into the city economic circulation decreased by 95.4 % as number of passing tourists through Ulaanbaatar city dropped by 93.1 %. Ulaanbaatar city profited from tourists by 20 billion 224 million MNT throughout the whole year and reached “direct loss” of 469 billion 654 million MNT as it had planned to gain profit from tourists in 2020 by 489 billion and 878 million MNT.

## B. Indirect loss level

In 2018, the GDP of Ulaanbaatar city reached 21,404,434 MNT, making up to 64.7 % of the total state GDP. In 2020, the city budget was confirmed at 915 trillion 347 billion 364 MNT and its total income was set at 889 trillion 896 billion 780 MNT. Analysis and research were conducted on each field and sector due to the far greater difference to the fact by estimating direct income loss and its influence to economy of Ulaanbaatar city.

**Motels** – There are 312 motels in function with 2,648 rooms and 3,636 beds in the capital city territory.[4] Mostly Mongolian residents visit motels in the city territory and annual room service is about 33.3 %.[5] As there is no research on monthly room service, this service was measured as 33.3 %. The average price of one room service in motels is 35,000–45,000 MNT.

Motels were made to halt their service from 26 February 2020 by the city mayor's order and even though they started to function progressively from 16 April 2020 by the order number A/521, this was a profitable period. Generally, motels' profitable period is from November to March but naturally Spring and Summer customers numbers decreased.

Also, due to the low capacity of people's income, the numbers of customers to motels were reduced considerably. And the following loss was estimated as considering motels that were unprofitable and closed almost 310 days of the year.

---

4 Ulaanbaatar Tourism Department, *Statistical data of hotels*, 2020.

5 E. Badelgaji, *Geographic research of service organizations in capital city*, Master's thesis, 2016.

**Tab. 2. Financial loss of motels**

| District | Total motels | Total rooms | Total beds | Daily loss (mill. tug) | Annual loss (mill. MNT) |
|---|---|---|---|---|---|
| Songinokhairkhan | 70 | 598 | 747 | 7.0–9.0 | 2,160–2,777 |
| Khan-Uul | 11 | 110 | 157 | 1.3–1.64 | 397–510 |
| Sukhbaatar | 35 | 209 | 308 | 2.4–3.1 | 755–970 |
| Bayangol | 79 | 673 | 905 | 7.8–10.8 | 2,431–3,126 |
| Bayanzurkh | 95 | 890 | 1,243 | 10.3–13.3 | 3,215–4,134 |
| Nalaikh | 2 | 20 | 31 | 0.23–0.30 | 72–92 |
| Chingeltei | 20 | 148 | 245 | 1.7–2.2 | 534–687 |
| Total | 312 | 2,648 | 3,636 | 30.8–39.6 | 9,567–12,300 |

Resource: Researcher's estimation

Daily economic loss of the motels in Ulaanbaatar is estimated as 30.8–39.6 million MNT and in 2020, due to the quarantine, annually its economic loss is 9 billion 576 million–2 billion 300 million MNT as they have closed for 310 days.

**Hotels** – Out of 290 hotels with 8,175 rooms and 11,075 beds in the city territory, 75 hotels use a classification or star-level.[6] Hotels charge more expensive rates but offer better service quality and more rooms. Generally, most of the customers of no-grade hotels are domestic travellers. According to 2014 statistics, 19.4 % of total customers of no-grade hotels were foreign travellers and remaining customers were domestic travellers.[7] However, most of the customers with star-grade hotels are foreign travellers and in unofficial data, it is mentioned that 90 % of total customers of graded hotels were foreign tourists. The average room price is 80–100 thousand MNT of non-graded hotels and least price of graded hotels' is 203 thousand MNT, with a highest price is 527 thousand MNT and an average price of graded hotels is 369 thousand MNT. Customers of non-graded hotels are 26.5 % and 38 % in graded hotels.

Although the coronavirus lockdown did not stop hotels from functioning, the measures taken against the virus, such as closed borders and recommendation to stay home, affected directly all hotel services. Research and survey show that, during this quarantine period, hotels'

6 Ulaanbaatar Tourism Department, *Statistical data of hotels.*

7 E. Badelgaji, *Geographic research of service organizations in capital city*, Master's thesis, 2016.

customers drooped to 1 %–10 % only.[8] Most of the hotels were closed and even if some hotels were functioning as isolation buildings, this was not for them a profitable solution. Following this, financial hardship set in considering that all hotels were with no income for between 3 days and 100 days or in low profitable time between September to November 2020: no foreign tourists during the summer and domestic travellers tended to go to the countryside. Estimates are that customers were 10 % for non-graded hotels and 5 % for graded hotels.

**Tab. 3. Loss estimation of hotels**

| District | Total hotels | Total rooms | Total beds | Daily loss (mill. MNT) | Annual loss (mill. MNT) |
|---|---|---|---|---|---|
| Non-graded hotels | 215 | 5,422 | 6,970 | 115–144 | 34,483–43,104 |
| Graded hotels | 75 | 2,753 | 4,105 | 386 | 115,807 |

Resource: Researcher's estimation

In Ulaanbaatar city, a total 215 non-graded hotels had daily losses of 115–144 million MNT and annual losses of 34 trillion 483 million to 43 trillion 104 million MNT. Besides, graded hotels had daily losses of 386 million MNT and 150 trillion 290 million to 158 trillion 911 million MNT of annual losses.

**Resorts and tourist camps** – In Mongolia, there are in total 576 resorts and tourist camps[9] and 151 out of these camps are in and around the city. Among them, 51 camps function throughout the whole year[10] (NAP, 2016). The remaining camps function between May and October seasonally. Camps' average price for each customer is 35,000–45,000 MNT.[11] Camps stopped functioning from 26 February 2020 by the city mayor's order, yet they started to function progressively from 16 April 2020 by the order number A/521, operating normally until 11 of November, then closed again due to the lockdown.

---

8 Mongolian Hotel Association. (2020). *Online meeting from hotel service field on 3rd April of 2020.*

9 Mongolian resort and tourist camp association. (2019). *Online meeting from hotel service field on 3rd April of 2020.*

10 NAP LLC. (2016). *Explanation of Gorkhi Terelj National Park.*

11 NAP LLC. (2016). *Explanation of General plan of Gachuurt village.*

Above 51 camps faced direct losses of 1,698–2,183 million MNT during the 100 days of lockdown however, 151 camps which worked during the summer season had low profits over only 150 days. In previous years, customers were over 38 % even though this percentage was decreased down to 15 %.

In other words, all camps and resorts profited in the Summer of 2020, on average, between 16 trillion 800 and 21 trillion 600 million MNT. This amounts to 11.1–14.4 million MNT for each camp during these five months of the Summer season. As first cases and data were unofficial and undefinable, research estimation could probably range over a ± 10 % of error. Due to this unofficial data, it is difficult to determine whether it's clear profit or overall income.

**Tab. 4. Capacity data of resorts and camps**

| | Total loss in 310 days | | | | Loss of camps which function during the winter in 100 days | | | |
|---|---|---|---|---|---|---|---|---|
| District | Total camps | Total rooms | Total beds | Mill. MNT | Total camps | Total rooms | Total beds | Mill. MNT |
| Songinokha-irkhan | 5 | 94 | 196 | 604–777 | 5 | 94 | 196 | 115–148 |
| Khan-Uul | 4 | 113 | 323 | 927–1,192 | 2 | 81 | 207 | 121–156 |
| Sukhbaatar | 9 | 466 | 792 | 2,442–3,139 | 9 | 466 | 792 | 465–598 |
| Bayanzurkh | 26 | 251 | 932 | 2,515–3,234 | 8 | 85 | 323 | 189–244 |
| Chingeltei | 4 | 24 | 61 | 188–241 | 4 | 24 | 61 | 35–46 |
| Nalaikh | 103 | 1,571 | 8,019 | 20,781–26,718 | 23 | 314 | 1,309 | 769–989 |
| Total | 151 | 2,519 | 10,323 | 27,459–35,304 | 51 | 1,064 | 2,888 | 1,698–2,183 |

Resource: Researcher's estimation

Resorts and camps which function throughout the year closed due to the Mayor's order and faced 1 trillion 698 million–2 trillion 183 million MNT of economic losses. Overall, considering all camps, resorts faced 25 trillion 761 million to 33 trillion 121 million MNT of direct losses during the Summer season. That is, the global picture is one whereby resorts and camps faced economic direct losses in 2020 of 27 trillion 459 million to 35 trillion 304 million MNT.

As for purchases by tourists, a certain amount of tour package spending went to the catering industry, to entertainment and transportation and to purchasing or shopping not included in the package price.

In the five years from 2010 and 2014, tourist purchasing amount was invested in the city economic circulation at a level of 1,272 million USD or 3 trillion 272 billion 876 million MNT.[12]

Based on this data, using dynamic analysis, tourist direct purchasing process invested in Ulaanbaatar city's economic circulation by 562.9 million USD or 1.562.610.0 million MNT. It was planned that in 2020, tourist purchasing investment would be increased by 10.1 % and would gain 619.8 million MNT. But considering that 93.1 % of this planned amount was unreached, the total city losses amounted to 577 million USD or 1 trillion 650 billion 201 million[6] MNT.

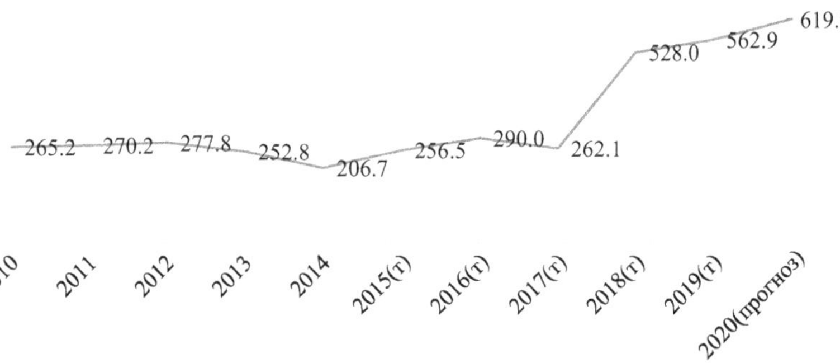


**Graphic 1.** Income from tourist purchasing process in Ulaanbaatar (mill.usd)
Resource: Researcher's estimation

## II. Food catering industry

In Ulaanbaatar city, there are 3,482 places of food-catering service and tourists who visit Ulaanbaatar use these services from restaurants, bars and coffee shops. Here are also included all restaurants and coffee shops which function inside the hotels. Tourists take service from 52.6 % of this total catering places in Ulaanbaatar city.

12 Marketmetriks. (2015). *Tourism impact on city economy, UB.*

**Tab. 5. Food catering places of Ulaanbaatar city**

| № | Type, category | BGD | BZD | SBD | SKD | ChD | KUD | BND | ND |
|---|---|---|---|---|---|---|---|---|---|
| 1 | Restaurants | 206 | 199 | 250 | 71 | 118 | 146 | 4 | 27 |
| 2 | Bars | 299 | 226 | 148 | 128 | 48 | 75 | 14 | 4 |
| 3 | Café, coffee shops | 25 | 54 | 71 | 26 | 13 | 34 | | 2 |
| 4 | Canteens | 116 | 517 | 143 | 209 | 109 | 130 | 52 | 18 |
| | Total | 646 | 996 | 612 | 434 | 288 | 385 | 70 | 51 |

*Resource: Governor's office Ulaanbaatar*

10.8 % of income from tourists in Ulaanbaatar city[13] goes to the tourist sector and based on this above estimation, the following indications are derived out income from tourists.

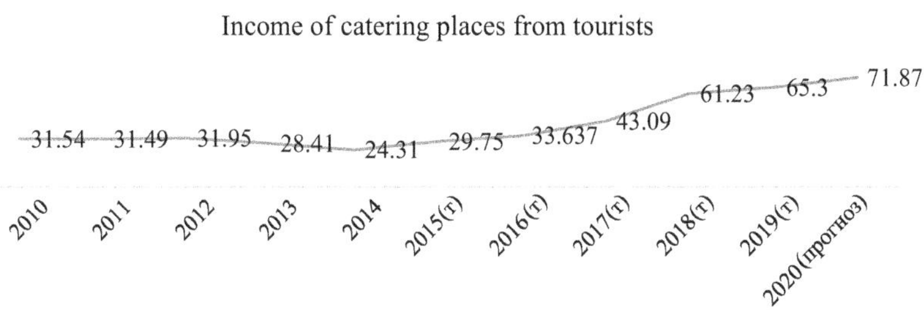


**Graphic 2.** *Total income from tourists to food catering places in Ulaanbaatar city (mill. MNT)*
Resource: Researcher's estimation

Between 2010 and 2014, catering companies made profits at the amount of 147.7 million USD or 410 billion MNT only from the tourism sector.[14] Based on this research, catering service companies gained 65.3 million USD or 181 billion 272 million[7] MNT of direct income from the tourism sector from 2015 to 2019 in Ulaanbaatar city, using a dynamic analysis method. By estimating conceptual increase to percentage, in 2020, estimation shown 71.87 million USD or 199 billion 511 million MNT of profit. But considering that tourists numbers

13 Marketmetriks. (2015). *Tourism impact on city economy, UB.*
14 Marketmetriks. (2015). *Tourism impact on city economy, UB.*

decreased by 93.1 %, the incomes of catering companies also decreased by 93.1 % and faced 669.2 million USD or 191 billion 386 million MNT of direct losses.

## III. Entertainment places

Between 2010 and 2014, 116.3 million USD or 322 billion 99 million MNT were gained from the tourism sector including museums, cinema theatres, art shows, entertainment service places, *Naadam* festivals for tourists and its organising independents and companies and other entertainment places.[15] This represents 8.4 % of total income from tourism sector to Ulaanbaatar city.

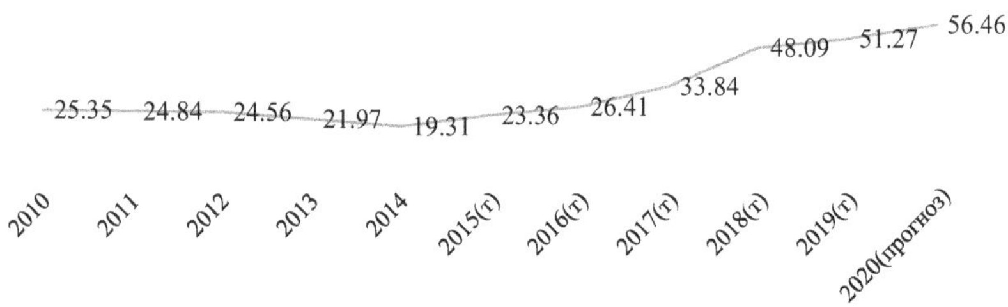


**Graphic 3.** Income estimation of entertainment places (mill.USD)
Resource: Researcher's estimation

Based on the above data, using dynamic analysis method, entertainment places gained 51.27 million USD or 142 billion 325 million MNT of profit from tourism. By conceptual analysis, in 2020, it was estimated that profit would have been 56.46 million USD or 156,732.0 million MNT from tourism sector. But considering that 93.1 % of this estimated profit is lost, this business field lost the profit of 35 million USD or 102 billion MNT.

15 Marketmetriks. (2015). *Tourism impact on city economy, UB.*

## IV. Transportation

In citywide, there are about 10,000 autobuses[16] and (in unofficial data) 2,000 vehicles participate in tourism transportation. In total, 760 vehicles were permitted in 2019 despite license number restriction in 2019 (CTA, 2020). Autobuses with more than 45 seats charge an average price of 150–200 thousand MNT daily. Buses with 25 seats charge an average of 150–200 thousand MNT. Minibuses' with 8 seats, such as Russian Furgon brand vehicle and Starex, charge 100–120 thousand MNT daily. Incomes of transportation service in tourism field is estimated below.

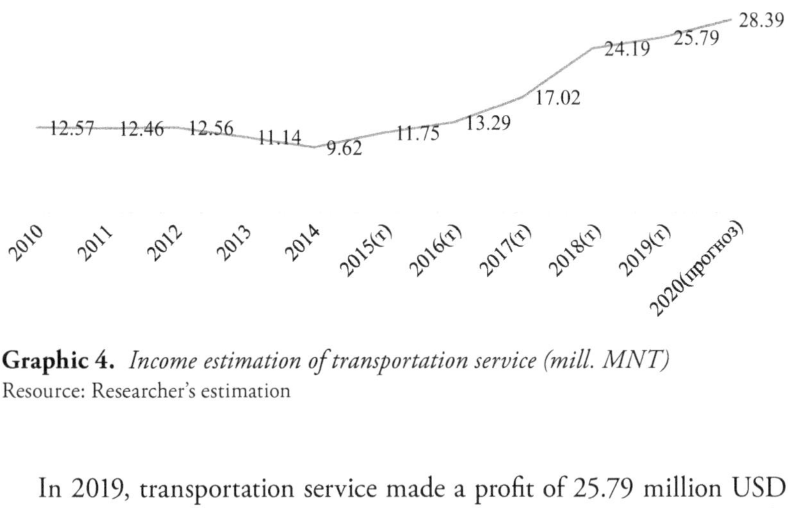


**Graphic 4.** *Income estimation of transportation service (mill. MNT)*
Resource: Researcher's estimation

In 2019, transportation service made a profit of 25.79 million USD or 71,593 million MNT. For 2020, research estimated that this profit would have increased to 28.39 million USD or 78 billion 810 million MNT. Yet, if we consider that this field lost 93.1 % of its income, this sector faces direct losses of 26.3 million USD or 75 billion 316 million MNT.

---

16 National Statistics Office of Mongolia. (2016). *Auto vehicles statistics and its structure of Ulaanbaatar city.*

## V. Events and activities

Every year, cultural and sport events and activities are organised for tourists in Ulaanbaatar city. Also, some package tours are included "mini *Naadam*" festival for tourists. Between 2010 and 2014, Ulaanbaatar city thus gained 37.3 million USD[17] (Marketmetriks, 2015) in income from events and activities held in the city. This represents 2.7 % of the total income of Ulaanbaatar city from the tourism sector. Based on this research, using regression analysis method, in 2020, Ulaanbaatar city was to gain a profit of 18.15 million USD only from such events and activities.

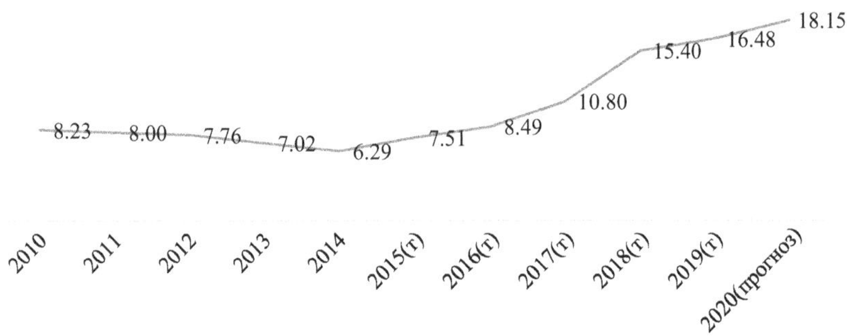


**Graphic 5.** *Income estimation of events and activities (mill. MNT)*
Resource: Researcher's estimation

In 2020, also considering this field lost 93.1 % of its income, directly faced losses of 16.9 million USD or 48 billion 340 million MNT were incurred.

*

In conclusion, due to the coronavirus pandemic, as Mongolia went under strict regulation since 26 February 2020, most of the organisations and companies were closed due to lockdown, causing most of the

[17] Marketmetriks. (2015). *Tourism impact on city economy, UB.*

business sectors to become stagnant. This mainly affected the tourism field because of this lockdown process that affected directly 88 thousand jobs.

Individuals and companies connected with tourism, such as motels, hotels, resorts, camps, museums, cinema theatres, entertainment service places, art shows, events and activities, *Naadam* festivals and its organising companies, transportation service individuals and companies faced the following direct losses.

| | |
|---|---|
| Motels | 9 billion 567 million–12 billion 300 million |
| Hotels | 34 billion 483 million–43 billion 104 million |
| Graded hotels | 115 billion 807 million |
| Food catering | 191 billion 386 million |
| Tourists' purchasing | 1 trillion 650 billion 201 million |
| Resorts | 27 billion 459 million–35 billion 304 million |
| Tour operators | Unavailable to estimate |
| Air transportations | Unavailable to estimate |
| Entertainment places | 102 billion |
| Tour transportations | 75 billion 316 million |
| Events and activities | 48 billion 340 million |

In 2020, city faced following losses. Direct income from tourists amounted to 469 billion 654 million MNT. Indirect losses from tourism field represented from 2 trillion 254 billion 649 million to 2 trillion 273 billion 848 million MNT. Out of this amount, 10–20 % of total income would have been collected to City budget fund by workers' social insurance payment, income tax payment of individuals and companies, 1 % city tax payment and other taxes in frame of direct and indirect economic circulation.

In other words, 225.4–454.7 billion MNT equivalent currency from tourism income was not made, which would have been collected to Ulaanbaatar city's budget fund[18] based on the estimate circulation of tourists for 2020. Basically, due to the stagnancy of the tourism

18 Budget income of 1,211.6 billion of Ulaanbaatar city, 2020.

field, Ulaanbaatar city faced a loss equivalent to 9.13–9.21 % of the city GDP.[19]

This gives the reader a very bold but quite realistic understanding of the concrete impact of a pandemic, in addition to learned and sophisticated political and legal accounts given by other chapters in this book.

19 GDP of UB city: 24,683,663.7 million MNT Resource: 1212.mn.

# General Conclusion

## Phoenix birds and international economic law

Ilya Lifshits

Almost every author of a general conclusion to a book, attempts to extract a general idea of all the contributed chapters. This book highlights i/ the changes in international economic law, ii/ in the wake of Brexit and the Covid-19 pandemic, iii/ in the Eurasian context. Chapter authors present their view of current developments in various fields of research and in light of these developments. Their multinational and interdisciplinary backgrounds provide a high quality of analysis.

Contemporary changes have brought several challenges to international law. It may seem that the hard-earned, complicated but manageable system of international relations that was instituted after WW-II could be dismantled in just a few years. Economic crises, trade and travel restrictions, and actions of populist governments inevitably rock the boat, or challenge the *status quo*, showing how fragile the system is, in particular the WTO multilateral trade system, EU solidarity or even human rights protection. However, the significant corpus of international norms that now covers almost all spheres of human life is still an excellent tool that serves as a *voetstok* (unified measuring level) for any event. Compliance or noncompliance, responsibility and liability, remedies and redress all exist and work in international legal coordinates. All actions, even breaches, are perceived and evaluated by means of international law. This notion is probably shared by all contributors to this volume.

The chapters of the first part of the book are devoted to trade and financial issues. The major challenge to the regulation of the multilateral trading system is considered by Remus Titiriga, who argues that US trade measures during the Trump Presidency were in line with the position of the Obama administration. According to the author, the interest of the US is to disrupt the international trade order and to switch to bilateral agreements. Despite particular declarations from President Biden, a real return to multilateralism will not happen.

Trade of particular products, especially food, has a vital importance in times of crisis. An overview of trade of corn and its legal regulation is presented by Zulfiya BAIMAGAMBETOVA and Assem AKHMETOVA. They provide an overview of corn trade regulations in different countries and international groupings. For example, Kazakhstan had to introduce 39 amendments to the law in view of WTO accession. The agricultural policy of this country was also influenced by the legal acts of the Eurasian Economic Union (EAEU), which comprises Kazakhstan and four other member states. Therefore, this example shows that legal regulation of a particular field comprises a combination of national, international and supranational norms.

Another aspect of international trade, namely, EU anti-trust law during a pandemic, is analysed by Marie DUMARÇAY. In particular, she notes that authorities tend to use the instruments of soft law more extensively. The issues of competition law are further addressed by Young-Hoa SON, who draws attention to the M&A market and possible new regulatory approaches to business mergers in the US, the EU and South Korea. For example, mergers during the current COVID-19 crisis may be approved in dealings with bankrupt companies even if the post-merger competition environment would be hindered by a particular deal. This relief is named 'failing firm-merger defence' and has been used to prevent a collapse of a particular industry.

Three chapters show how usual financial instruments (namely, settlements, short selling and state aid) work in times of crisis. The issue of the balance between health security and financial security is addressed by Géraldine LE LABOURIER-FLEURY LE GROS. Distant and contactless payments prevent contamination, but they also increase the risk of fraud. Hence, payment security in the EU should be strengthened, and this could be achieved by the use of several payment instruments included in the new project named EPI (European Payment Initiative). COVID-19 aggravated another old problem of the finance industry – short selling. Hye-Hwal SEONG studies regulatory changes and offers improvements for short-selling regulations in Korea. The selling of shares that a seller does not own has always been an issue for security regulations since it gives an opportunity to put substantial pressure on the shares' price and creates a risk of manipulative practices. The coronavirus crisis demands special regulation of short selling; for the time being, it is banned in

Korea except for that of medium- and large-sized stocks, which resumed on 3 May 2021. The author argues that short selling has certain positive effects and asserts that a total ban makes the Korean stock market less attractive to investors. The finance section is concluded by a chapter by Pierre FLEURY LE GROS, who comments on the French ordinance that created a solidarity fund. The author explains the controversial status of the general manager of a firm when pursuing a right to coronavirus state aid.

The chapters in the second part of the book address regional and interregional issues that mainly cover several kinds of challenges: BREXIT, COVID-19 and regional cooperation. Three chapters touch upon the problems following BREXIT: private international law in civil and commercial matters, international commercial litigation and transfer of personal data. Catherine GOLHEN admits that London is a privileged city regarding the resolution of commercial disputes, but she also questions whether this privileged status is due to membership in the EU. After BREXIT, the UK obtained the status of the third country in the EU, and Rome-I Regulation on the law applicable to contractual obligations as well as Brussels-I-bis Regulation on the recognition and enforcement of judgements in civil and commercial matters is no longer binding in the UK. However, on 29 March 2019, the UK incorporated provisions of the Rome-I Regulation into English national law. This decision will limit the impact of BREXIT and facilitate the harmonised application of conflict rules between the UK and EU members. The author notes that provisions of British national law incorporating the Rome-I Regulation will be interpreted by British courts (not the Court of Justice of the European Union), which may in the future result in different judgements. Catherine then concludes that BREXIT is a source of uncertainty and complexity related to judicial cooperation in civil matters.

This point of view with regard to commercial litigation is supported by Guillermo PALAO MORENO, who emphasises that the Trade and Cooperation Agreement between the UK and EU does not entail provisions devoted to cross-border commercial disputes. The author asserts that national private international law rules based on the principle of reciprocity must be followed now, which is the reason for great uncertainty.

Personal data transfer to the UK after BREXIT is discussed by Fanny ROGUE. Such transfer is subject to provisions of the GDPR (General Data Protection Regulation) of the transfer of personal data to third countries. The protection of personal data in the third country is to be equivalent to that provided by the GDPR, and this equivalence should be confirmed by the Commission. Such a decision is currently being negotiated between the UK and EU. The author concludes that EU legislation and its strict interpretation by the CJEU urge data controllers and processors to be settled in the EU. This legislation also directs third countries to bring their laws into conformity with the GDPR.

Two chapters touch upon GATT/WTO problems: export restrictions on face-masks and public procurement. According to Chan-Mo Chung, export restrictions on face-masks during Covid-19 can be justified under WTO/GATT provisions only when imposed temporarily at the time of a critical shortage. In any case not all exceptions could be applied due to the author's citing of article XXI, which for example, cannot be applied since the coronavirus situation does not fall under the term 'emergency in international relations'. Three studies, those by Sagyngaliy Aidarbayev, Aizat Bekzhan and Bakhyt Uderbayeva, compare public procurement in the EU and the EAEU. The EAEU's situation differs from that of the EU since the latter is a collective member of the WTO and a participant in the Agreement on Government Procurement (AGP); however, the EAEU is not a WTO member. Moreover, only 4 out of 5 EAEU members are WTO members, and only Armenia is an AGP participant. The authors conclude that this situation creates a number of uncertainties.

Another comparative study is devoted to taxation in the EU and the EAEU. Ilya Lifshits argues that abundant references to OECD recommendations in EU legal acts help the EU substantiate its own competence and adherence to the principles of subsidiarity and proportionality. The EU has clear competence in the harmonisation of indirect taxes. In contrast, the volume of legislation of the EAEU in the tax field is rather modest at present. However, the unions of states are in a better position to implement a single or harmonised tax regime, and the logic of integration demands a greater degree of central bodies' tax competence.

A conceptual chapter devoted to the EU internal market from the Eurasian perspective was written by Michel Bruno. The author questions the sovereignty of EU members states due to their dependence on Asian countries. The author asserts that trade agreements with Asian states jeopardise European trade, leading to deindustrialisation and breaches of labour law in Asian countries and in Europe. The real beneficiaries of these agreements are multinational corporations only. Bruno concludes that the economic and financial interests of big business took precedence over humanitarian values, and he welcomes the recent European Parliament call for the corporate social responsibility of European companies in Asia. This call may help to establish a path towards the objectives of the founding fathers of the European Communities.

Regional challenges are further addressed in two chapters on the Chinese Belt and Road Initiative (BRI) and on the US military presence in Korea. Kuralay BAIZAKOVA and Fatima KUKEYEVA consider the pros and cons of the BRI for Central Asian states and Kazakhstan in particular. The authors suggest that this project could be an open inclusive platform for multilateral cooperation. However, certain political risks and the threat of international terrorism may be a real challenge for the BRI. The opposite views for the US military presence in South Korea are considered by Tai-Uk CHUNG. Proponents of one position advocate the restoration of Korean military sovereignty, while others believe that the US army will protect the security of South Korea.

The third part of the book comprises chapters on sectoral and socio-economic issues, including health, intellectual property and tourism. The protection of the right to health is vital in times of global epidemics according to the research of Gulmira MASHIMBAYEVA and Aidana OTYNSHIYEVA. Authors touch upon a problem of 'vaccine nationalism', and they reiterate that only international cooperation can save us from the coronavirus crisis.

The other actual issue in times of pandemic – digital health – is discussed in the chapter by Amandine CAYOL. The development of distant medical services began in the 1990s, and the main legislative framework was prepared by 2019. However, until the onset of the COVID-19 pandemic, the use of telemedicine had remained at a rather low level. In 2020, the number of teleconsultations soared to 20 million from 60 thousand in 2019. This rise has brought several ethical and legal questions concerning the protection of health data and respect of patients' rights. The latter issue first of all relates to the quality of medical aid. The author comments on various French legal instruments applied to address these issues.

Legal consciousness with regard to COVID-19 is a subject of the chapter written by Yesbol OMIRZHANOV and Almagul TUSUPOVA. The authors provide an overview of actions to combat the pandemic in Kazakhstan and conclude that legal consciousness plays a key role in the effectiveness of any measure of the authorities taken in times of emergency. The coronavirus section is written by Odgerel Purevdorj and Erbakhit Badelgaji, who show the influence of Covid-19 on the tourist sector of the Mongolian capital, Ulaanbaatar, which faced a loss equivalent to 9.13–9.21 % of the city's GDP.

Three chapters cover intellectual property issues: one about the general issue of the evolution of IP rights and two on particular issues on implementing WTO IP standards in Kazakhstan's legislation and on copyright in Korea. Philippe Gast provides an overview of the development of IP protection from ancient times until now. In particular, the author underlines the significance of article 17 of Directive (EU) 2019/790 of the European Parliament and of the Council of 17 April 2019 on copyright and related rights in the Digital Single Market. This provision imposes the obligation on EU Member states to ensure that online content-sharing service providers are liable for granting unauthorised public access to copyright-protected works or other protected subject matter uploaded by their users. Philippe mentions that this norm was included in the directive despite the efforts of leading providers – GAFAM (Google, Apple, Facebook, Amazon, and Microsoft).

A thorough review of amendments to IP legislation in Kazakhstan in the framework of WTO accession was performed by Zhuldyz Sairambaeva and Madina Nurtay. The authors especially discussed the TRIPS coronavirus waiver which has been discussed in the WTO over the last several months. The legal status of film and theatre directors is considered by Sung-Kee Hong in the broad context of the development of the Korean IP industry. The author asserts that according to Korean law, a film director can be qualified as an author of audiovisual work, while a theatre director can hardly be qualified as the creator of new work. However, on the international level, WIPO allows theatre directors to enjoy copyright protection if theatrical production differs substantially from the script. This outcome especially matters in pandemic times when theatrical works are often performed in front of cameras.

*

The following concluding remarks attempt to provide a general overview of this book. Current events, including the Covid-19 pandemic,

Brexit and regional changes, have undoubtedly posed a great challenge to the international economic order. The authors admit this and try to articulate their personal view on possible responses to these challenges. What may unite all authors is the core of such a response. The world community should react using the instruments of international law on the solid basis of true equality, mutual trust and respect for regional differences. It would be a good pledge to the world's quick recovery and strengthen our belief that *Phoenix bird* can survive again.

# Postface

Kyeong-Ju LEE

It's a great pleasure to write a few words of encouragement towards these international research efforts that have led and still will lead to substantive international conferences, notably this $5^{th}$ Kazakh-Franco-Korean International Law Conference of May 2021.

Indeed, since 2014, several authoritative scholars in legal and social sciences of the *al-Farabi* Kazakh National University in Almaty, of Le Havre and Caen universities in France and of the Inha Law School in Korea have developed this cycle of academic meetings. The main themes of these conferences have been the cooperation and collaboration among European and Asian countries toward a more clear and focused globalised world.

Over two days, this $5^{th}$ meeting dealt with all these issues. During the first four encounters (2014, 2016, 2017, 2019), the recognition that globalisation is in progress was dominant, and the general environment was also open to globalisation. However, at this time with the development of a completely different environment from the past, questions about globalisation have been raised.

The present unfavourable environment makes the mission of the joint conferences stand out even more: analysing mutual cooperation for globalisation. It is expected that the original research by these dedicated scholars participating will greatly contribute to paving the way for a better future in difficult times. In addition to Kazakhstan, France, and Korea, scholars from China, Russia, Spain and Mongolia participate in this conference, so we expect to gain more diverse and valuable insights.

I would like to end this postface with appreciations. First of all, a word of thanks to Pierre Chabal of Le Havre University, to Amandine Cayol of Caen University also in France, to Zhuldyz Sairambaeva of *al-Farabi* Kazakh National University in Almaty and to Hye-Hwal Seong and Remus Titiriga in InHa Law School, for meticulously and thoroughly preparing this international meeting. Also a special thanks to the Lexfeim Centre directors Le Havre University and Demolombe Institute directors of Caen University for hosting this 2021 event and many of the previous ones. In addition, I would like to express my deep appreciation to the participating professors who took the valuable time to present their research topics.

When we finally overcome Covid-19 and the victory of mankind is declared, I hope to see you face-to-face in Korea, as planned in 2023. I wish all of us health and happiness. Thank you.

# Afterword

## Data flow and data protection: Actual and future challenges to reconcile antagonisms

Louis-Philippe GRATTON

The unprecedented health crisis that the world witnesses has significant impacts on trade and commerce, as the contributors to this book demonstrate. The pandemic also begets other consequences in Eurasia on competition, finance, performing arts, tourism, or data-management. The crisis, along with other factors such as the 'datafication' process,[1] actually contributes to the increase of the flow of data inside and among countries,[2] especially health data. This leads to a need to reconcile the economic growth potential of information circulation with the protection of individuals' rights to privacy.

## I. Hindrance of data flow in Eurasia

The geopolitics of data is a reality and it has rising importance in international commerce negotiations, as evidenced by the position adopted by India in talks around the *Regional Comprehensive Economic Partnership* (RCEP). New Delhi withdrew from the negotiations for

---

1 Datafication refers to the rendering into data of previously unquantifiable aspects of the world, like the location of a person: Kenneth Cukier and Viktor Mayer-Schoenberger, "The rise of big data – How it's changing the way we think about the world", *Foreign Affairs*, May/June 2013, p. 28, 29, 34–35.

2 See Edward D. Mansfield and Nita Rudra, "Embedded liberalism in the digital era", (2021) 75 *Int'l Organ.* 558, 562–563; and International Bank for Reconstruction and Development/World Bank, *Data for Better Lives – World Development Report 2021* (2021), pp. 91–111.

multiple reasons,[3] but the question of data localisation[4] was at the heart of the discussions.

India, with one of the fastest-growing technology industries in the region, insisted on locating servers hosting data within its borders, while 14 other of its negotiating partners opposed it.[5] Indian representatives also pushed for exceptions to prevent cross-border transfers of information. They virtually foresaw the importance to retain control on local data – a sort of data nationalism[6] – against the background of a health crisis.

If the final text of the RCEP prevents a Party to require businesses to use or locate computing facilities in its territory[7] and to adopt provisions preventing the cross-border transfer of information,[8] it also contains exceptions to these rules. A Party may adopt such measures "to achieve a legitimate public policy objective"[9] or "for the protection of its essential security interests".[10] Exceptions are almost *de facto* the norm because the objective, in the first case, is to be determined solely by the concerned Party[11] and, in the second case, the measures taken cannot be disputed by other Parties.[12]

---

3 Emeka Adibe *et al.*, "RCEP, CPTPP and the changing dynamics in international trade standard-setting", (2019) 16 *Manchester J. Int'l Econ. L.* 425, 434–435.

4 Data localization refers to national requirements to store data locally or respect local provisions before transferring data abroad: Anupam Chander and Uyên P. Lê, "Data nationalism", (2015) 64 *Emory LJ* 677, 680; and John Selby, "Data localization laws: Trade barriers or legitimate responses to cybersecurity risks, or both", (2017) 25 *Int'l JL & Info. Tech.* 213, 214–215.

5 Dinesh Narayanan and Kirtika Suneja, "India wants data localisation in RCEP for security interests", *The Economic Times*, 12 October 2019.

6 A. Chander and U. P. Lê, "Data nationalism", *op. cit.*

7 *Regional Comprehensive Economic Partnership*, 15 November 2020, art. 12.14 (2), hereinafter RCEP.

8 *Ibid.*, art. 12.15 (2). There is also another limited provision – that applies only to financial services – prohibiting Parties to adopt measures that prevent *"transfers of information […] necessary for the conduct of the ordinary business of a financial service supplier"* (*ibid.*, Ann. 8a, art. 9 (2) (a)).

9 *Ibid.*, art. 12.14 (3) (a) and 12.15 (3) (a).

10 *Ibid.*, art. 12.14 (3) (b) and 12.15 (3) (b).

11 *Ibid.*, f.n. 12 and 14. Other Parties may challenge the measure on the ground that it is arbitrary, it constitutes unjustifiable discrimination or it establishes a disguised restriction on trade (*ibid.*, art. 12.14 (3) (a) and 12.15 (3) (a)).

12 *Ibid.*, art. 12.14 (3) (b) and 12.15 (3) (b).

The Parties agreed to consider further current and emerging issues, such as the cross-border data flow, in future negotiations.[13] Less restrictive provisions on the transfer of information will have to wait as the general review of the Agreement is planned to start five years after the date of entry into force of the text,[14] a text that has not yet come into effect.

Parties may also have to consider a more comprehensive regime for data protection, a necessity exacerbated by the Covid-19 situation.

## II. Lack of a comprehensive data protection system

Asian countries saw the first concrete use of data to track the coronavirus epidemic, reduce its spread, and control the population's movement. Applications on smartphones even became passports to access the workplace, public transport, or commercial centers.

Applications such as these consume a wide range of personal data to achieve their goals, among them are geolocation and health data. If health data are needed to monitor and curb the pandemic, they are also considered sensitive information under regional and international[15] data protection frameworks and deserve special protection.

In the *General Data Protection Regulation* (GDPR), health data belong to special categories of personal data[16] because their processing poses "significant risks to the fundamental rights and freedoms"[17] of an individual. The European regulation even prohibits as a rule the processing of such information, unless an exception applies.[18]

The RCEP does not include similar detailed provisions. Data are mostly considered from an economic point of view and the agreement

---

13 *Ibid.*, art. 12.16 (1) (b).

14 *Ibid.*, art. 20.8 (1). The "Dialogue on Electronic Commerce" – the broader topic that includes data flow – is to be held through the RCEP Joint Committee consisting of senior officials of each Party (*ibid.*, art. 18.2 and 18.3 (1) (j)).

15 UN, General Assembly, Human Rights Council, Special Rapporteur on the Right to Privacy, Task Force on Privacy and the Protection of Health-Related Data, *Recommendation on the Protection and Use of Health-Related Data* (2019).

16 *Regulation (EU) 2016/679 of the European Parliament and of the Council of 27 April 2016 on the protection of natural persons with regard to the processing of personal data and on the free movement of such data*, OJEU L 119, 4 May 2016, art. 9 (1).

17 *Ibid.*, recital 51.

18 *Ibid.*, art. 9 (2).

does not contain commitments other than the obligation for each Party to have a legal framework to ensure the protection of personal information in the limited context of electronic commerce.[19]

The sensitive nature of health-related data is not considered *per se* and Parties are invited to take into account standards, principles, guidelines, and criteria developed by international bodies and organisations.[20] They are left to themselves to balance individual rights and the collective objective of preserving public health.

As solutions experienced first in Asia to solve the coronavirus crisis are implemented in Europe and elsewhere, data flow and data protection concern not only the Eurasian region, but the whole world. It opens up possibilities for dialogue on the concrete experiences of some and the legal rules of protection of others.

So it is of particular value for this book and its readership to have anticipated on so many of these pressing issues.

*

19 RCEP, *op. cit.*, art. 12.8 (1).

20 *Ibid.*, art. 12.8 (2).

# Notes on contributors

**Sagyngaliy** Aidarbayev, Dr. of Law, Professor, Dean of I.R Faculty, *al-Farabi* Kazakh National University, vice-president of Kazakhstan Association of International law, member of Arbitration court (National chamber of commerce "Atameken") and Russian Association of International law, honorary Prof. of the Russian Academy of Foreign Trade (Moscow, Russia).

**Assema** Akhmetova, PhD student, *al-Farabi* Kazakh National University.

**Erbakhit** Badelgaji, graduate research student, School of Geography, the National University of Mongolia, expert in Tourism Studies with Odgerel Purevdor.

**Zulfiya** Baimagambetova, PhD in international law, Associate Professor of International Law Department of *al-Farabi* Kazakh National University. Director of the Center of WTO and International trade law. Author of over 50 scientific publications on legal problems of International trade law.

**Kuralay** Baizakova, Doctor of History, Professor of International Relations dpt, Director of Institute for Security and Cooperation Studies, Director of European Information Centre. Editor-in-chief of the Eurasian Journal of Social Sciences and Humanities. Holder of the Medal of the Ministry of Education and Science "Honored person in education" for high achievements in the field of education.

**Aizat** Bekzhan, PhD student, International Law department, the *al-Farabi* Kazakh National University. Scientific interests "Public international law", "Diplomatic and consular law", "International legal regulation of government procurement, including international legal regulation of government procurement".

**Michel** Bruno, state Doctorate in Law, associate professor, director of the LexFEIM research Center and former dean of the Faculty of

International Affairs, Université Le Havre Normandie. Research interests: EU material law, EU's disunion and institutional reforms. His publications focus on EU law, EU common policies and human rights.

**Amandine CAYOL**, PhD in Law (Paris I Panthéon-Sorbonne), associate professor, Université Caen Normandie. Author of *Le contrat d'ouvrage* (Ed. IRJS, 2013) and "L'adaptation du système de santé français face à la pandémie de COVID-19 par le développement des usages de la télémédecine", *JML Droit, santé et société*, No. 3–2020, pp. 25–30.

**Pierre CHABAL**, Sc. Dr. Habil. (Pol. Science & I.R., Paris IEP), co-director LexFEIM Research Centre (Université Le Havre), associated to Sciences-Po Europe-Asia campus and visiting professor at *al-Farabi* Kazakh National University. He founded the Kazakh-French-Korean law research network in 2014. <https://caa-network.org/archives/21105>.

**Chan-Mo CHUNG**, PhD in Law (Oxon), Professor at Inha University Law School, Former President of the Korean Society of International Economic Law.

**Tai-Uk CHUNG**, PhD in Law, Professor of Law and Philosophy of Law at Inha University Law School. Co-organiser of the Kazakh-Franco-Korean conferences in 2017 and 2019.

**Marie DUMARÇAY**, PhD in Private Law devoted to companies that are victims of anti-competitive practices. And associate professor at the Université Caen Normandie. She has published numerous articles on antitrust law, including one on sustainable development and competition law.

**Pierre FLEURY LE GROS**, PhD in Private Law (Caen university), director of Law Dpt, of the BA-1 in Law and of the 'préparation CPGE' 1st/2nd years (Le Havre university), Member of the LexFEIM research Centre. <https://www.lefigaro.fr/vox/societe/fin-de-vie-le-droit-n-avalise-en-rien-l-assistance-au-suicide-20210326>.

**Philippe GAST**, PhD in private law (Paris II Panthéon-Assas university), associate professor of law at the Université Le Havre Normandie, formerly attorney at the Paris Bar, author of *Expérience spirituelle, conscience* *et droit* ['Experiencing Spirituality, Conscience and Law], Paris, published by Librairie de l'Inde, 401 pages.

**Catherine GOLHEN**, PhD in law, associate professor in Private law, Université Caen Normandie, Member of Demolombe Institute, Co-director of the University Diploma VIB (*Valorisation of biological innovations*) of Caen University. Author of: "Facebook: right to respect for private life versus right to proof", *Receuil Dalloz*, No. 42, 2020, p. 1353.

**Louis-Philippe GRATTON**, PhD in Law (Toulouse 1), LL.M. (Laval), LL.M. (Lausanne), practicing lawyer (Québec Bar) and data protection y consultant (Minsk). Editor of exculturae.com, Authored (with A. Ziegler), "Article IX", in H. Hestermeyer *et al.*, *WTO – Trade in Goods – M. Planck Commentaries on World Trade Law*, Brill/Nijhoff.

**Sung-Kee HONG**, PhD in Law, former Dean of the Inha University Law School, Professor in InHa law School specialising on Intellectual property Law.

**Fatima KUKEYEVA**, Doctor of history, Professor. Director of Resource center for American and Democratic studies. al-Farabi Kazakh National University. Medal of the Ministry of Education and Science "Honored person in education" for high achivments in the field of education.

**Kyeong-Ju LEE**, PhD in Law, Dean of Inha University Law School.

**Géraldine LE LABOURIER-FLEURY LE GROS**, PhD in Private Law (Caen university), is associate professor, member of LexFEIM, acting director of Master-2 'Judicial careers' at Le Havre university. Author of (in French) *'Consenting' to contact-less payment* [Le consentement du porteur à l'exécution d'un paiement par carte sans contact].

**Ilya LIFSHITS**, Doctor of legal sciences in International and European law, professor at the Russian Foreign Trade Academy. Scholarly interest International Financial Law, International Trade Law, EU Law, International Tax Law. Member of Advisory Board of the Russian Federal Antimonopoly Service (financial services), of European Society of International Law, of Russian Association of International Law.

**Gulmira Mashimbayeva,** Candidate of Jurisprudence, associate professor of International Law Department of al-Farabi Kazakh National University. Member of the Kazakh Association of International law. Chairperson of the Methodological Bureau of the Faculty of International Relations.

**Innocent Mutabazi**, PhD in Physics (Paris 7 university), professor and acting president of Normandie Université, formerly director of Physics research centre LIA CNRS1092 ISTROF (2013–2020), expert for the French ministry's HCERES, has edited three books and authored over a 100 articles (google scholar: h=21, 1,480 citations).

**Madina Nurtay**, PhD student at International Law department, the *al-Farabi* Kazakh National University. Research interest: dispute resolution issues in the field of intellectual property rights protection.

**Yesbol Omirzhanov**, PhD in law, associate professor, *al-Farabi* Kazakh National University, Candidate of Jurisprudence. Author of two textbook, four tutorials on theory and history of state and Law, Human rights and Islamic law.

**Aidana Otynshiyeva**, PhD in law. Senior Lecturer of the Department of International Law of *al-Farabi* Kazakh National University. Visiting scholars of Pennsylvania state University.

**Guillermo Palao Moreno**, Professor of Private International Law, Universitat de València (Spain). Member of MedARb GIUV2013-090 and of PROMETEO GV 2018/111. Has conducted research in Universitá La Sapienza (Rome), Harvard Law School, Max-Planck Institut für Ausländisches und internationales privatrecht (Hamburg), Institut Sussie de Droit Comparé (Lausanne). Author in five monographs, co-author in over 10 collective books, published both in Spain and outside.

**Odgerel Purevdorj**, defending PhD research student (2021) and senior lecturer, School of Geographical sciences, the National University of Mongolia, also associated to the Europe-Asia research network for its 2022 conference.

**Fanny Rogue**, PhD in law, associate professor in Private law, Université Caen Normandie. Member of Demolombe Institute, author of

"Violations du RGPD par Google: la sanction de 50 millions € est confirmée par le Conseil d'État!", note sous Conseil d'État, 19/6/2020, No. 430810, in *L'essentiel du droit des personnes et de la famille*, oct. 2020.

**Zhuldyz Sairambaeva**, PhD in law, Candidate of Jurisprudence, associate professor of International Law Department of *al-Farabi* Kazakh National University. Member of the Kazakh Association of International law. Executive Secretary of the Eurasian Journal of Social Sciences and Humanities. Author of 2 tutorials and about 30 scientific articles.

**Hye-Hwal Seong**, SJD in Law, Professor at Inha University Law School. Co-organiser of the Kazakh-Franco-Korean conference in 2021.

**Young-Hoa Son**, PhD in Law, Professor at Inha University Law School.

**Remus Titiriga**, PhD in Public Law of University Nancy 2, Professor at Inha University Law School. Co-editor of this volume of the Kazakh-Franco-Korean conference.

**Almagul Tusupova Candidate of Jurisprudence**, associate professor of International Law Department of al-Farabi Kazakh National University.

**Bakhyt Uderbayeva**, PhD in law, Associate Professor, Candidate of Jurisprudence, associate professor of Narxos University, Kazakhstan. She has more than 50 publications on various aspects of criminal law, international criminal law.

*

## Cultures juridiques et politiques

Vol. 1 Stephanie Rohlfing-Dijoux (éd)
La Transmission de Terminologie et de Concepts Juridiques dans l'espace Européen. Allemagne / France / Russie
2012, ISBN 978-3-0343-1094-9

Vol. 2 Otmar Seul & Tomas Davulis (éds./Hrsg.)
La Solidarité dans l'union Européenne / Solidarität in der Europäischen Union. Actes de la 5ème Université d'été franco-germano-lituanienne et européenne en sciences juridiques Vilnius, 3-10 juillet 2008 / Tagungsband der 5. Deutsch-Französisch-Litauischen und Europäischen Sommeruniversität in den Rechtswissenschaften,Vilnius 3.-10. Juli 2008
2012, ISBN 978-3-0343-1122-9

Vol. 3 Ralf Alleweldt, Raphaël Callsen, Jeanne Dupendant (eds.)
Human rights abuses in the contemporary world. Tri-National Workshop,Tbilisi, September 2011
2012, ISBN 978-3-0343-1147-2

Vol. 4 Stefanie Bouquet
La réglementation européenne relative à la discrimination fondée sur l'âge: conséquences sur le droit du travail français. Préface du Professeur Joachim Gruber, Université Paris Ouest - Nanterre La Défense
2012, ISBN 978-3-0343-1174-8

Vol. 5 Izabela Krasnicka & Magdalena Perkowska (éds.)
How to Become a Lawyer?
2013, ISBN 978-3-0343-1290-5

Vol. 6 Kerstin Peglow et Géraldine Demme (dir.)
La protection des intérêts privés sur le marché intérieur. La situation des consommateurs et entrepreneurs.
2015, ISBN 978-3-0343-1615-6

Vol. 7 Sam Lyes
Crimes internationaux et immunité de l'acte de fonction des anciens dirigeants étatiques.
2015, ISBN 978-3-0343-1690-3

Vol. 8 Fabien Bottini, Harold Gaba et Pierre Chabal (dir.)
Le régionalisme et ses limites. Regards croisés franco-kazakhs.
2016, ISBN 978-2-87574-335-0

Vol. 9 Otmar Seul, Kaïs Slama, Kerstin Peglow (Hrsg.)
Kulturvermittlung und Interkulturalität, ein deutschfranzösisch-tunesischer Dialog. Politische, rechtliche und sozio-linguistische Aspekte
2017, ISBN 978-2-8076-0133-8

Vol. 10 Stephanie Rohlfing-Dijoux (ed./dir.)
Developing Intraregional Exchanges through the Abolition of Commercial and Tariff Barriers. Myth or Reality?
L'abolition des barrières commerciales et tarifaires dans la région de l'océan Indien. Mythe ou réalité?
2017, ISBN 978-2-8076-0126-0

Vol. 11 Sagyngaliy Aidarbayev, Pierre Chabal, Zhuldyz Sairambaeva (dir.) Mutations de société et réponses du droit.
Perspectives franco-asiatiques comparées.
2017, ISBN 978-2-8076-0187-1

Vol. 12 Tomas Davulis (ed.)
Labour Law Reforms in Eastern and Western Europe.
2017, ISBN 978-2-8076-0416-2

Vol. 13 Tai-Uk Chung, Zhuldyz Sairambaeva, Pierre Chabal (eds.)
On the Asian and European Origins of Legal and Political Systems. Views from Korea, Kazakhstan and France
2018, ISBN 978-2-8076-0732-3

Vol. 14 Manuel Goehrs
Coopération transfrontalière et intégration européenne. Contribution à l'étude du principe fédéraliste
2018, ISBN 978-2-8076-0409-4

Vol. 15 Amandine Cayol, Zhuldyz Sairambaeva, Pierre Chabal (eds.)
The challenge of change for the legal and political systems of Eurasia. The impact of the New Silk Road
2020, ISBN 978-2-8076-1382-9

Vol. 16 Christine Canazza, Stéphanie Rohlfing-Dijoux, Otmar Seul (eds.)
L'Union européenne face au vieillissement de la population active. Analyse et perspectives autour de la discrimination sur la base de l'âge et des conditions de travail.
2020, ISBN 978-2-8076-1454-3

Vol. 17 Patric Kra
Ehe und Familienschutz in Zeiten des demografischen Wandels. Ein Rechtsvergleich zwischen dem deutschen und ivorischen Einkommensteuerrecht.
2021, ISBN 978-2-8076-1469-7

Vol. 18 Amandine Cayol, Hye-Hwal Seong, Remus Titiriga, Pierre Chabal (Eds.)
Eurasian challenges to international economic law. New developments after Brexit and in the context of the COVID-19.
2022, ISBN 978-2-87574-467-8

www.ingramcontent.com/pod-product-compliance
Ingram Content Group UK Ltd.
Pitfield, Milton Keynes, MK11 3LW, UK
UKHW020153290926
15471UKWH00005B/856

9 782875 744678